Anthropology of Vi
Conflict

Violence is a key feature of human social relations, yet has received comparatively little attention from social scientists. With increasing levels of conflict and violence in the modern world, *Anthropology of Violence and Conflict* offers a timely contribution to this growing area of anthropological research. The authors provide a balanced approach to the causes of violence and the human experience behind it, examining how violent conflict is often represented differently by perpetrators, victims and observers, as well as by winners and losers in war. To what extent are the conditions that lead to conflicts commonly experienced across cultures?

From each discussion emerges the importance of viewing contemporary violence as grounded in long-term antagonistic processes. Drawing on examples from North and South America, Africa and the recent civil strife in Sri Lanka, Albania and the former Yugoslavia, this volume examines well-known conflicts, past and present, and provides ample evidence of the fact that violence is never an isolated event. All conflict is reliant on perpetrators, victims and witnesses.

The authors all agree on the dialectical nature of violence: conflict is both imagined and performed, and this duality is crucial when examining the nature of violent conflict. By providing an anthropological perspective on this important subject, this volume is a crucial addition to the literature of violence and warfare.

Bettina E. Schmidt and **Ingo W. Schröder** are research associates at the Department of Social Anthropology, University of Marburg, Germany.

European Association of Social Anthropologists

Series Facilitators: Jon P. Mitchell, *University of Sussex*
Sarah Pink, *University of Loughborough*

The European Association of Social Anthropologists (EASA) was inaugurated in January 1989, in response to a widely felt need for a professional association that would represent social anthropologists in Europe and foster co-operation and interchange in teaching and research. The series brings together the work of the Association's members in a series of edited volumes which originate from and expand upon the biennial EASA Conference.

Titles in the series are:

Conceptualizing Society
Adam Kuper (ed.)

Other Histories
Kristen Hastrup (ed.)

Alcohol, Gender and Culture
Dimitra Gefou-Madianou (ed.)

Understanding Rituals
Daniel de Coppet (ed.)

Gendered Anthropology
Teresa del Valle (ed.)

Social Experience and Anthropological Knowledge
Kirsten Hastrup and Peter Hervik (eds)

Fieldwork and Footnotes
Han F. Vermeulen and Arturo Alvarez Roldan (eds)

Syncretism/Anti-syncretism
Charles Stewart and Rosalind Shaw (eds)

Grasping the Changing World
Václav Hubinger (ed.)

Civil Society
Chris Hann and Elizabeth Dunn (eds)

Anthropology of Policy
Cris Shore and Susan Wright (eds)

Nature and Society
Philippe Descola and Gisli Pálsson (eds)

The Ethnography of Moralities
Signe Howell (ed.)

Inside and Outside the Law
Olivia Harris (ed.)

Anthropological Perspectives on Local Development
Simone Abram and Jacqueline Waldren (eds)

Recasting Ritual
Felicia Hughes-Freeland and Mary M. Crain (eds)

Locality and Belonging
Nadia Lovell (ed.)

Constructing the Field
Vered Amit (ed.)

Dividends of Kinship
Peter P. Schweitzer (ed.)

Audit Cultures
Marilyn Strathern (ed.)

Gender, Agency and Change
Victoria Ana Goddard (ed.)

Natural Enemies
John Knight (ed.)

Anthropology of Violence and Conflict

Edited by

Bettina E. Schmidt and
Ingo W. Schröder

London and New York

First published 2001
by Routledge
2 Park Square, Milton Park, Abingdon, Oxon, OX14 4RN

Simultaneously published in the USA and Canada
by Routledge
270 Madison Ave, New York NY 10016

Routledge is an imprint of the Taylor & Francis Group

Transferred to Digital Printing 2005

Typeset in Galliard and Gill Sans by
Exe Valley Dataset Ltd, Exeter, Devon

British Library Cataloguing in Publication Data
A catalogue record for this book is availabe from the British Library

Library of Congress Cataloging in Publication Data
Anthropology of violence and conflict/edited by Bettina E. Schmidt and Ingo W. Schröder.
p. cm.
Includes bibliographical references and index.
1. Violence. 2. Culture conflict. 3. Social conflict. 4. Political violence.
5. Ethnic relations. I. Schmidt, Bettina, 1958–. II. Schröder, Ingo.
III. European Association of Social Anthropologists.

GN494.5 A58 2001
303.6—dc21 00–045705

ISBN 0–415–22905–7 (hbk)
ISBN 0–415–22906–5 (pbk)

Contents

List of figures vii
List of contributors ix
Acknowledgements x

1 Introduction: violent imaginaries and violent practices 1
INGO W. SCHRÖDER AND BETTINA E. SCHMIDT

2 The violence in identity 25
GLENN BOWMAN

Violence as everyday practice and imagination **47**

3 Socio-cosmological contexts and forms of violence: war, vendetta, duels and suicide among the Yukpa of north-western Venezuela 49
ERNST HALBMAYER

4 The interpretation of violent worldviews: cannibalism and other violent images of the Caribbean 76
BETTINA E. SCHMIDT

5 The enactment of 'tradition': Albanian constructions of identity, violence and power in times of crisis 97
STEPHANIE SCHWANDNER-SIEVERS

Violence and conflict **121**

6 Violence and culture: anthropological and evolutionary-psychological reflections on inter-group conflict in southern Ethiopia 123
JON ABBINK

7 Violent events in the Western Apache past: ethnohistory and ethno-ethnohistory 143
INGO W. SCHRÖDER

Violence in war **159**

8 When silence makes history: gender and memories of war violence from Somalia 161
FRANCESCA DECLICH

9 A turning point? From civil struggle to civil war in Sri Lanka 176
PETER KLOOS

10 Predicament of war: Sarajevo experiences and ethics of war 197
IVANA MAČEK

Index 225

Figures

3.1 Identity versus difference among the Yukpa 56
3.2 Levels of inside/outside among the Yukpa 58
3.3 Social levels of identity/difference 59
9.1 Conceptualisation of escalation to civil war 179
9.2 Two basic schisms in Sri Lankan society 186
9.3 From ethnic difference (stage 1) to regular civil war (stage 6) 193

Contributors

Jon Abbink is Research Associate at the African Studies Center, Rijksuniversiteit Leiden, the Netherlands.

Glenn Bowman is Lecturer in Anthropology at Rutherford College, University of Kent, Canterbury, UK.

Francesca Declich is Professor of Anthropology at the University of Urbino, Italy.

Ernst Halbmayer is Research Associate at the Laboratoire d' Anthropologie Sociale, Paris, France.

Peter Kloos was Professor of Anthropology at the Free University of Amsterdam, the Netherlands. He passed away after finalising his contribution in August 2000.

Ivana Maček is Research Fellow at the Department of Anthropology, Uppsala University, Sweden.

Bettina E. Schmidt is Research Associate at the Department of Social Anthropology, University of Marburg, Germany.

Ingo W. Schröder is Research Associate at the Department of Social Anthropology, University of Marburg, Germany.

Stephanie Schwandner-Sievers is Nash Fellow for Albanian Studies at the School of Slavonic and East European Studies, University of London, UK.

Acknowledgements

We would like to thank all those who participated in the workshop 'Worldviews and Violence' at Frankfurt, in particular Erdmute Alber, Christophe Anthoine, Anton Blok and Ida Hydle, whose papers could not be included here for various reasons.

We also gratefully acknowledge the financial support of the Department of Anthropology at the University of Marburg in preparing the manuscript for publication and Andreas Hemming's assistance in proof-reading.

Chapter 1

Introduction

Violent imaginaries and violent practices

Ingo W. Schröder and Bettina E. Schmidt

Almost one hundred years ago Georg Simmel published his seminal study of the fight (Simmel 1908). With this work he was the first to transcend the confines of evolutionist thinking about violence that had viewed intergroup conflict mainly as an instrument of evolutionary selection. From the evolutionist perspective, war was something that had developed along with the rest of the cultural inventory from unregulated primordial aggressiveness 'in the depths of mankind'[1] to modern, mechanised warfare as described by Clausewitz. Simmel looks at violence as a synchronic event, as a type of social relations between individuals and collectivities that serves specific ends at intergroup as well as intragroup levels. With this functional approach he set the stage for the modern anthropological study of violent confrontations that views them as social action relative to the interests and convictions of conscious actors.

While this basic assumption continues to be held in common by social scientists researching conflict, war and violence,[2] the field has become increasingly fragmented, particularly in the 1980s. Today, three main approaches can be distinguished:

1 the operational approach, focusing on the etics of antagonism, in particular on the measurable material and political causes of conflict;
2 the cognitive approach, focusing on the emics of the cultural construction of war in a given society;
3 the experiential approach that looks at violence as not necessarily confined to situations of intergroup conflict but as something related to individual subjectivity, something that structures people's everyday lives, even in the absence of an actual state of war.

These are ideal types, of course, and there is hardly any study that does not contain elements of all three, but a tendency can be observed in each of them to pull away in a different direction from the basic consensus on the social nature of violence.

The aims of this introduction are two-fold: first, we discuss the dichotomy of practice and imaginary that is, in our view, crucial to the understanding of violence as a total social fact and which runs as a common thread through the book. Second, we want to elaborate on the three above-mentioned facets of violence. Not only is each of these indicative of a different research perspective, but all of them together make up the whole spectrum of violence as it presents itself to anthropological analysis. Also, we will reflect upon the value of different theoretical approaches that have been brought to bear on the subject by different authors. Just as the various foci on the substance of violence have served to expand the notion of its phenomenological complexity, so the multiple theoretical approaches represented in this collection demonstrate that violence can, and in fact should, be viewed from a variety of angles. While not claiming to reintegrate the field of violence research, we believe the focus on the imaginary–practice dialectic outlined in this introduction presents a fruitful approach to violence as a multifaceted, yet ultimately comparable phenomenon all over the world.

This introduction should be read in concert with Bowman's chapter that approaches the subject from yet another slightly different angle, focusing on the socially constructive qualities of violence.

Violent practice

From Simmel's time to the present, the anthropological notion of conflict has usually been derived from the biological concept of competition. In its most succinct form, a definition of competition reads as follows: 'Competition occurs when two or more individuals, populations, or species simultaneously use a resource that is actually or potentially limiting' (Spielmann 1991: 17).[3] Violence results from competition neither automatically nor inevitably. As a large body of research from biological anthropology demonstrates, there are numerous non-violent avenues to conflict solution (relocation, exchange, territoriality). In fact, conflicts are much more often settled by preventive or compensatory strategies than by violent confrontation. They may not be as immediately effective as violence, but they are also much less costly and entail a much lower risk of wasting lives or energy (cf. Albers 1993; Jochim 1981). Under specific circumstances, however, none of these options may be feasible. This is where violence can prove a highly efficient way to influence the competition's outcome in favour of one's own group. Violence, in other words, has been shown to confer clear adaptive benefits to the successful party, be they short-term (replenishing the resource base) or long-term (sustaining a given population level through time). It has been argued (cf. Abbink, this volume pp. 123–42) that these advantages of the application of violence as a long-term strategy have been instrumental in shaping a group's psychological proneness to the use of force in the evolutionary process.

By linking violent acts to a basic state of conflict we are making three implicit but important statements about their social ramifications:

1 Violence is never completely idiosyncratic. It always expresses some kind of relationship with another party and violent acts do not target anybody at random (although the individual victim is likely to be chosen as representative of some larger category).
2 Violence is never completely sense- or meaningless to the actor. It may seem senseless, but it is certainly not meaningless to victim or observer. As social action, it can never be completely dissociated from instrumental rationality.
3 Violence is never a totally isolated act. It is – however remotely – related to a competitive relationship and thus the product of a historical process that may extend far back in time and that adds by virtue of this capacity many vicissitudes to the analysis of the conflictive trajectory.

As the several caveats implicit in the above suggest, however, violence is more than just instrumental behaviour. As historically situated practice, it is informed by material constraints and incentives as well as by historical structures and by the cultural representation of these two sets of conditions.

But what, then, is violence? It is the assertion of power or, to paraphrase David Riches' important discussion of the subject, an act of physical hurt deemed legitimate by the performer and by (some) witnesses (Riches 1986: 8). Since the violent act is relatively easily performed and, at the same time highly visible and concrete, it is a very efficient way of transforming the social environment and staging an ideological message before a public audience (1986: 11). The great advantage of Riches' definition lies in its abstractness which allows for cross-cultural comparability, and in its addressing the essential ambivalence of violence as instrumental and expressive action.

Even if violence can ultimately be traced to a condition of conflict, not all competition must be solved by violent means. If violence is resorted to or not has little to do with human nature and is only in rare instances enforced by structural factors that make all non-violent avenues of conflict solution impracticable. It has everything to do with cultural factors. Conflicts are mediated by a society's cultural perception that gives specific meaning to the situation, evaluating it on the basis of the experience of past conflicts, stored as objectified knowledge in a group's social memory. How this process of social legitimation of violence is accomplished will be discussed below; let us first consider the important subject of power. At some point, conflicts can no longer be avoided or negotiated, but escalate to a long-term antagonistic relationship – a condition usually termed war by anthropologists. The concept of war describes a state of confrontation in which the possibility of violence is always present and deemed legitimate by the perpetrating party, and in which actual violent encounters occur on a regular basis. It also means a relationship of political collectivities above the family level, ranging from bands or segmentary lineages to states (or even multiple-state alliances). In none of these collectivities, even in the most 'egalitarian' band societies, is the decision to go to war reached unanimously by all group members. It is made by those who hold power in the society. As R. Brian Ferguson puts it, 'wars occur when those who make the decision to fight estimate that it is in their material interests to do so' (Ferguson 1990: 30).

The élite's interests are usually encoded in a moral idiom relating the imminent violent confrontation to anything from revenge obligations to religious imperatives, 'traditional' animosity or 'the good of the nation'. The ways and means by which this moral idiom is inculcated upon the minds of those who actually march into battle varies greatly between bands and states, of course. The important point remains, however, that while conflicts are caused by structural conditions like the unequal access to resources, population shifts or external pressures, wars do not automatically result from them. Wars are made by people who can be supposed to have based their decisions on some sort of rational evaluation.[4] More particularly, wars are made by those individuals, groups or classes that have the power successfully to represent violence as the appropriate course of action in a given situation. But war as a long-term period of antagonistic practice and ideology could not be sustained if only a small élite were to profit from it. Violence can prove a successful strategy for many different kinds of perpetrators.

'War is like a delicious piece of cake', writes the Croatian novelist Dubravka Ugrešić, 'that everybody wants a piece of: politicians, criminals and speculators, profiteers and murderers, sadists and masochists, the faithful and the charitable, historians and philosophers, and journalists' (Ugrešić 1995: 126; translation by IWS).

Georg Elwert (1997, 1998, 1999) has proposed the term 'markets of violence' to describe those arenas of long-term violent interaction, unrestrained by overarching power structures and mitigating norms, where several rational actors employ violence as a strategy to bargain for power and material benefits.[5] In this view, war is a game played by strategically planning leaders or élites in which those who actually commit acts of violence are no more than pawns who – at least momentarily – forgo detached refletion in favour of highly emotionally charged action. Still, at both levels, motivation follows a specific cultural grammar that defines the value and relative importance of material and social benefits (honour, prestige). This cultural grammar gives a more permanent meaning to the violent confrontation and thereby offers an additional motivational framework that holds out incentives beyond the individual actor's immediate interests. With all these rational considerations involved in the decision to use violence, once unleashed it still has a strong tendency to generate its own dynamic. Military confrontations are governed by their own logic of short-term tactical or strategic imperatives that are likely to be completely unrelated to the original causes of the conflict. The detailed descriptive analysis of how decision-making processes evolve, which cultural models are employed to assess a situation as calling for violent action and what kinds of social relations are invoked in order to reach a conclusion among the power-holding élite that is making the decision has been much neglected in anthropological research on war.

One additional feature of violence that needs to be mentioned is its performative quality. Violence without an audience will still leave people dead, but is socially meaningless. Violent acts are efficient because of their staging of power and legitimacy, probably even more so than due to their actual physical results. In other words, war as a long-term process only now and then culminates in real acts of violence, and both parties include lots of individuals who are not confronted with real violence at all, but violence as performance extends its efficacy over space and time and gets its message across clearly to the large majority of people who are not physically affected by it. Also, its performative quality makes violence an everyday experience (with all the consequences to society) without anybody actually experiencing physical hurt every day.

The symbolic dimension of violence, on the other hand, may also backfire against its perpetrators and make it contestable on a discursive level, not as a physical but as a performative act. As Peteet's (1994) research on the Israeli–Palestinian conflict has shown, the experience of violence can be framed quite differently by the victims and perpetrators. The victims can take the opportunity to subvert the dominant group's intention to intimidate them through the use of violence by attaching a cultural meaning of their own to the suffering (in this case, as a male *rite de passage*), a meaning that allows them to reclaim agency and political identity. This case reminds us that, even in a situation of clearly uneven distribution of power, violence must not automatically be considered the most efficient strategy of conflict resolution. It is a complex social phenomenon that under certain circumstances may not be a good strategic choice at all.

Comparing violence

Violence is never so specific and culturally bounded that it cannot be compared. There is a long tradition in anthropology of linking types of collective violence to types of society and arranging them on an evolutionary scale (cf. Otterbein 1994; Reyna 1994). Riches' definition lends itself very well to broad comparisons on a functional level. Violence is a basic form of social action that occurs under concrete conditions, targets concrete victims, creates concrete settings and produces concrete results. All of these dimensions are clearly accessible to comparative analysis. More specifically, violence can be compared in relation to its causes, the event itself and its results.

Causes: as already mentioned, violence results from confrontations caused by the competition over (social and/or material) resources. Part of this antagonistic relationship can be explained historically, but in order to persist to the present day there must also be more recent incentives for perpetuating the conflict. The causes are generally accessible to historical and ethnographic research.

Events: violent acts are highly visible and usually take place in a public arena, which makes it easy to document or reconstruct their processual aspects. Moreover, long-term confrontations explode in violent clashes that can be described and analysed as events, forms of social action clearly marked off in space and time from everyday practice or, in other words, as a 'ramified sequence of occurrences that is recognised as notable by contemporaries and that results in a durable transformation of structures' (Sewell 1996: 844).[6] Events take place in well-defined locales and within a recognisable timespan. Due to these features they can be easily inscribed in any form of cultural archive and are easily recalled and recreated. Unlike perpetually culturally mediated everyday practice, events stand out because of their historical qualities of notability and transformativity as uniquely suited for comparison across time and cultural boundaries.

By focusing on events as categories of analysis we do not follow the current postmodernist shift in anthropological research on violence. Many recent studies (cf. Daniel 1996; de Silva 1995; Feldman 1991; Nordstrom 1997; Nordstrom and Robben 1995; Poole 1994) privilege 'experience' as the most authentic form of knowledge and have abandoned an analytical approach in favour of a subjectivist focus on the impact violence has on the everyday life of individuals (including the researchers themselves). While we do not dispute that experience constitutes an important aspect of violence as a social phenomenon, as is demonstrated by many of the contributions in this collection, we are not convinced that a true understanding of violent acts can only be achieved by being exposed to it (directly or indirectly, through the narratives of those who are). A strongly subjectivist approach will also ultimately interfere with any effort to view one specific violent confrontation from a historical or comparative perspective. We argue that no violent act can be fully understood without viewing it as one link in the chain of a long process of events each of which refers to a system of cultural and material structure that can be compared to similar structural conditions anywhere else.

Results: violence produces unique experiences that are culturally mediated and stored in a society's collective memory. Their representation forms an important resource for the perception and legitimation of future violence. Yet it also produces tangible results ranging from dead bodies to the redistribution of space, the relocation of people or the occupation of new territory. These are empirical facts that can be discerned physically or reconstructed from the historical record, but these facts also become malleable in cultural discourse. There exists no more important resource for an ideology of violence than the representation of past violence, of former dead, former loss and former suffering.[7] On the other hand, the individual's material gain held out by the successful application of violence is a highly important incentive for people's active participation in violent conflicts.

Clearly, violence can be interpreted as an instrumentally rational strategy of bargaining for power. Yet by limiting our view to its operational properties in conflict solution we fail to grasp the dialectic nature of violence. It is also a form of symbolic action that conveys cultural meanings, most importantly ideas of legitimacy. Based on Weber's classic definition, the concept of legitimacy entails that a social order is accepted as valid either due to its historicity, to its emotional value or to instrumental reasoning (1972: 19). The legitimacy of violence can be based upon each (and usually all) of the three aspects: it presents itself as recreating ideas and behavioural models from the past; it appeals to strong feelings of social closure based on the experience of either superiority or suffering, as generated by this very tradition of confrontation; and it offers itself as the most direct route to asserting the interests of those collectivities established by the above two mechanisms.

This is obviously a highly abstract description. One must guard against essentialising notions of the legitimacy of violence, which may rather be described as the legitimate use of force *in a specific context*. The tricky question is how this context can be specified, if at all. In practice, the notion of legitimate violence is highly contestable even among members of the same society.[8] On the other hand, particularly the close relationship between religion and violence (cf. Girard 1977), from female circumcision to human sacrifice, has always challenged our relativistic tolerance and our modern understanding of violence as meaningful action. Notions of legitimacy and ideas of meaningful action are obviously much more elusive and culturally bounded than are the causes of conflicts – and thus, much less suitable for comparison. Still the anthropologist must address this cultural dimension of violence as part of any serious holistic inquiry.

Violent imaginaries

Violence needs to be imagined in order to be carried out. Groups do not strike out at random at the next accidental bystander but follow cultural models of appropriate action. War is framed in a code of legitimation that declares the assertion of interests to be related to moral imperatives. The most important code of the legitimation of war is its historicity. The symbolic meaning of prior wars is re-enacted and reinterpreted in the present, and present violence generates symbolic value to be employed in future confrontations. Wars are fought from memory, and they are often fought over memory, over the power to establish one group's view of the past as the legitimate one. From this perspective violence is not only a resource for solving conflicts over material issues, but also a resource in world making, to assert one group's claim to truth and history against rival claims, with all the social and economic consequences this entails. The important question is: how does the discursive link between past violence and present-day violence work? By what means is the legitimacy of violence impressed upon those who are to march into battle and those who are to cheer them on? Not even modern state élites with modern media apparatuses at their disposal can invent confrontations out of nothing. While in non-state societies war is usually a consensual endeavour, even in modern states there usually exists a hegemonic accord among the people that the violent course of action laid out by the élite is justified.

Violent imaginaries, the emphasising of the historicity of present-day confrontations, can be represented through narratives, performances and inscriptions. Each of these representational strategies are easy to manipulate and are highly fragmented in any larger social context. New versions of 'authoritative' representations proliferate in war, contingent on the position and strategic interests of those who disseminate them. As Campbell (1998: 43) stresses, it is particularly important to distinguish between the 'micronarratives' of the 'participant-observers' (the political actors) and the 'macronarratives' of the 'observer-interpreters' (the media and outside academics). There are even among the conflict parties wide variations in the degree of people's actual physical and emotional involvement in the conflict and of their acceptance of the hegemonic message. Neither a group's violent imaginary nor its interests must be considered as monolithic. They correspond with one another on a general level, but in practice each conflict party is made up of numerous subgroups pursuing their own agendas.

Narratives: these keep the memory of former conflicts and past violence alive in stories, either by glorifying one's own group's achievements and benefits (cf. Meeker 1979; Rosaldo 1980) or by the perceived injustices, losses or suffering incurred by one's own group (cf. Malkki 1995; Swedenburg 1995). This type of social memory can be easily capitalised upon by state élites and elaborated into a hegemonic ideology of violence (cf. Čolović 1995).

Performances: performative representations of violent confrontations are public rituals in which antagonistic relationships are staged and prototypical images of violence enacted. Different kinds of 'war ceremonies' play an important part in the preparation and aftermath of war expeditions in non-state societies, but such rituals have also been preserved or reinvented among groups in modern societies (cf. Jarman 1997; Zulaika 1988). In fact, a performative quality is part of most public appearances of leaders in wartime (for a classic example, one need only think of the staged arousal of war frenzy in fascist Italy and Germany).

Inscriptions: violent imaginaries can also be inscribed in the cultural landscape as images displayed on banners or murals (cf. Jarman 1997; Peteet 1996). In a time of dramatically increasing influence of visual media, the broadcasting of TV images serves the same purpose. The role of these visual displays of antagonisms has received fairly little attention from anthropologists as compared to textual representations.

The symbolism of these violent imaginaries contains several characteristic elements (cf. Zulaika 1988: 32–4):

- a strictly polarised structure of 'we : they' that no individual can escape and that leaves no room for ambiguity;
- the application of the principle of totality to all aspects of this dichotomy: any action or expression by the other party of the confrontational relationship is taken to be a threat or aggressive act that calls for defensive action;

- the identification of 'our' side with the survival and well-being of every single individual: the struggle is of vital importance for the life of the group and the lives of each of its members;
- the moral superiority of 'our' cause is not affected by the outcome of the struggle. A defeat will not eliminate the rightness of 'our' position;
- post-war society is portrayed in dire terms: there can only be complete victory or total defeat. The winning party will do everything to eliminate the losers physically or politically.

Elements of history are decontextualised and reinterpreted as part of a communal legend of confrontation, creating an imaginary of internal solidarity and outside hostility. Antagonistic discourses are not invented or discontinuous with history, but fragments of memory are shifted in order to constitute new definitions of collective identity.

In late modernity the most common currency of violent imaginaries are nationalism and/or ethnicity (cf. Appadurai 1998; Kapferer 1988). Given the highly fluid and vague nature of these categories, it seems ironic that they should have gained such deadly relevance in an age of globalisation when identities tied to space or history are becoming increasingly fragmented under the onslaught of new socio-economic imperatives. Indeed, many of today's 'ethnic conflicts' seem completely irrational at first sight. Yet as Appadurai suggests, there may be a certain logic behind these efforts to create a 'macabre form of certainty' (1998: 229) under these conditions by violently asserting an increasingly elusive local identity against 'others'. As the post-communist scenario shows, after the collapse of grand narratives and overarching power structures there is a need to create new bonds of loyalty, even if this involves redefining one's neighbour as an ethnic antagonist. The fact that ethnocidal violence can break out so suddenly in settings of former long-term peaceful coexistence, indicates that it is not the result of blind hatred but rather is perpetrated (or organised, anyway) by actors who are fully aware of what they are doing and who are pursuing concrete current interests. Ethnic cleansing may not be a viable strategy of achieving the goals it was intended to achieve, but it is, none the less, the result of planned, purposive action. Violent imaginaries do not turn into violent practices on their own account, they are always implemented through human agency.

The relationship between imaginaries and practices is complicated further by the fact that imaginaries are inherently positioned in social space. Perspectives on violent events can never be 'neutral' or 'objective'. The fundamental 'triangle of violence' includes perpetrators, victims, and observers, all of whom are caught up in their own interpretive frameworks and their own agendas (Riches 1986: 8–10). As Christian Krohn-Hansen reminds us, studies of violence tend to focus on the victim's perspective, often missing out on the perpetrator's view altogether. Yet, 'if we are to understand violence as performance, we must look at the motives and the values of the uses of violence' (1994: 367). A holistic interpretation of any violent event must be based on all three perspectives, at least theoretically. In reality, it has to rely on the one or two perspectives accessible to the researcher, most likely the victim's *or* the perpetrator's plus the observer's. Even this last – in theory the most detached – party's testimony will usually lean towards one side or the other. Moreover, the roles of perpetrator, victim, and observer – as useful as they are for highlighting one specific violent event – are not static over time. As conflicts escalate or new confrontations are built upon old antagonisms, victims may turn into perpetrators and vice versa, and observers may become active participants.

To take matters one step further, even the categorisation of action as violence tends to be contested (which, as Riches points out, is an essential property of violence). Cultural performances like human sacrifice, which seem extremely violent and revolting to the Western mind, are considered completely legitimate and ordinary by members of other cultures (possibly even by the victims, as some anthropologists suggest). Closer to home, the opinions about the death penalty as a common instrument of justice differ widely from Texas to Germany. Obviously the contestability of violence from a multiplicity of emic perspectives remains something to be incorporated even in the reconstruction of conflict's operational properties.

This finally leads us to the collecting of data about violence. As Nordstrom and Robben have shown in their book *Fieldwork Under Fire*, conditions of violence tend to confront us as anthropologists with our own humanity. Heike Behrend, writing about her research on war in northern Uganda, notes the lack of words to describe accurately her experiences (1993: 22). She calls the methods of anthropological fieldwork into question: ethnographic research on war provokes one to think and to act in opposition to someone, and no longer be an outside academic (1993: 18). Violence forces the 'neutral' researcher to take sides and makes detached 'participant observation' extremely problematic. Philippe Bourgois who conducted fieldwork among street-level drug dealers in East Harlem, one of the toughest ghetto neighbourhoods in the United States, describes in detail his personal difficulties in experiencing everyday violence and relates his changing attitudes during the three and a half years of his research. Like Behrend, he challenges the relevance of the anthropological tenet of cultural relativism ('cultures are never good or bad; they simply have an internal logic') that makes ethnographers 'never want to make the people they study look ugly' (1997: 15).[9]

In most cases, however, anthropologists are not in a position to observe violent events directly. Thus, we are usually dealing rather with a 'quadrangle of violence' in practice, adding the role of interpreter. Detached from the synchronicity of the participant observer, the academic analyst extracts his information from participants' narratives *after the fact* (maybe even decades or centuries later). As an outsider to the collectivities engaged in violent confrontation, he hardly ever runs the risk of turning into either a victim or perpetrator at a later stage. This does not mean, however, that the researcher is immune to the vicissitudes of the polysemantics of violence. He does not extract the truth, he just adds another – although usually more detached – perspective. He is likely to be in a position better suited to demystify earlier narratives about conflicts than those who were actively involved, or at least, physically exposed to the violent event. Still this may not keep the results of his research from being instrumentalised by future perpetrators to fuel another violent confrontation.

On the phenomenology of violence

Let us return in more detail to the three phenomenological dimensions of violence outlined at the beginning. To repeat, violence as a social fact can be viewed from three angles: as violence understood more narrowly as a form of interpersonal relations in everyday cultural reality, as conflict, and as war.

Thus, the focus on violence turns our gaze to the interpersonal level of legitimate physical hurt and its quotidian aspect as reflected in social reality and its cultural representation. The main intent of the implementation of violence from this perspective lies in its being harnessed to strategies of social closure, of defining 'us' and 'them' as clearly and diametrically opposed entities. The form and content of these strategies may vary widely across culture, time, and circumstances. Three typical cases are described by the contributors to this volume:

- Violence may constitute an integral element in a group's ideology of self-definition, creating a social imaginary as well as its anti-social/'outside' counterpart. This is demonstrated by Ernst Halbmayer's analysis of the various form of violent interaction and the symbolic value of cannibalism among the Yukpa of Venezuela.
- The same symbolic value is accorded cannibalism under very different circumstances, as shown by Bettina E. Schmidt. The image of culturally legitimate violence, embellished with all the horrific details of the colonial imagination, can be instrumental in establishing a faultline not only between 'own' and 'other', but between civilisation and savagery as well. This perspective clearly underlines the imaginary quality of violence, which may serve the same purpose of social in- and exclusion, no matter if its discursive representation reflects any real acts of physical hurt or not.
- Violence is not a mere exercise in discursive construction, however. As Stephanie Schwandner-Sievers's discussion of the everyday use of violence in present-day Albania shows, it is also a form of pursuing very real material interests. Yet, violent practice in Albania operates through the recourse to a tradition of feuding, reflecting and recreating cultural models of behaviour. It does not simply follow a short-term individualistic logic of instrumental rationality (although this does surely play a part in its recent upsurge in Albanian social relations), but generates its own ideology of legitimacy – in this case by tapping into the resource of traditional imaginaries of the social world.

Obviously, the dialectic of practice and imaginary in this perspective is most closely related to the notion of violence as elaborated by Riches. The act of physical hurt reflects a concept of legitimacy – the expression of an ideology of the social world and its boundaries, and of the different modes of behaviour toward different constituencies in this world, sanctioned by their historicity (reified as 'culture' or 'tradition').

The focus on conflict looks beyond everyday relations of violence and their discursive legitimation to the underlying causes for the establishment of this form of behaviour. Violence is identified as a strategy generated by competition over scarce resources, as a means to overcome or prevent situations critical for the survival of a given population.

- Under these circumstances, violence may become established as a viable long-term strategy of group maintenance and of a populations's physical and social reproduction. Notions of competition and resulting adaptive responses underlie the approaches of Jon Abbink and Ingo W. Schröder. Abbink, in particular, brings concepts derived from evolutionary psychology to bear on his study of Suri warfare to demonstrate how violence as an established strategy of external relations enhances the chances for group survival.
- Moreover, violence also offers short-term benefits of material gain, social recognition and the attainment of culturally defined goals (like revenge) outside the realm of material incentives. These goals must be viewed as expressions of a long-term cultural adaptation to a social reality characterised by competitive social relations, but they tend to develop a situative rationality of their own, reinforcing the selection of violence as the appropriate way of conflict solution at one specific point of time. The interplay of long-term and short-term aspects of conflict, along with other structural constraints (like colonialism) in the development of a historically documented 'war complex' is analysed by Schröder for the case of nineteenth-century Western Apaches.

As these analyses show, competition results from objective material conditions, but violence does not follow automatically, and it is not the only available option under these circumstances. Conflicts are perceived as such by actors guided by culturally prescribed criteria of evaluation and rationality. These imaginaries charter a course toward (or away from) violence by translating historical trajectories of experience into a moral code of appropriate behaviour under specific circumstances.

War, finally, is viewed as a long-term condition of violent interaction between clearly established groups of actors. A focus on violence from this perspective entails the notion that war is the result of a process of escalation, propelled (in part) by a dynamic of its own that tends to reproduce violence as dissociated from a condition of material conflict, through the reproduction of an ideology of antagonism. Although these properties of violent relations can be observed at all levels of social integration, the quality of war as a social reality of its own (as separate from everyday, 'civil' reality) is particularly typical of war in the world of modern state systems – be it between or within sovereign states. The contributions highlight three crucial characteristics of this kind of legitimate long-term mass violence:

- War's ability to make history and to be recreated through memory. Francesca Declich demonstrates through the analysis of refugees' tales from the war in Somalia that organised violence dramatically impinges upon the life of its victims, and how these experiences are used to represent the image of violence in social memory.
- War's ability to escalate and de-escalate, but always to progress along a historical trajectory of events. This quality is clearly shown by Peter Kloos' analysis of civil war in Sri Lanka, the development of which followed a course marked by several critical 'turning points', where the next step of escalation was initiated through a specific event.
- Its very quality of establishing a separate social reality that enforces its unique forms of social relations. Ivana Maček describes three modes of individual existence under the conditions of civil war in Bosnia (soldier – deserter – civilian) that are clearly set apart from everyday reality under conditions of peace and that draw everybody into the specific logic of life under violence.

Once again, these examples show that wars do not happen at random on their own accord but are made by reflexive human actors who may follow their own interests, but are as a majority manipulated (or even forced) by the state system's ruling élite. These élites reproduce or produce imaginaries of closure, of violent 'otherness', to mobilise the actual fighting squads.

On theoretical approaches

Cross-cutting these phenomenological foci, there is a triad of theoretical perspectives on violence which have been stated on pp. 1–2.

1 An operational approach that links violence to general properties of human nature and rationality and to general concepts of social adaptation to material conditions. It aims to explain violent action by comparing structural conditions as causes affecting specific historical conditions. Examples of this approach are the materialist perspective favoured by Schröder, Abbink's recourse to evolutionary psychology and the decision-making model applied by Kloos.
2 The cognitive approach is the most widely used to explain violence, and also the broadest – all of this volume's contributions subscribe at least to parts of it. It portrays violence as first of all culturally constructed, as a representation of cultural values – a fact that accounts for its efficacy on both the discursive and the practical level. Thus, violence is seen as contingent on its cultural meaning and its form of representation. It should be approached with careful attention to the sociocultural specificity of the historical context. Halbmayer's and Schwandner-Sievers' contributions demonstrate how ethnographic methodology can be employed to elucidate cognitive models of actors in violent confrontations. Schmidt, on the other hand, approaches the cultural discourse about violence from a literary perspective.
3 The experiential approach focuses on the subjective qualities of violence. It views violence as something the basic impact of which on life can only be grasped and is only reflected through individual experience. Violence, here, is highly contingent on individual subjectivities, and its meaning unfolds mainly through the individual's perception of a violent situation. This approach lends itself best to the type of post-modernist ethnography exemplified by the contributions of Declich and Maček that aim to elucidate the fragmented world of individual experiences of violence, of how worlds of war are refracted through the narratives of men and women who have been exposed to or threatened by violence.

The degree of compatibility that we have identified earlier as one of the pillars of an anthropological approach to violence, decreases from the first to the third of the above-mentioned foci. While the operational perspective looks for parameters transcending cultural specificity and the boundedness of violent events in time, space and society, the cognitive perspective derives its parameters from the social construction of the world by a collectivity bounded in time and space – which, after all, contains elements well suited for comparison. The experimental perspective tends to neglect cultural generality in favour of pure fragmented subjectivity. As we have stated above, the extreme proponents of this post-modernist view subscribe to a randomising view of violent events that negate the possibility and usefulness of anthropological comparison.

As it should have become apparent by now, we are wary of the idea of any simple, one-dimensional approach to violence. The dialectical perspective we have outlined above highlights the basic properties of violence as a social resource and points the way, as we believe, toward a fruitful analytical framework, but it does not preclude a wide variety of theoretical and methodological viewpoints to be successfully applied. This should be the message sent out by this volume.

Future directions: an anthropological approach to violence

In conclusion, we urge that research must strongly focus on the processual character of violent practices, linking them both to conflicts and to their cultural imagining and thus bridging the gap between the different anthropologies of conflict, war and violence. Clearly, violence and its various forms of social realisation represent a highly complex phenomenon that can be reduced to neither a mere mechanical reaction to resource stress or impulse of human nature nor to the random flexibility of discourse or individual subjectivity. Violence must be understood as a form of practice mediating between the historical boundedness of action in response to specific structural conditions and human creativity and the cultural quest for meaning.

An anthropological approach should adopt an analytical, comparative perspective in order to contribute to the understanding and explanation of violence, making it clear that:

- acts of violence are no sudden outbursts of aggressiveness devoid of historicity, meaning and reflexivity;
- violent imaginaries are no ephemeral constructions of fragmented subjectivities, nor are they the inevitable products of reified concepts such as 'cultural models' or 'traditions';

- violence is performed as well as imagined by reflexive, socially positioned human beings under specific historical conditions for concrete reasons.

Moreover, an anthropological approach should provide a clear description of overarching parameters for explanation: an understanding of the social imaginaries that shape the collective practice and representation of violence and a description of the subjective experience of violence and its narrative construction. And finally, it should pay special attention to the processual characteristics of violent action. These can be described through a four-stage model:

1. Conflict – the socio-economic contradictions at the base of intergroup competition.
2. Confrontation – the perception of these causes by the parties involved as relevant, creating an antagonistic relationship.
3. Legitimation – the official sanctioning of violence as the legitimate course of action through the imagining of violent scenarios from the past and their social representation. Questions such as the direction, timing and framing of violent acts are decided at this point.
4. War – if these three stages have been passed, violence is finally put into practice as a means to achieve specific ends.

It must be stressed again that violence as a cultural resource is employed only at the final stage of the process. None of the steps leading up to it are inevitable or irreversible. At the transition from one stage to another there are always alternative, non-violent courses of action for solving the conflict open to both parties. At each stage de-escalation may occur for a number of reasons and conflict parties may revert to peaceful interaction. Once again we stress here that violence is a resource in social relations. Just like in any other context, social relations are characterised by their diachronicity and are always likely to be renegotiated and redefined.

To the anthropological eye the above model may seem overly abstract (it does in fact owe a lot to models from political science; cf. Jung 1995), and we do indeed urge our fellow researchers not to stop at the mere description of the processual properties of conflicts. Anthropological models designed to explain the creation of a meaningful social universe are, in our view, uniquely well suited for the analysis of the social implementation of violence. The recourse to violence under specific conditions results from decisions that have narrowed down the number of options for conflict resolution to one. Anthropologists should try to understand the cultural mediation of real-world conditions that bring these decisions about. Examining the contributions to this volume, we find that a number of crucial questions have been raised: Why do intergroup relations in some cases oscillate between co-operation, coexistence, and confrontation over extended periods of time? Is it a question of power games being played by rational actors, the simple inability to cope with conflict through arbitration due to the lack of overarching institutions, or are 'cultures of violence' driven by motives not immediately related to instrumental reasoning? And what are the cultural concepts of war and violence through which these processes of confrontation are experienced, and by what means is violence implemented in one specific context? In other words, how exactly are conflicts thought and executed by those involved? Finally, by what means are histories of violence turned into agendas for (legitimate) violence? History does not present itself to a mnemonic community as 'given', history is made out of social memory by members of the community who have the legitimation to externalise notions of the past in public. Who are these individuals? What are the ideas and interests that motivate them?

Moreover, there may be no other form of social relations that has the propensity to recreate and reimagine collectivities and loyalties, to redraw or strengthen social boundaries as radically as violent confrontation. Invoking Simmel one more time, we suggest paying close attention to this dynamic property of violence that cannot only destroy lives and social bonds but is also a powerful instrument in the creation of social worlds (cf. Bowman, this volume pp. 25–46). Both sides of this Janus-faced quality of violence have only recently become painfully obvious to the world watching the horrors of war in the Balkans.

One final note of caution to our fellow anthropologists regarding research on violence: in the narratives generated by violent confrontations, to a greater extent than in most other social contexts, truth quickly falls by the wayside. True motives tend to be camouflaged by the aggressors, just as their suffering tends to be exaggerated by the victims. In fact, the dynamics of violence are very likely to create their own motives that in the minds of those involved easily take precedence over their original motivations and conceptions. Our call for attention to the cultural construction of violence notwithstanding, we do not believe that conflicts as historically generated trajectories can be properly understood simply by piecing together accounts from perpetrators, victims, and observers. All of these narratives of violence become salient only before the backdrop of the material and diachronic properties of conflicts. By bringing together these two divergent yet ultimately dialectically related aspects of violent confrontations, by viewing historical practice as reflecting cultural imaginaries and cultural modes of expression as structured by specific historical conditions, can anthropology make a unique contribution to our understanding of violence in the world.

Notes

1 In reference to the title of a popular book by the German anthropologist Karl Weule, '*Der Krieg in den Tiefen der Menschheit*' (Stuttgart 1916).
2 Although obviously closely interrelated, these three labels are by no means congruent and may, with some reservations, stand as representatives for the three types of approaches noted below.
3 cf. Jochim 1981 for a detailed discussion of the ecological approach to conflict. The same concept can be detected behind definitions of social conflict from sociology and political science (cf. Blalock 1989; Ross 1993).
4 Even if this rationality is also culturally mediated and may not be the same as the observer's.
5 The rationality of violence becomes especially apparent in Tilly's (1997) analysis of the creation of the modern nation state; for another recent rational-choice approach, cf. Kalyvas 1999.
6 We refer to Sewell's study for a thorough description of the sociohistorical analysis of events; cf. also Sahlins 1991.
7 This has been strikingly demonstrated by the recent conflicts in the former Yugoslavia (cf. Bowman 1994; Bax 1997; Hayden 1996; Verdery 1999).
8 This becomes especially apparent in relation to violent crime (a topic outside the scope of this book). At the Frankfurt Workshop, Ida Hydle's paper 'Murder without Motive?' (not included here) challenged notions of seemingly 'senseless violence' in our own society. In the summer of 1998 the case of a French policeman almost beaten to death by German hooligans made headlines, pointing toward the question if illegitimate violence becomes more acceptable in Western society if commited in a state of intoxication.

9 This attitude is relevant in the study of many violent subcultures. On the other hand, if we regard violence as contagious illness, as Girard notes for the Chukchi, maybe we should keep a watchful eye on anthropologists returning from research under violent conditions.

Bibliography

Albers, P. (1993) 'Symbiosis, merger, and war: contrasting forms of intertribal relationships among historic Plains Indians', in J. H. Moore (ed.) *The Political Economy of North American Indians,* Norman: University of Oklahoma Press.

Appadurai, A. (1998) 'Dead certainty: ethnic violence in the era of globalization', *Public Culture* 10: 225–47.

Bax, M. (1997) 'Mass graves, stagnating identification, and violence: a case study in the local sources of 'the War' in Bosnia Hercegovina', *Anthropological Quarterly* 70: 11–19.

Behrend, H. (1993) *Alice und die Geister: Krieg im Norden Ugandas,* Munich: Trickster.

Blalock, H. M., Jr. (1989) *Power and Conflict. Toward a General Theory,* Newbury Park and London: Sage.

Bourgois, P. (1997) *In Search of Respect: Selling Crack in El Barrio,* Cambridge and New York: Cambridge University Press.

Bowman, G. (1994) 'Xenophobia, phantasy and the nation: the logic of ethnic violence in former Yugoslavia', in V. Goddard, J. Llobera and C. Shore (eds) *Anthropology of Europe: Identity and Boundaries in Conflict,* London: Berg.

Campbell, D. (1998) *National Deconstruction. Violence, Identity, and Justice in Bosnia,* Minneapolis: University of Minnesota Press.

Clausewitz, C. von (1980)[1832–4] *Vom Kriege: hinterlassenes Werk des Generals Carl von Clausewitz,* Bonn: Dümmler.

Čolović, I. (1995) *Bordell der Krieger. Folklore, Politik und Krieg,* Osnabrück: Fibre.

Daniel, E. V. (1996) *Charred Lullabies. Chapters in an Anthropology of Violence,* Princeton: Princeton University Press.

de Silva, P. L. (1995) 'Studying Political Violence and Its Cultural Constructions', *Folk* 36: 61–89.

Elwert, G. (1997) 'Gewaltmärkte. Beobachtungen zur Zweckrationalität der Gewalt', in T. von Trotha (ed.) *Soziologie der Gewalt,* Opladen: Westdeutscher Verlag.

—— (1998) 'Gewalt als inszenierte Plötzlichkeit', in J. Koehler and S. Heyer (eds) *Anthropologie der Gewalt. Chancen und Grenzen der sozialwissenschaftlichen Forschung,* Berlin: Verlag für Wissenschaft und Forschung.

—— (1999) 'Markets of violence', in G. Elwert, S. Feuchtwang and D. Neubert (eds) *Dynamics of Violence. Processes of Escalation and De-*

Escalation in Violent Group Conflicts, Sociologus, Supplement 1, Berlin: Duncker & Humblot.

Feldman, A. (1991) *Formations of Violence. The Narrative of the Body and Political Terror in Northern Ireland,* Chicago: University of Chicago Press.

Ferguson, R. B. (1990) 'Explaining war', in Jonathan Haas (ed.) *The Anthropology of War,* Cambridge: Cambridge University Press.

Girard, R. (1977) *Violence and the Sacred,* Baltimore: Johns Hopkins University Press.

Hayden, R. M. (1996) 'Imagined communities and real victims: self-determination and ethnic cleansing in Yugoslavia', *American Ethnologist* 23: 783–801.

Jarman, N. (1997) *Material Conflicts. Parades and Visual Displays in Northern Ireland,* Oxford: Berg.

Jochim, M. A. (1981) *Strategies for Survival. Cultural Behavior in an Ecological Context,* New York: Academic Press.

Jung, D. (1995) *Tradition – Moderne – Krieg. Grundlegung einer Methode zur Erforschung kriegsursächlicher Prozesse im Kontext globaler Vergesellschaftung,* Münster: Lit.

Kalyvas, S. N. (1999) 'Wanton and Senseless? The Logic of Massacres in Algeria', *Rationality and Society* 11: 243–84.

Kapferer, B. (1988) *Legends of People, Myths of State. Violence, Intolerance, and Political Culture in Sri Lanka and Australia,* Washington, DC: Smithsonian Institution Press.

Krohn-Hansen, C. (1994) 'The anthropology of violent interaction', *Journal of Anthropological Research* 50: 367–81.

Malkki, L. H. (1995) *Purity and Exile. Violence, Memory, and National Cosmology Among Hutu Refugees in Tanzania,* Chicago: University of Chicago Press.

Meeker, M. E. (1979) *Literature and Violence in North Arabia,* Cambridge: Cambridge University Press.

Nordstrom, C. (1997) *A Different Kind of War Story,* Philadelphia: University of Pennsylvania Press.

Nordstrom, C. and Robben, A. C. G. M. (eds) (1995) *Fieldwork under Fire. Contemporary Studies of Violence and Survival,* Berkeley: University of California Press.

Otterbein, K. F. (1994) *Feuding and Warfare. Selected Works of Keith F. Otterbein,* Langhorne: Gordon and Breach.

Peteet, J. (1994) 'Male gender and rituals of resistance in the Palestinian Intifada: a cultural politics of violence', *American Ethnologist* 21: 31–49.

—— (1996) 'The Writing on the Walls: The Graffiti of the Intifada', *Cultural Anthropology* 11: 139–59.

Poole, D. (ed.) (1994) *Unruly Order. Violence, Power, and Cultural Identity in the High Provinces of Southern Peru,* Boulder: Westview.

Reyna, S. P. (1994) 'A mode of domination approach to organized violence', in S. P. Reyna and R. E. Downs (eds) *Studying War: Anthropological Perspectives*, Langhorne: Gordon and Breach.

Riches, D. (1986) 'The phenomenon of violence', in D. Riches (ed.) *The Anthropology of Violence*, Oxford: Basil Blackwell.

Rosaldo, R. (1980) *Ilongot Headhunting, 1883–1974. A Study in Society and History*, Stanford: Stanford University Press.

Ross, M. H. (1993) *The Culture of Conflict. Interpretations and Interests in Comparative Perspective*, New Haven: Yale University Press.

Sahlins, M. (1991) The return of the event, again; with reflections on the beginnings of the Great Fijian War of 1843 to 1855 between the kingdoms of Bau and Rewa, in A. Biersack (ed.) *Clio in Oceania. Toward a Historical Anthropology*, Washington: Smithsonian Institution Press.

Sewell, W. H., Jr. (1996) 'Historical events as transformations of structures: inventing revolution at the Bastille', *Theory and Society* 25: 841–881.

Simmel, G. (1908) 'Der Streit', in *Soziologie. Untersuchungen über die Formen der Vergesellschaftung*, Leipzig: Duncker & Humblot.

Spielmann, K. A. (1991) *Interdependence in the Prehistoric Southwest: An Ecological Analysis of Plains-Pueblo Interaction*, New York: Garland Publishers.

Swedenburg, T. (1995) *Memories of Revolt. The 1936–1939 Rebellion and the Palestinian National Past*, Minneapolis: University of Minnesota Press.

Tilly, C. (1997) 'War making and state making as organized crime', in *Roads from Past to Future*, Lanham: Rowman & Littlefield.

Ugrešić, D. (1995) *Die Kultur der Lüge*, Frankfurt: Suhrkamp.

Verdery, K. (1999) *The Political Lives of Dead Bodies. Reburial and Postsocialist Change*, New York: Columbia University Press.

Weber, M. (1972) [1921/22] *Wirtschaft und Gesellschaft: Grundriss der verstehenden Soziologie*, Tübingen: J. C. B. Mohr.

Zulaika, J. (1988) *Basque Violence. Metaphor and Sacrament*, Reno: University of Nevada Press.

Chapter 2

The violence in identity[1]

Glenn Bowman

'Violence', in its everyday usage, shares meaning with a term – 'violate' – which is etymologically derived from it. 'Violate', as a verb, means variously

> 1 To break, infringe, or transgress unjustifiably.
> 2 To ravish or outrage (a woman).
> 3 To do violence to; to treat irreverently; to desecrate, dishonour, profane, or defile.
> 4 To vitiate, corrupt, or spoil, esp. in respect of physical qualities.
> 5 To treat (a person) roughly or with violence; to assail or abuse.
> 6 To break in upon; to interrupt or disturb; to interfere with rudely or roughly.
>
> (OED 1971: 3635)

Implicit in all the above senses of the term 'violate' is the concept of an integral space broken into and, through that breaking, desecrated. Thus, in its passive grammatical sense, 'violate' indicates something 'characterised by impurity or defilement' as in, to use the *Oxford English Dictionary*'s own example, 'Take home the lesson to thee. . . . Who makest of this lovely land, God's garden, A nation violate, corrupt, accurst'.[2] The primary *Oxford English Dictionary* definition of the noun 'violence' – 'the exercise of physical force so as to inflict injury on, or cause damage to, persons or property; action or conduct characterised by this; treatment or usage tending to cause bodily injury or forcibly interfering with personal freedom' (ibid.) – relays with it this sense of an assault of one entity upon the integrity of another.

Other definitions of 'violence', however, cohabit with what the *Oxford English Dictionary* categorises as the primary one, specifically,

> force or strength of physical action or natural agents; forcible, powerful, or violent action or motion (in early use freq. connoting destructive force or capacity). Now often merging into next, with an intensive sense . . . great force, severity, or vehemence; intensity of some condition or influence.
>
> (ibid., definitions 3 and 4)

Etymologically it is these 'secondary' meanings which have precedence. Skeat, in *A Concise Etymological Dictionary of the English Language*, derives 'violent' through the French from the Latin *uiolentus*, 'full of might', which is formed as an adjectival form from *uiolus*, 'due to *uīs* (force)' (Skeat 1927: 594).[3] The *Oxford English Dictionary* derives 'violence' from the Latin adjective *violentia* (vehemence, impetuosity, etc.), itself derived through the Latin *violentus* from *violens* (forcible, impetuous, vehement, etc.) from *vīs*, strength (OED 1971: 3635). The noun 'violence' – which in its everyday connotation always presumes an object in relation to which it manifests itself – thus appears to be intransitive in its originary form, signifying a force or strength – a potential for action – pre-existing and independent of whatever object it may or may not act upon in the future. The etymology, in other words, foregrounds what the *Oxford English Dictionary* suggests is no more than a peripheral meaning. Violence, at least semantically, does not need a victim.

These philological burrowings may seem trivial at the beginning of a collection of essays examining, from a number of revealing perspectives, not only the ways violence manifests itself in different cultural contexts but also the roles our perceptions of the violences of others have played in forging our European cultures and the disciplines we wield in our examinations of others's cultures. The contributors have brought a substantial conceptual armoury to bear on the question of whether or not 'violence' can be examined comparatively, and a retrospective investigation of the pre-history of the term they are mobilising may seem regressive in light of the ground they have taken. My 'retreat' into European philology may seem even more pointless in light of David Riches' assertion – articulated in an earlier foray into the anthropology of violence (Riches 1986a) – that European terms do not always fit non-

European contexts and describe the practices developed therein.[4] Although Riches continues to use the term 'violence' in his study, he attempts to ground his usage in nuanced empirical investigations of various contexts – European and non-European – in which violence can be seen, and he substitutes for the culturally limited 'Anglo-Saxon meanings of violence' a definitional model he terms 'superior'. Riches focuses his analysis 'on the act of violence itself' (Riches 1986b: 8) and thus redefines 'violence' as 'an act of physical hurt deemed legitimate by the performer and illegitimate by (some) witnesses'[5] (ibid.). In both Riches' *Anthropology of Violence* and this volume the term 'violence' is forced to do analytical and conceptual work beyond the bounds of its normal employment, and we as anthropologists can only benefit from the new perspectives on an old topic these books have offered. Why, then, do I insist on dragging out the etymological dictionaries?

Riches' insistence on defining violence as 'an act of physical hurt' and on methodologically focusing on 'the act of violence' shifts the analytical emphasis of an anthropology of violence away from the source of violence (that which is capable of violence because it is 'full of force') and towards the socially embedded performance of a specific type of violence (that which acts upon a recipient). Schröder and Schmidt, who at least nominally adopt Riches' perspective,[6] are compelled by his definition to anchor their investigations on the observable performance of acts of violence against others who are subjected to that violence. While such a focus is indubitably appropriate to a discipline which bases its hypotheses on empiricist observation, the anthropology of violence's tendency to restrict its attention to acts in the course of which one integral entity violates or attempts to violate another's integrity prevents it from attending to other arenas in which violence operates, some of which I will argue are the *fora* in which the agents which threaten violence and are in turn threatened by violence are shaped. I will suggest in the following that violence is a force that not only manifests itself in the destruction of boundaries but as well in their creation, and that 'intransitive violence' (which may operate conceptually prior to manifesting itself in action) serves to create the integrities and identities which are in turn subjected to those forms of violence which seek victims. Violence – rather than being a performance in the course of which one integral entity (person, community, state) violates the integrity of another – may as well serve to generate integral identities by inscribing borders between something in the course of becoming an entity and its surroundings. Attention to etymology draws our attention to the context out of which a particular usage emerges at an historical moment, and in leading us to examine the process of differentiation that produces a particular meaning compels us as well to think of the meanings excluded and the reasons for those exclusions. In this case, the etymology of 'violence' foregrounds aspects of the term's semantic field which are not overtly manifest in the acts we define as violent. To see 'hurting' as an aspect of violence rather than as its core will compel us to ask 'what else does violence do'?

An examination of Pierre Clastres' anthropology of pre-state societies is provocative, in spite of the criticisms which have been directed at its 'primitivism',[7] because Clastres reveals the deep implication of violence towards other communities in the self-understanding of the Amerindian communities he worked with. In *The Archaeology of Violence* (Clastres 1994 [1977]) and elsewhere Clastres conceives of 'primitive society'[8] as a face-to-face community inherently antagonistic to any moves towards dissolving its unity and effecting a 'division . . . between those who command and those who obey' (Clastres 1994: 156):

> At its actual level of existence – the local group – primitive society . . . is at once a totality and a unity. A totality in that it is a complete, autonomous, whole ensemble, ceaselessly attentive to preserving its autonomy...A unity in that its homogeneous being continues to refuse social division, to exclude inequality, to forbid alienation. Primitive society is a single totality in that the principle of its unity is not exterior to it: it does not allow any configuration of One to detach itself from the social body in order to represent it, in order to embody it as unity.
>
> (Clastres 1994: 155)

At the core of the sociality informing 'primitive society' is thus not only an antipathy to any figure of power distinguishing himself or herself from the collectivity through impressing his or her individual will upon the rest but as well a consensus around the necessity to mobilise against any actions which would dissolve that face-to-face society into any larger collectivity:

> Primitive communities maintain a certain distance between each other, both literally and figuratively: between each band or village there are their respective territories, allowing each group to keep its distance. . . . [T]he hypothesis of friendship of all with all contradicts each community's profound, essential desire to maintain and deploy its being as single totality, that is, its irreducible difference in relation to all other groups, including neighbors, friends, and allies.
>
> (Clastres 1994: 157)

Clastres argues that primitive societies are inherently antagonistic to any extra-communal logics of generalised exchange (whether logics of friendship, kinship, or economic trade) because such logics call on the members of autonomous communities to identify with others beyond the bounds of that community and, through that identification, initiate a process of unifying 'the multiplicity of partial We's into a meta-We . . . [which would lead to] the elimination of the difference unique to each autonomous community' (ibid.). Clastres' 'primitives' see social concourse beyond the demographic limits of their immediate communities as antagonistic to the 'We' in which they find their identities, and implicitly recognise in this antagonism not only a threat to the intimate sociality which grounds their identity but as well the possibility of the emergence of an autonomous power to rule over them. From this recognition follows a profound social proclivity to warfare against 'the Other':

> Primitive society refuses: identifying with others, losing that which constitutes it as such, losing its very being and its difference, losing the ability to think of itself as an autonomous We . . . [T]here is, inherent in primitive society, a centrifugal logic of crumbling, of dispersion, of schism such that each community, to consider itself as such (as a single totality), needs the opposite figure of the foreigner or enemy, such that *the possibility of violence is inscribed ahead of time* in the primitive social being; *war is a structure of primitive society and not the accidental failure of an unsuccessful exchange.*
>
> (Clastres 1994: 157, 158, emphases mine)

Violence is not here an act which impinges upon a social context from a space outside of community (either that of deviance or of an

Other) or through the workings of contingency, but is a fundamental aspect of that context. The social is structured and maintained by the inherent promise (often realised) of violence at its borders.

Exchange between groups, which stands in the history of anthropology as the matrix out of which the social emerges,[9] is in Clastres' analysis predicated upon violence rather than threatened by its subsequent emergence:

> Primitive society constantly develops a strategy destined to reduce the need for exchange as much as possible: this is not at all a society for exchange, but rather a society against exchange. . . . [It is only] the state of war between groups [which] makes the search for alliance necessary, which [in turn] provokes the exchange of women.
>
> (Clastres 1994: 161, 163)

For Clastres such exchange – initially provoked by the need for (tenuous) alliances which the war-producing logic of difference brings about – will, if allowed to run its course, lead in time to the concentration of power in the hands of individuals or cliques who reorient violence so that it no longer serves to maintain the integrity and autonomy of the group but instead works violence *against* the community in furthering the transformation of the community into something other than what it had been. Such individuals or cliques come into being as a consequence of the necessity of co-ordinating the society's increased complexity, which itself devolves from the unification of previously distinct populations, from the institutionalisation of means of effecting exchanges between peoples who are not in daily face-to-face contact, from the articulation of new modes of communication and legitimation for binding communities which do not share the same histories or *habituses,* and from the mobilisation of hostile activities against societies bordering on the new social regime. In this instance violence, which had previously served as a force guaranteeing the perpetuation of a community's integrity through the warlike marking of a border between that in-group and others outside of it, begins its transformation into a bifurcated force for refashioning the character of the in-group and protecting the integrity of that new society it constructs. This violence acts on and for the group in the name of the group from sites of power (those occupied by priests, chiefs and royal families) easily distinguished from the spaces on and against which power works.

This development culminates in the emergence of modern state formations wherein some agents of the state appropriate to themselves the power to perform violence against outsiders as well as against 'deviant' forces within the society the state controls while others constrain and direct the non-deviant citizenry so that it serves to perpetuate and reproduce the order characteristic of the state.[10] With the emergence of such formations the process of discursively reconfiguring the 'violence' of authority so that it no longer appears as violence *as such* is in large part completed; henceforth 'constructive' violence comes to be seen as pedagogy and conformity while repressive state violence appears as the legitimate expression of the 'will of the people' which is rendered necessary by the state's responsibility to protect the citizenry it represents from the illegitimate violence of the peoples' enemies (external enemies of the state, criminals, revolutionaries, mad persons, etc.).[11] The 'transgressive' violence of the enemies of the state is seen to threaten the integrity of the state and its citizenry from places beyond the boundaries of the social even when, as is often the case, that violence emerges from within the population ruled over by the state (hence the discursive formulation of the locales of deviance, criminality, and insanity by legislative, academic and medical institutions). As the visible violence of the state is popularly accepted as defensive and as carried out by persons and institutions representing the will of the citizenry, the state is strengthened in its power when 'called upon' to manifest its violence against 'enemies of the state'. Often the threat of the 'other' (national enemies, spies, criminals, ethnic or religious minorities, the insane) will be amplified (if not invented) by organs of the state so that it can expand its power over those it claims to protect.

Few anthropologists would argue that it is our job to overthrow the state, but most would still argue that it should not be our role to strengthen its power. None the less, the focus on violence as a violative act – as 'an act of physical hurt deemed legitimate by the performer and illegitimate by (some) witnesses' – emphasises the deviance of violence (whether, as in classical sociology, of the criminal, or, as in the popular discourses analysed by Schmidt in this volume, the violence of the cultural other) and thereby masks what the violence of the state and the violence of enemies of the state share in common.[12] While few would object to the assertion that there are substantial differences between state and anti-state violences demonstrable in their means, their motives and their ends, fewer still would recognize that the perpetrators of these violences share, despite those differences, an intention to reshape the worlds of the people those violences touch, whether directly or through processes of memorialisation. In recognition of these facts, this volume focuses on the performative aspects of violence and of narratives of violence, and that emphasis, like that of Eileen Scarry's powerful study of torture (Scarry 1985), stresses that violence is 'world-making'. It is important that we focus on the fact that it is not simply violative violence (torture, rape, cannibalism, acts of war and the transgressive like) which makes and unmakes worlds in which humans act or fear to act. 'Defensive' and 'constructive' violences (RSAs and ISAs), which shape a world of rules, rights, and regimes and people that world with imagined communities of 'us' and 'others', are deeply invested in the work of playing images of integrity off against the threat of images of violation, and we must attend in our analyses of social formations and deformations to the ways violences – violative and as well as 'defensive' and 'constructive' – shape and reshape our identities.[13]

Dean closes his review of *Chronicle of the Guayaki Indians* by accusing Clastres of 'unabashed pristinism' and by stating that Clastres' work is a latter-day manifestation of 'anthropology's intellectual legacy of primitivism, which needs to be checked before the discipline can continue to fulfil its mission as a critical voice in the shaping of contemporary local and global affairs' (Dean 1999: 11). It is true that Clastres' fascination with what appears to him to be the *zero degree* of state organisation gives his work a neo-Rousseauian flavour which is very much out of fashion in the current day.[14] I am forced, however, to move beyond Clastres' material not because, like Dean, I feel it is 'romantic . . . [and] essentializ[ing]' but because Clastres, in showing the Guayaki to be a paradigmatic case of absolutely non-statist organisation, does not show identities being formed but presents them as simply – and perhaps primally – already in place. When Clastres writes that,

> for a Guayaki tribe, relations with Others can only be hostile. . . . There is only one language that can be spoken with them, and that is the language of violence. This stands in

> surprising contrast to the Atchei's clear and consistent desire to eliminate all violence from relations among companions (Clastres 1998: 237)

he presents us with a social condition which can only be opposed to those of other societies already caught up in developing in the direction of 'proto-statist' and 'statist' formations. We can imagine (and today witness) the Guayaki being violated (rendered impure, defiled) by movements to reify political authority within and over their community, but we cannot conceive of how their idea of community came into being in the first place.[15] If violence against others is a structural principle of community, how could community exist before others were encountered? Yet, how could there be others to encounter if there wasn't already a community existing in terms of which to think otherness? Clastres shows, synchronically as it were, that violence and identity are profoundly interwoven in Amerindian society. His opposition of primitive non-statist societies to proto-statist and state societies enables us to think of a genealogy of violence within which two sorts of violence emerge within the space of the social – one normative and defensive, the other deviant and violative. What Clastres' ethnography does not show is identity arising out of violence, and this – rather than simply the intermingling of violence and identity – must be demonstrated if violence is to be seen as a force that is creative as well as destructive.

Simon Harrison, in *The Mask of War: Violence, Ritual and the Self in Melanesia*, contends that amongst the villages of the Manambu lineages in the middle Sepik region of Papua New Guinea 'peaceful sociality within and between communities is [normally] taken for granted' (Harrison 1993: 149). However, the intrasociality (characterised by trade and gift exchanges between communities) which links persons across a wide and potentially unbounded social field is periodically shattered by rituals performed by the men's cults of the region which discursively compel members of the communities within which those cults operate to perceive peaceful exchanges between communities as acts of aggression rather than co-operation. Manambu men's cults 'create' a threatening 'outside' by dividing a terrain which was previously the 'inside' of sociality into two opposed sectors – that of 'us' and that of 'them'. In the Manambu region this division is effected by positively valorising certain types of social interaction (those pertaining to kin and ritual relations) and condemning others as collaborations with the enemy (trading relations with neighbours, hospitality towards guests, gift exchanges with members of adjacent communities). Because peaceful sociality within and between communities is normally taken for granted:

> The only way that bounded groups can form is through purposive action *against* that sociality. The sociality itself cannot be extinguished, only transformed into a sociality of a different kind. There is no choice whether to have social ties with other communities; they can only have such ties. The only possibilities are that these social ties may be peaceful or violent.
> (Harrison 1993: 149)

In reinterpreting elements of intrasocial interaction manifesting co-operation between communities as signs of violence committed against the ingroup by its enemies the members of these cults – who are in effect 'warriors in waiting' – are able to dominate the communities through creating a shared perception of the necessity for mobilising for war. The men 'transform a conception of themselves as simply a coresident collectivity of kin and neighbours interacting in various ways with each other and with outsiders into a conception of a specifically political entity independent of others' (ibid.: 150). Identities are thus not only formed for the men, but new modalities of identity are generated for all the members of the community (as well as for those in the communities warred against). War thus produces particular crystallisations of sociality out of what had previously been larger networks of interaction. The men's cults, by propagating violence, produce new realities:

> The Melanesian men's cults were not simply cultural responses to a violent world, but attempts, specifically by men, to prescribe such a world whether or not it actually existed at the level of behaviour. The cults were not simply functional adaptations to war but were male organisations for 'producing' war and for producing the bounded groups to wage it.
> (Harrison 1993: 149)

In some ways of course the situation described by Harrison in Melanesia could be seen as a transformation of (or development out of) that presented by Clastres for Paraguay; the Manambu of Avatip village may well be acting as would the Guayaki were the latter, lured by trade and exchange into peaceful relations with their neighbours, to have subsequently rebounded from that sociality and returned to their autonomous groupings. Certainly Harrison says of the Manambu that:

> [t]hey fought and fostered war in their cult, not because they lacked normative ties beyond the village but, quite the opposite, *precisely because they had such ties* and could only define themselves as a polity by acting collectively to overcome and transcend them.
>
> (Harrison 1993: 150)[16]

Certainly it is the case that the boundaries inscribed by the activities of the Avatip men's cults activate territorial divisions which pre-existed the initiation of antagonistic relations. While peacetime Manambu sociality draws together spatially distinct communities by establishing trade and gift exchange relations between them, there none the less remains a discrete 'inside' which engages the 'outside' on friendly terms; Harrison describes his generalised sociality as a 'sociality between groups' (ibid.: 23). In a situation of inter-communal warfare these groups render themselves once more distinct by changing the sorts of 'goods' which pass through the territorial boundaries between them from goods which assert mutual dependency (trade objects, gifts, guests) to those which assert antagonism (bellicose rhetorics, raiders, cut-off heads). In this systolic and diastolic movement between open and restrained sociality one finds resonances with the structural oscillation Leach described between *gumsa* and *gumlao* modes of social organisation among the Kachin people of Highland Burma (Leach 1954).

It is not, however, the structural constraints and limited social play of tribal communities which I want to evoke in my final example of the creative powers of violence. It seems, throughout the previously discussed examples, as though a dynamic force has mobilised the various social formations we have observed. In both the Guayaki and Manambu instances, violence against others is consequent on perceptions by the war-making communities of a profound threat offered to their being by the presence of the others. The Guayaki are presented by Clastres as living with a perpetual awareness that sustained interactions with others will mortally wound the way of living that the members of the isolate community share, and this sense of the threat of sociality with the other leads, in the shorter rather than longer term, even to the violent termination of alliances with groups with whom they have banded together to war against others. Similarly the men of the Manambu men's cults are literally divided from the forces which maintain them and their communities during times of peace. In situations of war, on the contrary, they reunite with the spirits from whom they were separated in mythical times:

> When men went on a raid all these beings were believed to go into battle with the men and fight invisibly alongside them. . . . [I]t was not just the men who went to war but the very resources for which they fought – their entire ritual system, their rivers, lakes and their total means of livelihood – took up arms and went with them.
>
> (Harrison 1993)

Like Bertrans de Born in Ezra Pound's 'Sestina: Altaforte', the men of the Avatip men's cult Harrison worked with were only men when they were at war:

> I have no life save when the swords clash . . .
> Then howl I my heart nigh mad with rejoicing . . .
> Hell grant soon we hear again the swords clash!
> Hell blot black for alway the thought 'Peace'!
>
> (Pound 1971: 1386)

In each of these cases, it can be argued that the 'threat' perceived as devolving from the situations the people war to escape is 'unreal' or 'illusory', but in terms of that powerful collocation of tradition, mythology, rumour and shared practice which makes up a lived world these beliefs are as real as the worlds they inhabit. They are, in other words, 'to die (or kill) for'.

The 'threat' which these people perceive as threatening to strike at the very core of their being is what I would, following Laclau and Mouffe, term an 'antagonism'. A confrontation with an antagonism is not a competition since, in a competition, both the winner and the loser emerge from their struggle as the subjects who entered into it; the only difference is that one will have acquired an advantage or object for his or herself which the other will have failed to grasp. An antagonism is different since in the case of an antagonism the subject is himself or herself put at risk by the confrontation; 'the presence of the 'Other' prevents me from being totally myself' (Laclau and Mouffe 1985: 125). In some instances – such as that cited by Laclau and Mouffe of a peasant who can no longer be a peasant because of the landlord who is evicting him from the land he works – the relationship is quite material. In others – and I think here of Brian Moeran's study of violent popular films in Japan wherein the fictional gesture of extreme and transgressive violence is an inscription that enables both audience and author to fantasise overcoming the antagonism of a mortality that will erase them and their mundane acts (Moeran 1986) – the perception of antagonism and the response to it may seem deeply subjective and even poetic. An antagonism is, furthermore, not something as easily evaluated as 'a matter of life or death'; many persons would feel that to carry themselves badly in battle and to survive it marked (even if only by themselves) as cowardly would be far more antagonistic to their selves than to die well in battle. An antagonism is perceived as a threat to the subjectivity of the person threatened, and for that reason its perception will depend strongly not only on cultural determinants but as well, and to varying degrees, on particular life histories. What antagonisms hold in common is that they put the self at risk, and that they are perceived as needing to be overcome if the subject is to endure. The Guayaki instance – where the dissolution of the face-to-face community into wider social networks threatens the world which enables the members of the group to be who they are – like that of the Manambu men – where the persistence of peace is antagonistic to identities which can only be sustained in situations of war – demonstrate the way perceptions of antagonism work in relatively uncomplex societies to stabilise identities and to create and sustain social groupings.

I would like in closing briefly to refer to a contemporary situation which I have studied, both through fieldwork as well as through books and newspapers, over the past ten years. Unlike the previously discussed examples, this situation involves modernised complex societies with a long experience of statehood. I would like to examine the period leading up to the past decade of warfare in the late Socialist Federative Republic of Yugoslavia, which we now refer to as 'Former Yugoslavia'. I do not intend to delve deeply into the history of the region or into ethnographic studies of it; the story of 'the death of Yugoslavia' is familiar to most readers, and I list below some of the ethnographic and historical work on the region which I have found useful (or have written).[17] Yugoslavia's peoples have been radically transformed over the past fifty years as varying experiences of antagonisms – individual and collective – have led to the constitution of numerous groupings and regroupings. There have been numerous advocates – with various agendas – testifying to the enduring and fixed identities of the people who make up Yugoslavia's national groupings,[18] but the evidence suggests instead that identities have – in the course of encounters with circumstances interpreted as personal and/or collective antagonisms – been reformulated and subsequently fixed into forms which differ radically from those which have preceded them. Here, we do not see the oscillation that was implicit in Harrison's work and, perhaps, latent but unobserved in the tribal societies examined by Clastres. We see instead radical disruptions of previous modes of life, and the articulation of strategies of opposition to perceived antagonisms which, in the course of being worked through amidst the contingency of events, result in the recognition of new solidarities which create new subject positions to defend. Violence, here, engenders identity.

Yugoslavia was a state born out of war, and the federation which emerged from the Second World War, under the leadership of Marshall Tito, was shaped by the region's experience of the war. 'During the Second World War the conquerors not only destroyed the state, but they set its components against each other in an unprecedented way, for never before had there been physical conflict among the Yugoslav peoples as such' (Pavlowitch 1988: 14). Over one million of a pre-war population of seventeen million were killed, and Paul Garde estimates that eighty per cent of the deaths were inflicted on Yugoslavs by Yugoslavs (Garde 1992). As a consequence of Tito's and the partisans' recognition that the state was vulnerable to external attempts to subvert and destroy it, especially through mobilising nationalist insurrection as the Germans and Italians had during the war, the state propagated a powerful ideology of *bratstvo i jedinstvo* ('brotherhood and unity') which promoted economic and political equality between the national elements making up the federation and which repressed, with all the necessary state violence, the emergence of any nationalist tendencies within the national groupings, tendencies which the government (and many of the people) saw as antagonistic to the survival of Yugoslavia. Through the development of a powerful state apparatus, focused on the Yugoslav National Army, and the careful playing off through the following twenty-five years of its non-aligned status as a means of garnering economic support from both Soviet and capitalist states, Tito and the Communist Party were able to maintain authority, provide a decent standard of living for most of the population (supported by massive loans from the IMF and elsewhere as well as by strong dependence on the export of Yugoslav *gastarbeiters* to Western European nations), and suppress and occasionally violently crush any emergence of nationalist mobilisation.

In the 1980s, however, the whole carefully constructed edifice began to crumble. The Arab Oil Embargo of the 1970s had seriously damaged the Western economies, and many of the loans which had so profligately been granted to Yugoslavia to lure it towards the capitalist road began to be called in. Simultaneously, Yugoslavia's ability to export both its labour and its goods was impaired. By 1984 Tito was dead and the economy was in tatters with an unemployment level of fifteen per cent, inflation at sixty-two per cent, and a drop in the average standard of living of thirty per cent from its 1980 level (Mencinger 1991: 76–9). A general disgruntlement began to set in throughout the country as state policies began to be seen not to defend the people and their standard of living but to be attacking them; in the early 1980s a wide range of assertions – expressed in idioms ranging from the economic and political to those of art and culture (Mastnak 1991) – began to articulate perceptions of the antagonism of *the state* to *its people* .

These expressions did not, however, fall 'naturally' into a nationalist idiom. Tito's anti-nationalist policies and the modernisation processes which had accompanied them had to a large extent submerged the idiom of national identity beneath a flood of contending discourses on selfhood. Rural migration to the cities and to areas outside Yugoslavia where money could be earned had eroded much of the pre-communist rural isolation. In the cities a trans-Yugoslav cosmopolitanism had developed around work, education and cross-marriage. The violence of the state was thus not initially perceived as inflicted upon one's national being but appeared to attack people's abilities to earn and save money, play or listen to rock music, call for greater representation in political forums, and so on. All Yugoslavians were afflicted by the declining standard of living and the clumsy moves of the state to enforce cultural and economic homogeneity during this period, and within the republics the state's antagonism to personal fulfilment struck at all residents, regardless of whether or not they were of the ethnic majority.

The discursive shift to nationalist discourse occurred through the intervention of republican politicians who created 'national' platforms from whence they could launch bids to increase their holds on power in a Yugoslav state characterised, after the death of Tito, by a vacuum at the political centre. To gain power they had to consolidate their holds on the dispersed dissatisfactions which had grown exponentially after the breakdown of Titoist hegemony (Ramet 1985), and many did so by inventing ethnically-defined constituencies to represent. The general strategy followed throughout the regions was to convince the people that the reason they could no longer live in Yugoslavia the way they believed they had a right to was because the communist state – aligned with other national groupings which benefited from depriving them of their rightful national heritage – was expressing towards them the antagonism with which it had treated other members of their national constituencies over the past forty-five years. People whose individual encounters with a collapsing economy and an increasingly paranoically repressive state convinced them that the state had produced a situation which was antagonistic to them as individuals were faced, as regional elections mobilised the federation in the late 1980s, with nationalist politicians (many of whom had been previous members of the communist bureaucracies) who told them that their sufferings as individuals who happened to be Slovenes, Serbs, Croats or whatever were in fact symptomatic of the sufferings that all of the respective national group's population – dead or alive – had had inflicted upon it over the past decades by an antagonistic state and/or antagonistic neighbouring national groups. Nationalist campaign rhetorics were grounded not on calls for reforms and changes in the Yugoslav constitution but on platforms which argued that the state was dedicated to the destruction of the nation and, for that reason, had itself to be destroyed. I was, for instance, in Ljubljana during the campaigns for the Slovene election and was struck by the sight of anti-state campaign stations bedecked with pictures of caves (*foibe*) filled with the bones of persons killed during the massacres which had taken place at the close of the Second World War. Although the persons the partisans and others had killed came from various national groupings and political movements, the captions on the photographs said simply 'This is what *They* did to *Us*'. The assertion was direct – 'the communists killed Slovenes *en masse* as they came to power' – and the implication needed no further elaboration – 'and subsequent policies from the communist state towards the Slovenes have been a continuation of national genocide by other means'. This rhetoric called on people *as Slovenes* to recognise that communist violence towards Slovenes in the past was *qualitatively the same as* the state's violence towards them in the present. Individuals encountered antagonisms which threatened them with the impossibility of being what they had previously been as individuals, and were subsequently taught, first of all that much worse was to come, and second that they now were sharing the experience of the state's antagonism with a nation of others. The explosion of nationalist rhetoric which accompanied the opening year of the war (which encompassed a massive production of revisionist, nationalist histories), along with prolific evidence of attempts by respective groups to wipe out others, provided people who responded to being addressed in national terms with evidence of the previously concealed violence which had afflicted 'their people's' pasts as well as irrefutable proofs of the need to kill others in order that they, and the nation with which they were now conjoined, would endure.

In Yugoslavia people whose experience of relative deprivation in relation to a more affluent and liberal past were easily convinced that violence had been performed against them by some agent who had 'stolen their pleasure'. Clever political manipulation, and the possibility of presenting an earlier period's 'defensive violence' (the repression of nationalism) as an example of a 'nation theft' (Zizek 1990) which was in fact a 'theft of being', enabled various political cliques to come to power on the back of a popular will to destroy the antagonism which they experienced. Out of that rage, and the will to destroy the other before it destroyed 'us', were forged strong collective identities which in time – and after extreme genocidal violence against previous neighbours – gave rise to a multitude of new nations. It is, I believe, important to acknowledge that these new nations, even when they took old names, were not resurgent identity formations brought back into being by the collapse of communism but new inventions of community – far less tolerant of alterity than had been previous ones – which had been imagined and then carved out of multi-ethnic communities in response to fantasies of the violence the others would carry out on 'us' if we did not first destroy them through pre-emptive violence.

I began this chapter by suggesting that violence was a force for creating integrities as well as one that simply violated, polluted and destroyed already existing entities. In the course of developing that idea I have shown that identity politics forms borders which enclose an 'I' or a 'we' and exclude – oft times violently – others. Through examining Pierre Clastres' material on Amerindians' war-based wills to autonomy and then Simon Harrison's men's cults which crystallise identities by attacking sociality I came to suggest that communities, like individuals, draw borders not so much to assert presence but to exclude the influence of that which is perceived as threatening to the persistence of that presence. I then suggested that an entity's perception of what Laclau and Mouffe call an 'antagonism' – a presence which is believed radically to threaten the persistence of that quiddity which marks the being of an entity – may precisely provide the spur that drives an entity to mark out the boundaries of its identity and to 'defend' them with violence – a violence often manifested aggressively (pre-emptively). It is important to stress that a perception of antagonism is sufficient to impel individuals and communities to boundary marking, maintenance and defence. Identity may be far more inchoate than is the sense of threat to its persistence that an antagonism provides. Attributions of antagonisms need not be groundable, and it is often the case that an enemy is sited and a programme of 'defensive' violence inaugurated without any 'real' justification. The instance of the bloody dissolution of Yugoslavia was cited as a situation in which the state – and later ethnic groups seen as antagonistically allied with the state against the interests of national communities – served as the *foci* around which nationalist politicians invented constituencies by mobilising generalised dissatisfactions and both directing them towards and attributing them to the antagonism of the other. In designating an other against which destructive violence must be mobilised, an entity realises – through the negation of that it would negate – what it is it fights to defend.

Notes

1 With apologies to Max Gluckman (Gluckman 1956) whose title, 'The Peace in the Feud', inspired mine.

2 Harriot Hamilton King, *The Disciples*. 1873, p. 300, quoted ibid.
3 'Violate' is from the past participle of the Latin *uiolāre*, 'to treat with force', formed – again – as if from the adjective *uiolus*, due to *uīs* (ibid., 593).
4 Riches 1986b: 1–3, see also Parkin 1986: 204–5.
5 His earlier 'commonsensical' and 'Anglo-Saxon' definition, which focused on the performer of violence as actor, saw violence as 'the intentional rendering of physical hurt on another human being' (ibid: 4).
6 On p. 3 they answer the query 'what, then, is violence?' with 'It is the assertion of power or, to paraphrase Riches' important discussion of the subject, an act of physical hurt deemed legitimate by the performer and by (some) witnesses'.
7 See, for an interesting debate on the contribution of Clastres (who died in an automobile crash in 1977) to anthropology, Bartholomew Dean's review of Clastres' *Chronicle of the Guayaki Indians* (1998, originally 1972) in *Anthropology Today* (Dean 1999) and Jon Abbink's response in the same journal (Abbink 1999). Clastres' *Chronicle* offers further insight into the issues of violence and identity, particularly in chapters five and six (Clastres 1998: 193–274).
8 For Clastres what characterises primitivity is the refusal of communities to allow power to separate itself from the collectivity and to – from that autonomous position – impose itself on the collectivity by claiming to represent it. Primitivism is, for Clastres, a strong virtue, and it is this valorisation which Bartholomew Dean – who wants to see indigenous people mobilise through media and political representation to fight for collective rights – finds objectionable.
9 See, for instance, 'The Principle of Reciprocity', chapter V in Lévi-Strauss' *The Elementary Structures of Kinship* (Lévi-Strauss 1969: 52–68).
10 Althusser, in his seminal 'Ideology and ideological state apparatuses' (Althusser 1971), distinguishes between RSAs (repressive state apparatuses) and ISAs (ideological state apparatuses), noting that the former – which includes military forces, police forces, judicial apparatuses as well as institutions dealing with mental health – mobilise literal violence against enemies of the state – both within and outside – whereas the latter work to enculturate and perpetuate subjects – obedient citizenry – whose acceptance of the state's discursive organisation of the real serves to naturalise the institutional powers which perpetuate the state's hegemony.
11 See, for a stimulating examination of the discursive reformulation of state violence into techniques of constraint and discipline, Foucault's *Discipline and Punish* (Foucault 1977).
12 Edmund Leach points out in an essay on terrorist violence that both 'anti-state' violence and the violence with which the state 'protects' itself and its people are extra-societal violences which come from

beyond the bounds of the communities through which, around which and over which they contend (Leach 1977).

13 The distinction Macek makes in this volume between 'soldiers' and 'civilians' on the one hand and 'deserters' on the other reflects the deserters' experiencing of the state's 'defensive' violence from a position outside of the ideological frame which, for both civilians and soldiers, provides that violence with its legitimacy and marks it as radically other than the violence of the society's enemies.

14 But see Abbink's defence of Clastres which criticises Dean's investment in 'emerging stereotype[s] in 'globalisation studies'' (Abbink 1999). Certainly Dean's implication in development – which leads him to celebrate the fact that 'private and public organisations are now providing critically needed financial support and technical support for the creation and on-going operation of indigenous advocacy organisations' (Dean 1999: 10) – sets him firmly in opposition to Clastres who would – rightly or wrongly – see such resourcing as a direct cause of the fatal division of egalitarian communities into 'those who represent' and 'those who are represented'.

15 Implicit in Clastres' argument, as in any presentation which argues from 'origins', is the problem of circular reasoning. I would take here the stimulating yet finally philosophically problematic arguments of Durkheim and Mauss about the origins of religion and of primitive classification (Durkheim 1912; Durkheim and Mauss 1903) as paradigmatic: how can society represent itself to itself if it only develops the idiom in which representation can occur in the course of representing?

16 Against the egalitarian tenor of Clastres' analysis is Harrison's point that when the Manambu communities are at war the men are empowered – as warriors and ritual leaders – over other members of the community.

17 See particularly Pavlowitch 1988; Allcock 1992; Feldman *et al.* 1993; Bowman 1994; Bringa 1995; Silber and Little 1995; Kirin and Povrzanovic 1996; Godina 1998; and Bowman forthcoming.

18 The myth of the eternal enmity between the peoples of the Balkans has a long history (see Glenny 1999 for a critical assessment of its usage by the Great Powers) but fell out of use between the latter part of the Second World War when the British threw their support behind Tito and approximately 1993 when most of the NATO countries decided that Yugoslavia should be divided along ethnic lines.

Bibliography

Abbink, J. (1999) 'Doing justice to Clastres', *Anthropology Today* 15: 21.

Allcock, J. (1992) 'Rhetorics of nationalism in Yugoslav politics', in J. Allcock, J. Horton and M. Milivojevic (eds) *Yugoslavia in Transition*, London: Berg.

Althusser, L. (1971) 'Ideology and ideological state apparatuses (notes towards an investigation)', in L. Althusser (ed.) *Lenin and Philosophy and Other Essays*, London: Verso.

Bowman, G. (1994) 'Xenophobia, fantasy and the nation: the logic of ethnic violence in Former Yugoslavia', in V. Goddard, L. Josep and C. Shore (eds) *Anthropology of Europe: Identity and Boundaries in Conflict*, Oxford: Berg Press.

—— (forthcoming) 'Constitutive violence and rhetorics of identity: a comparative study of nationalist movements in the Israeli-Occupied Territories and Former Yugoslavia', *Social Anthropology* (forthcoming 2000).

Bringa, T. (1995) *Being Muslim the Bosnian Way: Identity and Community in a Central Bosnian Village*, Princeton Studies in Muslim Politics, Princeton: Princeton University Press.

Clastres, P. (1994) [1977] 'Archaeology of violence: war in primitive societies', in P. Clastres (ed.) *Archaeology of Violence*, New York: Semiotext(e).

—— (1998) [orig. 1972] *Chronicle of the Guayaki Indians*, New York: Zone Books.

Dean, B. (1999) 'Critical re-vision: Clastres' chronicle and the optic of primitivism', *Anthropology Today* 15: 9–11.

Durkheim, E. (1912) *Les Formes Élémentaires de la Vie Religieuse: le Système Totémique en Australie*. Paris: Alcan.

Durkheim, E. and Mauss, M. (1903) 'De quelques formes primitives de la classification: contribution à l'étude des représentations collectives', *Année sociologique* 6: 1–72.

Feldman, L., Prica, I. and Senjkovic, R. (eds) (1993) *Fear, Death and Resistance: An Ethnography of War, 1991–1992*, Zagreb: Matrix Croatica.

Foucault, M. (1977) [1975] *Discipline and Punish: The Birth of the Prison*, London: Allen Lane.

Garde, P. (1992) *Vie et Mort de la Yougoslavie*, Paris: Fayard.

Glenny, M. (1999) *The Balkans, 1804–1999: Nationalism, War and the Great Powers*, London: Granta Books.

Gluckman, M. (1956) 'The Peace in the Feud', in M. Gluckman (ed.) *Custom and Conflict in Africa*, Oxford: Basil Blackwell.

Godina, V. (1998) 'The outbreak of nationalism on former Yugoslav territories: an historical perspective on the problem of supra-national identities', *Nations and Nationalisms* 4: 409–422.

Harrison, S. (1993) *The Mask of War: Violence, Ritual and the Self in Melanesia*, Manchester: Manchester University Press.

Kirin, R. and Povrzanovic, M. (eds) (1996) *War, Exile and Everyday Life: Cultural Perspectives*, Zagreb: Institute of Ethnology and Folklore Research.

Laclau, E. and Mouffe, C. (1985) *Hegemony and Socialist Strategy: Towards a Radical Democratic Politics*, London: Verso.

Leach, E. (1954) *Political Systems of Highland Burma: A Study of Kachin Social Structure*, London: Athlone Press.

—— (1977) *Custom, Law and Terrorist Violence*, Edinburgh: Edinburgh University Press.

Lévi-Strauss, C. (1969) [1949] *The Elementary Structures of Kinship*, Boston: Beacon Press.

Mastnak, T. (1991) 'From the new social movements to political parties', in J. Simmie and J. Dekleva (eds) *Yugoslavia in Turmoil: After Self-management?*, London: Pinter.

Mencinger, J. (1991) 'From a capitalist to a capitalist economy?', in J. Simmie and J. Dekleva (eds) *Yugoslavia in Turmoil: After Self-management?*, London: Pinter.

Moeran, B. (1986) 'The beauty of violence: Jidaigeki, Yakuza and eroduction films in Japanese Cinema', in D. Riches (ed.) *The Anthropology of Violence*, Oxford: Basil Blackwell.

OED (1971) *The Compact Edition of the Oxford English Dictionary*, Oxford: Oxford University Press.

Parkin, D. (1986) 'Violence and will', in D. Riches (ed.) *The Anthropology of Violence*, Oxford: Basil Blackwell.

Pavlowitch, S. (1988) *The Improbable Survivor: Yugoslavia and its Problems, 1918–1988*, London: C. Hurst and Co.

Pound, E. (1971) [1926] 'Sestina: Altaforte', in E. Pound *Personae: The Collected Shorter Poems of Ezra Pound*, New York: New Directions.

Ramet, P. (1985) 'Apocalypse culture and social change in Yugoslavia', in P. Ramet (ed.) *Yugoslavia in the 1980s*, Boulder: Westview.

Riches, D. (ed.) (1986a) *The Anthropology of Violence*, Oxford: Basil Blackwell.

—— (1986b) 'The Phenomenon of violence', in D. Riches (ed.) *The Anthropology of Violence*, Oxford: Basil Blackwell.

Scarry, E. (1985) *The Body in Pain: The Making and Unmaking of the World*, Oxford: Oxford University Press.

Silber, L. and Little, A. (1995) *The Death of Yugoslavia*, London: Penguin and BBC Books.

Skeat, W. (1927) *A Concise Etymological Dictionary of the English Language*, Oxford: Clarendon Press.

Zizek, S. (1990) 'Eastern Europe's republics of Gilead', *New Left Review* 183: 50–62.

Violence as everyday practice and imagination

Chapter 3

Socio-cosmological contexts and forms of violence

War, vendetta, duels and suicide among the Yukpa of north-western Venezuela

Ernst Halbmayer[1]

It was Reichel-Dolmatoff who stated in an early paper that the Yukpa[2] Indians are not only warriors because of hate, envy, or pleasure, but rather that war is 'a fundamental necessity for them' (Reichel-Dolmatoff 1945: 62). In his chapter on 'war' Reichel-Dolmatoff does not elaborate further on this statement, but describes certain aspects of warfare (1945: 62, 64), pre-warfare ritual dance-fighting (1945: 64), fighting that occurred during maize-beer celebrations (1945: 65) and the resulting vendetta (1945: 66). Since the publication of Reichel-Dolmatoff's paper, anthropological observations of violent behaviour have been refined, masses of data have been collected and a broad theoretical discussion on violence and warfare in Lowland South America has taken place. The latter was pioneered by the scientific battle on Yanomami warfare (e.g. Albert 1989, 1990; Alès 1984; Chagnon 1968, 1983, 1988, 1989, 1990a, 1990b; Ferguson 1990, 1995; Harris 1984; Lizot 1989, 1994).[3] Compared with those intellectual endeavours, in which some of the outstanding anthropologists working on the continent have been engaged, the aim and scope of this paper on violence[4] among the Yukpa is limited and mainly socio-cosmological in its focus. I do not try to give a final or monocausal explanation as to why war or violent behaviour occurs, nor is it my aim to provide statistical data ordered by 'etic' western categories on the frequencies of different forms of violent behaviour. Rather, my question is how institutionalised forms of violence are structured according to socio-cosmological contexts.

War, blood-feuding and ritualised duels among the Yukpa were carried out until the 1960s and then disappeared due to the increased establishment of formal leadership, introduced by Capuchin missionary activities.[5] Isolated events where the practice of war becomes evident,[6] or blood-feuding occurs, may still take place. Also violent confrontations and fighting in situations which once involved ritualised duels are still frequent, as is suicide. Today, however, the symbolic notions of violence, which are based in the Yukpa sociocosmology and related to different levels of their social organisation, are more significant than these violent practices. These notions of violence relate this north-western outpost of Carib-speakers to a broader spectrum of lowland South American societies. Their general logic has been described variously as a constitutive element of the reproduction of the social structure (Alès 1984: 111), in terms of the local construction of identity and alterity (Menget 1985), the cannibalistic predation of enemies (Vivieros de Castro 1993), or a structural instability of the consanguine/affine polarity, produced by a double concentric englobement (Descola 1993: 186–7).

My interest in violent behaviour as a specific form of human communication and interaction is three-fold: (1) in which contexts specific forms of violence are carried out, (2) how these different institutionalised forms of violence may be explained within their socio-cosmological context and (3) how these forms of violence may be related to definitions of violence, which are based on the distinction of legal and illegal violence.

One of the basic refinements in the analysis of the social contexts of violent behaviour and a common point of departure for a long time has been the distinction between internal and external warfare. This distinction obviously refers to the identity/alterity difference. It was Cariage (1979, 1980) who demonstrated the relevance of this distinction for the Yukpa and distinguished external war from internal vendetta.

This chapter tries to go beyond the existing analysis of Yukpa warfare and violence as – besides war and vendetta – it will consider other forms of violent behaviour such as duels and – maybe surprisingly – suicide.[7] It will focus on basic distinctions present within cosmology and social organisation and show how action and social organisation are related to and are dependent upon each other, produce and reshape, make and re-make each other in a process of permanent co-production (Dupuy and Varela 1992). From this point of view violent actions have – as do, for example, marriages, or residence decisions – the potential to reproduce *and* transform social organisation.

Before I focus on the aspects of identity and difference in the Yukpa worldview, I will present some basic ethnographic information on the Yukpa. The Yukpa are the north-western outpost of the Carib-speaking Indians and live in the Sierra de Perijá, which forms the international border between north-western Venezuela and north-eastern Columbia. They are located south of the Arawak-speaking Guajiros (Wayú), north of the Chibcha-speaking Barí and west of the also Chibcha-speaking Kogi, Ica and Sanhá of the Sierra Nevada de Santa Marta. There are about 6,700 Yukpa, about 4,200 (OCEI 1993) of them live in Venezuela and about 2,500 in Columbia (Lizzaralde 1988: 170). Kenneth Ruddle (Ruddle 1971) has shown that the Yukpa consist of sixteen different subgroups living in different river valleys. Linguistic research, however, questions that the northernmost Japreria are a Yukpa-subgroup and rather gives them the status of a related group speaking an autonomous Carib language (Durbin 1977: 24; Oquendo 1998). Important anthropological descriptions of the Yukpa include those of Bolinder (1917, 1958), Wavrin (1953), Reichel-Dolmatoff (1945, 1960), Reichel-Dolmatoff and Clark (1950), Rivet and Armellada (1950), Wilbert (1960, 1962, 1974), Ruddle (1971, 1974), and an ethnographic overview based on these accounts by Ruddle and Wilbert (1983). Furthermore, there exists a number of unpublished dissertations (Cariage 1979; Lhermillier, A. 1980; Lhermillier, N. 1980; Paolisso 1985). My own research among the Yukpa (Halbmayer 1998) has mainly been carried out among the Irapa of the Tukuko-valley.[8]

Yukpa economy is based on shifting cultivation, hunting, gathering, and today on the cultivation of coffee as a cash crop[9] (Ruddle 1970, 1974; Paolisso 1985; Paolisso and Sackett 1985). Kinship is bilateral and of a Dravidianate South American type (e.g. Viveiros de Castro 1993; Henley 1996; and contributions in Godelier, Trautmann and Tjon Sie Fat 1998). The classificatory bilateral cross-sex cross-cousins are the marriageable affines. According to the existence of oblique marriages, the ♂ZD/♀MB[10] are terminologically fused with the bilateral cross-sex cross-cousins. In G+2 and G−2 a replication of younger and elder sibling terms may be found, which leads to a terminology with alternate generations.[11] Residence is, in practice, ambilocal whereas a preference for (temporal) uxorilocality and bride-service is stressed. Settlement patterns are fairly dispersed and traditionally range from single households, based on (polygamous) marriage(s) and the unmarried children of such relations, up to agglomerations of twenty houses. Today a territorially based distinction between communities, which nowadays may exceed the above-mentioned agglomerations, is established throughout the territory.

The establishment of primary distinctions according to Yukpa origin myths

According to Yukpa mythology, the creation of the world is not a creation *ex nihilo* but a series of transformations by a mythical transformer who is called either Armouritsha or Tamoryayo. The transformation of the world into its present state is based on a differentiation of the originally undifferentiated. This process is described as follows:

> At the beginning there was no life on earth. The firmament and the earth were very close to each other, and therefore it was very hot. The earth was surrounded by two suns, so it never became dark. The seas and the rivers boiled, as water boils, standing in a pot over the fire. There was no life on earth. Tamoryayo was the only one who existed, he was living on the other side of the firmament over the fog. He lived alone, but was upset to be alone and decided to come to the earth. But he found the earth incredibly hot and it was impossible to live there. Tamoryayo couldn't stand the horrible heat which was burning down everything. So he took bow and arrow, aimed them at the sun and shot her into the eye. At this moment the firmament rose a little and as the arrow hit the sun it became darker. He shot again and at this moment the firmament rose again to the position where it is today.
>
> (translated from Armato 1988: 9)

The sun Tamoryayo hit turned dark and became the moon, and the world and the firmament were separated. That is how the difference between day and night, cold and hot came into existence and changed the world's condition into a tempered and liveable one. David Guss described this sort of mythical operations for the Ye´kuana by stating that 'these myths of origin serve as the perfect paradigms of transformation, symbolically depicting the daily operation of culture. The action they describe is inevitably one of movement from darkness to light, from chaos to order, from cannibal to human' (Guss 1991: 112). In the case of the Yukpa, not darkness but the extreme double brightness is the state associated with chaos and cannibalism.

This becomes even more clear if one takes into account other myths which characterise the untransformed sun as an aggressive enemy representing danger and standing in a relationship of predation towards the Yukpa, who as a consequence, become the hunted prey. The moon, on the other hand, is portrayed as gentle and helpful, representing safe relations of reciprocity and becoming a mythical father-in-law,[12] who gives his daughter and food to the Yukpa (Wilbert 1974: 84–6, 131–5; Armato 1988: 49–50; Halbmayer 1998). These differences, which transformed the former chaotic world into a liveable one, distinguish safe and socialised from wild and potentially dangerous relationships. Safety in this logic goes hand in hand with a harmonious exchange of reciprocal relations and identity, whereas danger is associated with negative reciprocity and difference.[13] It was Claude Lévi-Strauss who pointed out that economic exchange and war are just two sides of the same social process (Lévi-Strauss 1943: 138). I agree with this general argument but prefer to distinguish reciprocity from negative reciprocity instead of war from economic exchange and will argue that violent interactions as well as economic transfers may both be structured either according to the logic of reciprocity or the logic of negative reciprocity. The distinction between negative reciprocity and reciprocity is at the core of the making and remaking of the distinction between identity and difference and finds its expression in different social fields such as marriage arrangements versus wife-stealing, peaceful exchange versus illegitimate or even violent appropriation, and, as I will try to show, even in different forms of violence.

A second important mythical differentiation in the Yukpa worldview separates humans from animals, an event which goes hand in hand with the establishment of the incest taboo and the transformation into animals of those Yukpa maintaining incestuous relations.

> In ancient times the earth was populated by animals. There was the family of parrots, the family of monkeys, the family of vultures, the family of sparrows, the family of jaguars, the family of tapirs [. . .].
>
> They were persons as we are today.
>
> These people began to behave badly. The fathers began to live with their daughters. The mothers were together with their sons. The brothers lived with their real sisters. All of them behaved badly.

One day Tamoryayo came as a person to the Yukpa and saw that they behaved badly. The men and the women were always drunk. This is why Tamoryayo said:

'You wanted it like that. This night, when the moon becomes red, all of you will be transformed into animals.'

In this night, when all of them were sleeping, the moon became red and all of them were transformed into animals. Those who had been brave were transformed into jaguars. Those who had been lazy were transformed into sloths. The singers were transformed into singing birds. The dirty ones into opossum. In this way Tamoryayo punished the first inhabitants of the earth because they behaved badly. In this way the Yukpa explain how the first animals had been created.

Tamoryayo said:

'The sun will lighten the day.

The moon will lighten the night.'

In this time he created day and night.

So Tamoryayo stayed to live on earth, but it is said that he was tired of being alone. That is why he looked for a way to find company. That was the moment when he created the first (two) women out of a tree trunk.[14]

Tamoryayo lived with these women and they had a lot of children which they called Yukpa. In this way the first inhabitants of the world appeared.

(translated from Armato 1988: 39–40)

So within the cosmology of the Yukpa we find at least two major distinctions: one between dangerous, predatory, negative social relations associated with the enemy, the sun, and safe, reciprocal relations for which the father-in-law moon stands. And it is *within* the domain of reciprocity that the difference between incestuous and non-incestuous relations was established.

Basic distinctions in the social organisation

A look at the etymology of the word *Yu'pa* and its central antonym *Yuko* may give a first idea of how the Yukpa conceive the distinction between identity and difference. *Yu'pa* usually is translated as 'people' and *Yuko* as 'enemy' (Armellada 1948: 135; Cariage 1980: 15; Paolisso 1985: 49; Vegamian 1978). These terms may be applied on various social levels, but, regardless of different levels, the term *Yu'pa* is always used to designate the group with which the speaker identifies himself, whereas *Yuko* pertains to the other, to the non-identical.[15] The content of *Yu'pa/Yuko* may vary and may include according to the context

- all the indigenous, if opposed to the non-indigenous *watia,*
- all the known Yukpa subgroups, if opposed to other indigenous groups such as the Bari or Wayú (Guajiro),
- the own Yukpa-subgroup, if opposed to the neighbouring subgroups.

The last and narrow meaning of *Yu'pa* was the traditional one. The Yukpa-subgroups live in different river valleys, separated by high mountain ranges, which impede frequent interactions between them. They generally see each other as enemies, as *Yuko.* Their relations have been characterised by negative reciprocity, war and wife-stealing.[16] There is no tribal or ethnic sense of common identity which would include all these sixteen subgroups and only the people of the same subgroup are included in the kinship system. In contrast to wife-stealing, marriages based on social agreement take place within the mainly endogamous subgroups. However, with increased reciprocal relations such as visits, friendly relations between subgroups may develop, which may lead to peace agreements (Wavrin 1948: 409) and to the establishment of marriage relations or even to a fusion of two groups if the topography of the territory will allow it. In contrast, internal conflicts can lead to the end of reciprocal relations and fission may occur and create new subgroups, as happened for example in 1949, when a deadly conflict in the Irapa-Yukpa settlement of Kanowapa led to the fission of the Viakshi, who moved south and started to live as an independent small subgroup at the sources of Rio Santa Rosa.

A closer look at the etymology of *Yu'pa* and *Yuko* shows – as already indicated by Cariage (1980: 15) – that *Yu-* means bodily and is used to designate body parts such as *Yu-wasa,* the head, or *Yu-aturu,* the heart.[17] Both *Yu'pa* and *Yuko* refer to bodily aspects: '*-pa*', means 'a group of the same class', whereas '*-ko*' means 'a group of another class' and implies otherness and non-identity.

The difference between people and enemies is, therefore, one expressed as the difference between people sharing the same *Yu-*, the same bodily aspects, or not. Among the Yukpa, as in many South American cosmologies, corporal identity is not considered a purely biological fact. It is rather a consequence of social processes. Most importantly, it is achieved through the incorporation and exchange of the same substances, expressed in the exchange and the consumption of the same food. By feeding each other and by consuming the same class of food, beings are progressively transformed into individuals of the same 'meat' or the same 'substance' (Rival [1996: 294] expressed this for the Huaorani). At the centre of identity and difference, we thus find an exchange theory that distinguishes people who share reciprocity, *Yu'pa*, and people who share and interchange relations of negative reciprocity, *Yuko* (see Fig. 3.1).

However, applying this distinction to a universe of people does not have the effect that the same people always end up in the same categories, as their relations may change according to social actions such as marriages, conflicts, war, and residence decisions. The relation between people may be transformed from reciprocity and sharing to non-reciprocity and vice versa. Therefore, the distinction between sharing a reciprocal or a non-reciprocal relationship applied to a social universe leads to a permanent contraction or expansion of the inner content of the social universe, and according to the relations enacted at a specific time more or less, and even different people will be included into the social context of reciprocal sharing.

From a formal point of view, the form of a distinction establishes an inner space (in our case *Yu'pa*) and a surrounding space (in our case *Yuko*) or social outside. The inner space may be further differentiated. The distinction between identity and difference may be introduced, may re-enter (Spencer Brown 1973) into the inner space of *Yu'pa*; into the area of people who share.

Differentiation in societies lacking clearly defined corporate groups, as do the majority of Carib-speakers, seems to be the effect of applying the basic distinction of identity/difference within the

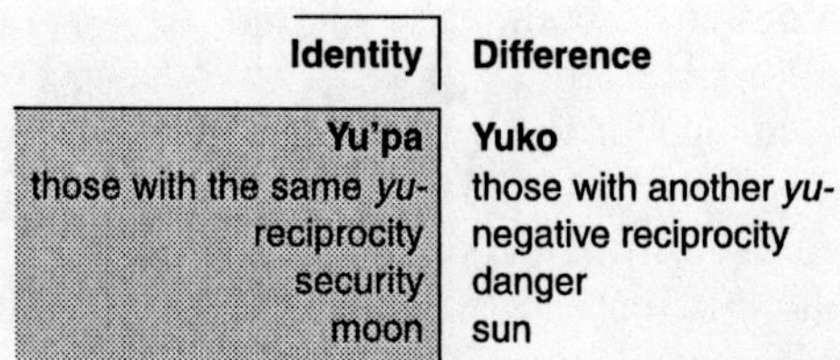

Figure 3.1 Identity versus difference among the Yukpa.

established inner space of *Yu'pa*. Thus we get a form containing the form, like Russian dolls, where the distinction between the doll and its surrounding is repeated within the doll itself. Maybe an onion would be a more appropriate metaphor, lacking the notion of entirely separated entities, but with a repetitive internal differentiation which establishes multiple social levels.

In the centre of this system we find a logic which in its simplest form may be characterised by at least two distinctions, whereby one is included in the other and these distinctions produce three levels or spaces: an outer space which may be called 'outside', an inner space called 'inside', and a space incorporated by the inside called 'internal outside'. The latter is a space which in relation to the outside is inside and in relation to the inside an internal outside.

These two distinctions are the same as they both distinguish inside from outside, identity from difference, but as they do this by using different criteria they are not entirely identical (see Fig. 3.2). Within the space of reciprocity the distinction between the inside/outside is reintroduced and reappears in a specific form, namely between people who may share marriage relations and those who may not. Within the group who may not share marriage relations, sexual relations between men and women fall under the incest taboo, whereas the men of this group are obliged to support each other in the case of conflict. This is the same distinction made by the mythical transformer Tamoryaya between incestuous relations and non-incestuous ones, and it finds its expression in two kinds of families distinguished by the Yukpa, namely *yipushno* and *opiyo*. This social area, as a whole, is surrounded by a non- or pre-social undifferentiated outside represented by the undifferentiated mythical state.

The core of males, which may not be connected through marriage relations, is formed by a father and his sons and can be extended by the logic of fraternal relations to include the father's brother and his sons. This is the group or family the Irapa-Yukpa call *yipushno*. The members of this group are kin to each other and their relations are based on generalised reciprocity or a mode of protection: they are obliged to revenge each other and the consequences of a violent act committed by one of this group falls back upon the perpetrator or any other person in that group (Cariage 1980). The women belonging to this group[18] fall under the incest taboo.

In other words, this is the minimal group where the distinction of identity and difference, expressed in incestuous versus non-

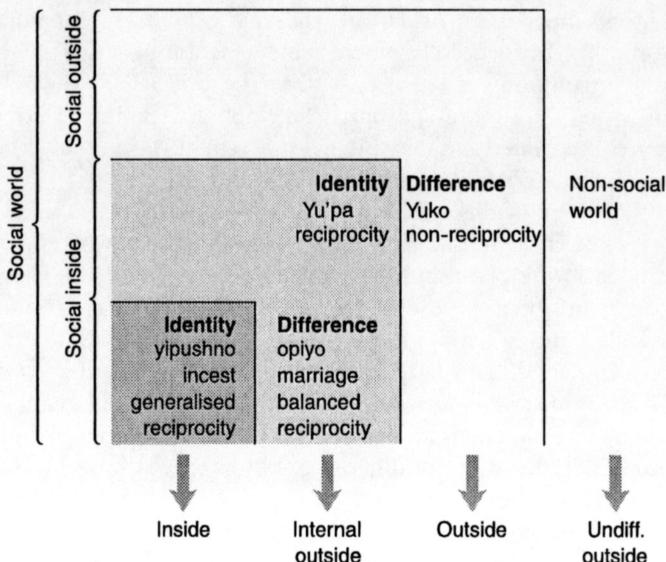

Figure 3.2 Levels of inside/outside among the Yukpa.

incestuous relations may not be reintroduced and therefore the necessary difference for non-incestuous marriage relations does not exist. This is the minimal inside, the smallest Papuschka doll, the core of the onion. The members of these unions are allies in relation to war and rivals in relation to marriage. These men who have to defend and revenge each other may at the same time have serious conflicts over women. Within the Yukpa kinship system[19] a man should marry *pahte*: this kinship category includes classificatory bilateral cross-cousins and the ZD. Therefore, not only brothers may compete for the same women, but also father's and son's since the father's ZD is the son's cross-cousin.

Marriage allies, in contrast to war allies, are people who stand in an affinal relationship and do not belong to the *yipushno* group. This distinction creates the difference necessary for non-incestuous marriage relations. In relation to the outside, established marriage relations create the security and the safety for which the mythical father-in-law moon stands. Within large Yukpa subgroups, this may produce an additional re-entry of the inside/outside difference between *opiyo* and the members of the subgroups which are included in the kinship system, but where hardly any close actual

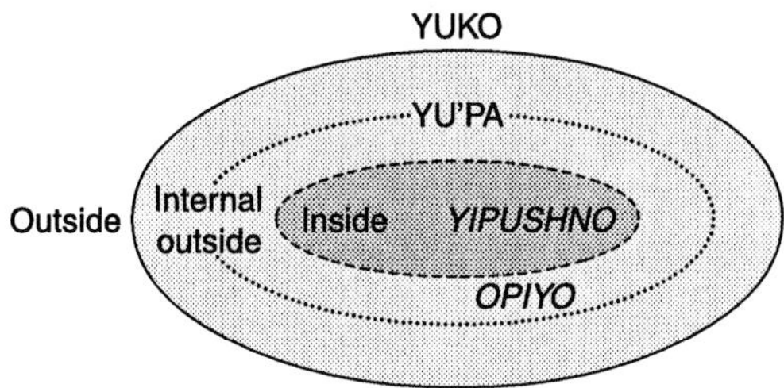

Figure 3.3 Social levels of identity/difference.

marriage relations exist. Within small subgroups the distinction between *opiyo* and the subgroup tends to be identical. In relation to the inside, *opiyo*, nevertheless, represents an outside, and informants stress the difference between this affinal family and the kin family (*yipushno*), as one between the problematic family (*opiyo*) and the family who gives support (*yipushno*). Persons included into the *opiyo* category may take part in war activities and support the *yipushno* group in conflictual situations as long as the opponents belong to a further outside, but they are not obliged to do so (see Fig. 3.3).

Forms of violence and their social context

The outlined double distinction between identity/difference within the social area relies on an exchange of negative reciprocity versus one of reciprocity and, within the latter, this distinction re-enters in the form of incestuous versus non-incestuous relations. These forms of relations define the social fields and possibilities of interaction and, as we will see, also the forms and consequences of violence.

The difference between an exchange of negative reciprocity and one of reciprocity in terms of violence is significant: within the area of negative reciprocity violence is an appropriate and standard way of communication. War raids and wife-stealing are carried out against Yuko people, whereas within the area of reciprocal exchange such relations will lead to fission.

According to Cariage (1980), external war is a violent conflict between persons who had no relation with one another up to this time. War expeditions are carried out by men of a region who attack another valley. These war excursions were preceded by a celebration during which a dance called *serémpa* was performed. Reichel-Dolmatoff describes it as follows:

> Two rows of men face each other in some 30 steps distance, each one with his bow and an equal number of arrows. The men of one row shoot their arrows against their opponents who wait their turn to return the shot. So each row shoots whereas the opposite row parades and exposes only its body profiles. . . . As all men shoot simultaneously and parade with the steps of a torero, this duel gets rhythm and movement. It is admirable to see the warriors on this occasion: in the moment of shooting the Indian lifts his right arm into the air and shouts shrilly and smacks his hand with a strong slap against his thigh. Naturally, injuries are very frequent during a *serémpa*, but that excites the participants even more, who are lucky to be rather inept because of their drunkenness.
>
> (translated from Reichel-Dolmatoff 1945: 63)

After this dance, women prepare *kuse,* maize balls which were eaten with *masaya*, a black wasp species, valued because of its aggressiveness and the painfulness of its bites. The people also continue to drink maize beer. Later, another dance is performed, during which agave leaves or a trunk of a banana plant symbolising the enemy is ritually killed by shooting it with a bow and arrow. The singing expresses the aggressiveness and fearlessness of the dancers, and by imitating the jaguar's roar they indicate their jaguar-likeness[20] and readiness for killing. During all this, men wear black-painted faces, a visible sign of aggressiveness and a state of war.

During the attacks, which are conducted as ambushes, they attempt to kill the enemies and, if possible, take their wives and young children with them. The wives and children will be integrated into the aggressors' own group. The people participating in these war expeditions are glorified and highly honoured, and the details of these attacks are told with enthusiasm (Cariage 1980: 16). Thus, aggressiveness and violence against the outside, against personally unknown people of another valley, is highly valued and provides the base for acquiring internal prestige, a warrior reputation, and consequently, respect and power.

In contrast, blood-feuding or the vendetta has quite a different image. The vendetta is not preceded by a public ritual, and no one involved wants to speaks about it or be identified as the perpetrator. Unlike war expeditions, the vendetta takes place within the same region, among personally known people. Consternation, not enthusiasm, is the emotion associated with it (Cariage 1980: 16), and no social prestige may be acquired by it. Rather one risks becoming a victim of revenge. If vendetta occurs it transforms the harmonic social relations, and opposes not only the persons directly involved but also their *yipushno* groups of war allies. Vendetta redraws the distinction between negative reciprocity and reciprocity. People who up to such an event have been inside the area of reciprocity may now become *Yuko* if no efforts for peaceful reconciliation is made. If one speaks openly about such events or expresses pride in having fought someone from the same group, one may risk re-establishing the conflict.

Thus the vendetta clearly has the connotation of introducing difference and negative reciprocity into a social context of reciprocity and harmony. It has the potential to divide a group and may lead to fission and the end of reciprocal relations. Like external war, vendetta is a form of violence based on negative reciprocity that leads to killing the victim, but in contrast to war, it is carried out within reciprocal relations and has, therefore, the potential to transform these into negative reciprocal ones. War, in contrast, is just the confirmation of an existing relationship of negative reciprocity. In the context of war an at least temporal transformation of the existing relationship may only be established through the creation of peaceful reciprocal relations and exchanges.

A third form of violence has already been mentioned in the description of the *serémpa* dance. It takes place within the area of reciprocal relations and seems to have an entirely different logic: duels. War and vendetta are forms of relationships guided by a logic of taking without offering any compensation. The exchange established by these forms of violence is obviously an indirect one where a long time may pass between the attacks and it is an exchange of uninvited 'taking' from the other group. Duels, in contrast, are a socialised and reciprocal form of violence and among the Yukpa killing in this context is an accident and not a goal.

More common than the *serémpa* duels before war expeditions were duels which took place during the maize beer feasts. During these still important events, different local groups gather and frequently violent conflicts arise due to increased alcoholic intoxication. Maize beer celebrations are situations symbolically associated with a state of emergency and violence. The arising conflicts traditionally culminated in duels where the opponents stood face to face and in turn struck their bows powerfully against each other's heads. The one who remained standing longest won. 'A right to response' (Carriage) is the concession to the opponent in duels and an expression of their symmetrical reciprocal character. Serious cicatrices and deformations of the skullcap are frequent results and are prestigious signs of courage shown with pride by old men. As long as these duels did not lead to very serious wounds and the danger that the injured person might die, such violence remained without further consequences.

Wavrin describes the day after such a fight in the following words:

> After a night of deep sleep, all the Motilones[21] awake refreshed and start with big words. In the most cordial tone one remembers the orgiastic scenes from the day before and congratulates each other:
>
> – You have been brave.
>
> – You too, you have been fighting well.
>
> – Ah! Ah! With whom?
>
> – With him.
>
> – Ah! (a smile of satisfaction).
>
> – You gave me a big blow with the club.
>
> – Ah! Ah! And why?
>
> – I don't know anymore but I got it, here I feel it.
>
> – And you (the other intervenes) you hit him strongly in return for his blow.
>
> – Good! Good! (a smile of satisfaction).
>
> The victim who was missed by Juan asks me:
>
> – And I, did I fight?
>
> – All the time, you were the worst, you were the most vehement.
>
> – Ah! Good! So I'm a man! But did I behave well with you? I didn't provoke you? I didn't want to fight with you?
>
> – No, you behaved well with me. But Juan, Marinte, Arichinachimu, Monaro, Seshkete, Maskachi, Khosetrera, everyone, you provoked a lot. You threatened them all the time and you wanted to fight.
>
> He smiles:
>
> – Good! Good! I'm a man! I'm brave and I fought! I'm a man!
>
> (translated from Wavrin 1953: 289)

Yukpa duels are not directed by a logic of non-reciprocal taking without direct compensation; rather, they are a form of direct reciprocal exchange: the stroke is given and the question is who will be able to better resist these 'gifts'. The loser is the one who is unable to return and to compensate for the stroke he received. Nevertheless, such events bear the risk of shifting from an reciprocal event to a negative-reciprocal one: this would be the case if a person is killed.

Forms of ritualised reciprocal confrontations also took place between villages of the same subgroup. Bolinder describes such an attack by warriors from a neighbouring settlement and labels it 'war games'.

> There they came, the husky, painted warriors, . . . It turned out that while this battle was only a matter of 'war games' it did serve a useful purpose by letting off the steam generated during the recent celebrations. Not only that but even though they were just corn cobs, they could smack an opponent a good hard blow. . . .
>
> The battle had begun. Indians from our village met the attack and in no time arrows were whining through the air. The battle lines curved forward and back in attack and defence. Even at 60 to 75 feet the impact of the corn-cob tipped arrows made sharp smacking sounds as they hit the bodies of the antagonists. I also noticed that the fighters swung around to take the impact of the blows on their backs instead of risking painful blows below the belt. And as there were not many misses, I imagine quite a few had difficulty sitting down for a couple of days when it was all over.
>
> A few hours after it had begun, both forces withdrew from the field and the women, who had been standing on the sidelines cheering their 'teams', took over their duties of binding up the wounds and cleaning up the mess before they started making hearty meals for their men.
>
> (Bolinder 1958: 171–2)

Another form of neither negative-reciprocal (war, vendetta) nor reciprocal (duels) but self-referential violence is frequent among the Yukpa: suicide. Obviously suicide is like war and vendetta, a form of violence that aims to kill, but in contrast to the previously-mentioned forms, under conditions of the abolishment of the offender/victim distinction, the offender himself becomes the victim. For the Peruvian Aguaruna, Brown (1986) has suggested that suicide takes place if there is no possibility of organising collective reactions to social conflict. Brown compares male and female suicide rates among the Aguaruna, and explains the higher female suicide rate with the women's inability to organise collective reactions to social conflict.

In contrast to the Aguaruna, suicide among the Yukpa is more frequent in males than females,[22] an inversion which cannot be explained by better female than male opportunities for collective reactions to social conflict. Men's opportunities for collective reactions are generally not worse than those of females. However, is this true for all men, in every context? Or are there contexts and situations in which men lack this ability, and are such situations especially linked to suicide?

Male suicide is mainly a reaction to matrimonial conflicts, to adultery and/or the elopement of the wife with another man. Normally, such a situation leads to major conflicts within the village or the villages involved. As such an event becomes public, the marriage is considered to be dissolved and now either the former situation has to be re-established or the new one formally accepted. Such a situation places the husband and the seducer in opposition, and it depends on the relationship between the husband and his parents-in-law whether they support a re-establishment of the former marriage or support their daughter's wish to marry another man.[23] Traditionally such situations led to duels and even killings (Wilbert 1960: 124), but today the formally appointed *caciques* try to settle such conflicts peacefully, through a rearrangement of marriage relations and the establishment of a new balance within the settlement. These processes may include the punishment of the unfaithful persons with short-time arrest and/or compensation payments.

If we accept the general part of Brown's thesis on the relationship between suicide and the ability to carry out collective reactions to social conflict, the core question is, what impedes collective male reactions against the seducer among the Yukpa? Under the current conditions of *cacique* leadership, one might rephrase this question slightly and ask, what impediment prevent men finding their cases properly supported within the public conflict-settlement hearings. The whole settlement participates in these hearings and such events sometimes last a whole day and night and may even continue the following day until an agreement is achieved. If the betrayed man is forced to accept an agreement through group pressure but without real conviction, it is very likely that he will leave for the forest in an unobserved moment and try to strangulate himself in a sitting position with his bow cord. Another, today rather rare *harakiri*-like way to commit suicide, is to stab one's own arrow into the stomach.

In my opinion the explanation for this kind of behaviour is closely related to the social nature of the *yipushno* group, whose members are war allies and who support each other in conflict, but at the same time compete for the same women. If the seducer is a parallel cousin, a brother, the father or a father's brother, that means a man belonging to the close kin group forming the war allies, the arising conflict is not one between opposing parties, rather it is a conflict within the minimal social unit of support and identity. This situation impedes collective reactions to conflicts and support from the *yipushno* group during the conflict settlement. As Cariage (1980) has pointed out, an attack against a member of this group affects the whole group. However, in such a situation the normal support and protection mechanisms are paralysed, as any support would at the same time represent an attack against a member of their own group. In these situations hardly any socially accepted possibilities for violent reactions against others exist. To fight the enemy in a situation where he is part of the *yipushno* group means to fight oneself, and suicide is the perfect expression of such a configuration.

In such a situation parts of the own core group become symbolically identified with the enemy *Yuko,* as adultery and elopement are considered a form of wife-stealing. Symbolically, violence in this context leads to a paradoxical situation where the core distinction established by the mythical creation of sun and moon, between negative reciprocity and reciprocity becomes blurred, and negative reciprocity is introduced into the very core of support and identity. Whereas at the level of *opiyo* and *Yu'pa*, negative reciprocity may be introduced and leads to a redefinition of group borders, a re-entry and redefinition of the identity/difference distinction within the core of the *yipushno* group is impossible. This situation leads to a state where, symbolically, the basic distinction between negative reciprocity and reciprocity is eliminated and the risk of a reverse transformation (Guss 1991: 112) into a mythical state of pre-differentiation, of non-differentiation between animals and humans, of two identical suns and an unliveable world becomes evident.

Such a reverse transformation and de-differentiation has to be avoided, as must violent actions within the *yipushno* group.[24] In this context, it seems significant that the Yukpa also committed suicide when they accidentally killed closely related people (Reichel-Dolmatoff 1945: 61; Bolinder 1958: 172).

Conclusion: social organisation, power and the notion of violence among the Yukpa

It has been shown that all forms of violence relate to an internally repetitive distinction of identity and difference. These distinctions, created in mythical differentiation processes, establish different social levels whose specific content may decrease or increase according to social processes.

Among the Yukpa, different forms of violence are related to the basic distinctions of social organisation and worldview. They are associated with local concepts of power and prestige. Power and prestige are attributed to those people who have the ability to integrate internal differences, to socialise parts of the outside and to fight the non-socialised others. Prestigious people establish relations through marriage, exchange of food, labour or even techniques of spiritual contact to a broad group of people and/or spirits in order to integrate and socialise them. Political leadership and shamanic power rely on an integrative skill, in the latter case on the ability to establish reciprocal contact to spiritual beings and animal spirits and to fight the dangerous and malicious ones. Violence against the outside following the prey/predator logic of negative reciprocity is highly prestigious, valued and collectively ritualised. Central values of male fearlessness and aggressiveness are enacted in the course of these violent actions, through which men may acquire social and symbolic capital for leadership. However, violent actions following this logic have these qualities only if directed against the outside, against *Yuko*. Within the inside, negative-reciprocal violence would lead to fission of the group and reduce the number of followers and therefore the leader's influence and power.

For that reason, vendetta, the other form of violence following the prey/predator logic, which is conducted within the inside against Yukpa, is regarded with consternation, and no public rituals are related to it.

Reciprocal violence, as enacted in public duels within the realm of reciprocity, may equally be used for acquiring social prestige and stress male fearlessness and aggressiveness, and the resulting marks are shown with pride. However, this form of violence is not a way to fight the different, non-integrated other, but is rather a way of finding the most valuable, aggressive and fearless individuals among a group of people. It does, however, bear the danger that reciprocal violence may turn into a negative non-reciprocal one and lead to fission.

Self-referential violence in the form of suicide takes place within the core-inside of generalised reciprocity, if negative reciprocity is introduced by adultery, which is symbolically equivalent to women's robbery. Suicide is a way to show fearlessness, to blame and attack the seducer in a situation where no real attack might be carried out and, last but not least, it is an expression of sorrow and mourning.

Prestige and power are attributed to those people who have the ability to deal with potentially dangerous outsiders by establishing reciprocal relations or fighting them. Depending on the form of violence and against whom it is directed, it may either be supportive or disastrous for the personal accumulation of power and prestige. As the social relation within which a violent action takes place ultimately provides its specific meaning and significance, there is no contextless abstract notion of offence among the Yukpa. The same action may be highly valued or deeply despised according to the social relation in which it takes place, and therefore a widespread notion of violence which already includes a moral evaluation is problematic. The common distinction between legal and illegal violence prominently inscribes a moral evaluation and affirmative relationship to existing power relations into the discourse of violence. It supports the tendency to view only the illegal use of methods of physical coercion as violent. Such a notion supports an established legal system, reinforces the 'state monopoly of physical violence' (Max Weber) and a political system whose functioning is based on the threat of violence.

This duplication of violence into legitimate and illegitimate realms tends to be related to social systems which had established institutionalised forms of domination but which were absent among the Yukpa. Neither the distinction between negative reciprocal, reciprocal or self-referential violence, nor its evaluation as valued or feared, is one which could be translated as legitimate versus illegitimate. Among the Yukpa an institutionalised inclusion of legal violence into society with the aim of punishing illegal forms of violence did not exist.[25] One may be attacked, one might defend oneself and organise a counterattack, or fight a duel, but the question is definitely not one that centres around the issue of whether a certain form of violence is legitimate or not. No one would doubt that revenge, a counterattack or just to strike back in a duel is an appropriate way of response. Therefore conceptions which inscribe a distinction between legal and illegal spheres into the notion of violence seem to have limited explanatory power for rather loosely organised, non-centralised societies without some sort of formal and standardised legal system. This is also true for the conception of violence as outlined by Riches, who states that the performer tends to see the violent act as legitimate and the victim conceives it as illegitimate. The author promotes a perspective 'which puts the focus on the act of violence itself' and defines violence as 'an act of physical hurt deemed legitimate by the performer and illegitimate by (some) witnesses' (Riches 1986: 8).

Such a focus on the single act and its different evaluation by performer and witness leads to a reification of the performer/victim distinction. If we look at sequences of inter-related violent acts as specific forms of dynamic relations between persons and groups, such a distinction, based on a single act and its different evaluation immediately (duels) or in the longer term (vendetta, war) becomes blurred.

Such an oscillation leads to two possible points of view. The first, frequently taken by anthropological reasoning, is one which depicts such societies as entirely fierce and violent. The inflicting of physical harm was the evidence for such a view and the causes for the violent behaviour were frequently based in sociobiological, ecological or materialist explanations. Such an approach, which takes the existence of relations of physical harm as an indicator for violence, is based on what I would call a first order notion of violence. A second order notion of violence would distinguish between legal and illegal forms of physical harm and would refer to the illegal forms of physical harm as violence. Such a view is, therefore, connected to some sort of legal evaluation. Societies lacking systems of legal evaluation may therefore be described as violent in the first sense or but hardly in the second sense, without referring to external standards. Such relations of physical harm are a constitutive and necessary element in the reproduction of these social systems, and may even be regarded as a functional equivalent to aspects of a legal system. That is why, for the Yukpa, violence was not a question which might be reduced to hate, envy or pleasure but a 'a fundamental necessity'. In other terms, it is not only the exchange of 'goods' which leads to a social order but also the exchange of different forms of physical violence. Associating such forms of violence a priori with non-legitimacy and therefore considering them as 'bad' comes close to stating that a certain system of social reproduction is illegal or illegitimate.

The expanding state, which tries to establish and expand its monopoly on physical violence, and missionary agendas, associate first order violence with non-legitimacy and thus transform these traditional forms of violence into illegal ones. As a consequence, the 'pacification' of indigenous peoples becomes a heroic act within a civilisational project. The installation of structures of formal leadership and the appointment of official *caciques* legitimated by missionaries and the state, equipped with power and authority for the administration of justice and punishment, introduced the duplication of violence into Yukpa society. Warfare, vendetta and ritualised duels have largely disappeared and many informants stress that the stories about these events are '*atancha*' stories, stories from the ancestors, even though the older men participated in these events.

Notes

1 The completion of this paper was supported by the Austrian Program for Advanced Research and Technology (APART) awarded by the Austrian Academy of Sciences. For comments in different development stages of this paper I am grateful to Ulrike Davis-Sulikowsky, Clemens Zobel, Georg Elwert, Bernhard Hadolt and Andrea Stoeckl.

2 Reichel-Dolmatoff uses the old term Motilones, which refers to both the Barí and the Yukpa, but his ethnographic data were collected among the Colombian Yukpa of the Maraca valley.

3 According to the respective theoretical orientations of the authors, this debate related explanations of Yanomami warfare to different aspects of social order: From the sociobiological perspective the emphasis was placed on the access to women (Chagnon), while from the ecological point of view the access to meat and game was privileged (Harris). In a historical-materialist perspective the access to goods in relation to the expanding state was stressed (Ferguson), and within a sociological and cosmological approach attention focused on the internal logic of social and cosmological relations (Albert, Alés, Lizot).

4 A preliminary and minimal working definition of violence understands violence as 'act(s) of intended harm'. These acts may either cause

physical, psychic, social or material harm. They may be intended by individual or collective, physical or spiritual actors or just ascribed as intended by victims or witnesses. Such acts may rely on directly observable physiological-material interventions or on only indirectly observable ones, based in spiritual means as e.g. shamanic warfare or sorcery. I have selected institutionalised forms of directly observable 'intended physical harm' among the Yukpa for further consideration in this paper.

5 I have published a more detailed description of these processes in Halbmayer 1998 (68–78).

6 This was obviously the case after the killing of three Yukpa in the village of Kasmera by the Venezuelan military in 1994. This event is also symptomatic of the fact that societies like those of the Yukpa once brought under control of state systems rather become victims of state violence than active agents of violence against the outside world.

7 A more detailed distinction between war, raid, vendetta, feud, vengeance killing as e.g. Black-Michaud (1975) has proposed seems inadequate for the Yukpa, as there is no clear-cut distinction between the general or specific choice of victims, and there may be a shift from individual to collective enterprises in the course of vendetta.

8 I conducted 13 months of field research among the Yukpa from 1991 to 1992 and spent an additional total of four months there in 1988, 1994, 1997 and 1999.

9 As the rivers and consequently the fish in these mountain areas are small, fishing is a rather secondary subsistence strategy.

10. ♂ and ♀ indicate the speaker's sex; Z=sister; D=daughter; M= mother; and B=brother.

11 However, there are significant differences between the kinship-systems of Yukpa subgroups. An analysis of these variations is in preparation.

12 Such a notion of a helpful father-in-law stands in contrast to many other South American societies where the father-in-law is rather associated with the dangerous outside.

13 The notions of reciprocity and negative reciprocity rely on Sahlins (1972). 'Reciprocity' without specification includes balanced as well as generalised reciprocity.

14 For the myth of the creation of the women see Armato (1988: 11–13). Among the Parirí Yukpa men and women are created by a being called 'God' by Wilbert (1962: 139f. 1974: 75)

15 This view is not generally shared: Reichel-Dolmatoff introduced Yuko as a self-referential term (1945: 18). He changed his interpretation on the meaning of the term in subsequent publications (Reichel-Dolmatoff and Clark 1950; Reichel-Dolmatoff 1960: 165), but did not explicitly modify his initial statement. That Yuko is a term of self-reference among indigenous people living on the Colombian side of

the Sierra de Perijá was reaffirmed by Ruddle (1971, 1974) who opposed them to the Venezuelan Yukpa. Also, Carriage, despite giving an appropriate description of the significance of the terms (yikpa/yiki), insists on the term Yuko as a self-designation (1980: 15). According to the available data, however, I doubt that Yuko (enemy) was used as a self-designation in the region and I will not use the term 'enemy' (Yuko) as an anthropological term for a group of people, as long as there is no empirically sound evidence for the inversion of the significance of Yukpa/Yuko among certain subgroups.

16 These subgroup divisions have weakened considerably with increased contact and interaction between them encouraged through missionary activities and the advancing integration into the national society (see Halbmayer 1998).

17 Among the Colombian Yukpa of the Casacare valley, where Carriage conducted field-research, due to dialectical differences, *Yikpa* means people, and bodily is expressed by Yi- instead of Yu-.

18 The Sister, Father's Sister and Father's Brother's Daughter.

19 For a detailed description, see Halbmayer (1998: 136–85).

20 'To be aggressive' or 'wild' *(iso)* is closely related to the word for 'jaguar' *(isho),* called 'tigre' in local Spanish.

21 The term Motilones was used to refer to the Yukpa and to their southern Chibcha-speaking neighbours the Barí. It became clear in the 1950s that there are two culturally distinct groups living in the area west of the Lago de Maracaibo.

22 The higher male suicide rate among the Yukpa has already been noted by Gusinde (1955: 425) nearly 50 years ago. Suicide seems not be common among all the Yukpa subgroups: Wilbert (1960: 128) mentions that suicide is not practised among the Pariri, whereas Reichel-Dolmatoff (1945: 61) states that suicide is very common among the groups living at the Rio Maraca, and also Bolinder (1958: 166) mentions suicide attempts. I was able to document 50 cases of suicide among the Irapa Yukpa of the Tukuko valley, 30 conducted by men and 20 by women (results based on a smaller sample of 33 cases, which show the same general direction have been published in Halbmayer 1997). A calculation of suicide rates, however, meets with several obstacles: (1) There is no proof that I have been able to document all cases. (2) There is no possibility of verifying exactly when these documented cases took place. However, each victim is remembered by name and their kinship relation can be specified. The Yukpa have a very shallow genealogical knowledge which generally goes back only to the grandparents. My calculation is based on the assumption that these suicides occurred during the last 60 years. (3) A significant population growth of over 40 per cent took place in the region between 1982 and 1992 (Halbmayer 1998: 84–5); however,

there are no reliable population data available for the period of 60 years. My calculation for the whole period is based on the population data collected in 1992. A significant underestimation of suicide rates might be the consequence of such a procedure. Therefore, the presented numbers can only provide a general indication if the suicide rates are high or low, but no value should be put in the numbers as such. Calculated on the base of 764 inhabitants of the Tukuko valley in 1992, the suicide rate in the region would be 109.1/100,000. In comparison, this number seems very high: the suicide rate in Venezuela is 5.1 (1994) and in Colombia 3.5 (1994). Data for other countries are: Great Britain 7.1 (1997), Netherlands 9.9 (1995), USA 11.8 (1996), Sweden 14.2 (1996), Germany 15.1 (1997), Austria 20 (1997), France 20.6 (1995), Switzerland 21.4 (1994), Finland 27.2 (1995), Latvia 36.9 (1996), Estonia 39.2 (1996), Russian Federation 41.2 (1995) Lithuania 48.2 (1996) (Source: WHO; all data per 100,000 inhabitants). For the Aguaruna, however, Brown mentions a suicide rate of 180/100,000.

23 Female adultery is frequently interpreted as the wish to end the marital relationship.

24 A more detailed analysis of these socio-cosmological aspects has recently been prepared (see Halbmayer 2000).

25 This also seems true for other Carib-speaking groups and Gillin (1934) previously had pointed out that 'little attention is paid to abstract ideals of right and wrong' and that 'law and justice are highly personal' (1934: 334). For the introduction of public punishment among the Yukpa, see Halbmayer 1998.

Bibliography

Albert, B. (1989) 'Yanomami violence, inclusive fitness or ethnographic representation', *Current Anthropology* 30(5): 637–40.

—— (1990) 'On Yanomami warefare: rejoinder', *Current Anthropology* 31(5): 558–63.

Alès, C. (1984) 'Violence et ordre sociale', *Etudes rurales* 95/96: 89–114.

Armato, J. (1988) *Lo que cuentan los Yukpa,* Maracaibo: Comisíon Presidentcial para el Bicentenario del Natalicio del General Rafael Urdaneta.

Armellada, F. C. d. (1948) 'Una aclación necesaria: ¿Todos los Indígenas de Perijá son Motilones? ¿Los Motilones son Karibes?', *Venezuela Misionera* X(112): 131–6.

Black-Michaud, J. (1975) *Cohesive Force. Feud in the Mediterranean and the Middle East.* Oxford: Basil Blackwell.

Bolinder, G. (1917) 'Einiges über die Motilon-Indianer der Sierra de Perija (Kolumbien – Südamerika)', *Zeitschrift für Ethnologie* 49: 21–51.

—— (1958) *We Dared the Andes. Three Journeys into the Unknown*, London, New York: Abelard–Schuman.

Brown, Michael F. (1986) 'Power, gender, and the social meaning of Aguaruna suicide', *Man (n.S.)* 21: 311–28.

Cariage, P. (1979) 'Contribution à l'Étude des Yuko: un groupe indigène du nord-est de la Colombie', unpublished Dissertation, École des Hautes Études en Sciences Sociales.

—— (1980) 'Guerre et guerre entre familles chez les Yuko', *Bulletin de la Société Suisse de Américanistes* 44: 13–16.

Chagnon, N. (1968) 'Yanomamö social organization and warfare', in M. Fried, M. Harris, and R. Murphy (eds) *War: the Anthropology of Armed Conflict*, New York: Natural History Press.

—— (1983) *Yanomamö: The Fierce People*, New York: Holt, Rinehart & Winston.

—— (1988) 'Life histories, blood revenge, and warfare in a tribal population', *Science* 239: 985–992.

—— (1989) 'Reponse to R. B. Ferguson', *American Ethnologist*, 16: 565–9.

—— (1990a) 'On Yanomamö violence: reply to Albert', *Current Anthropology* 31(1): 49–53.

—— (1990b) 'Reproductive and somatic conflicts of interest in the genesis of violence and warfare among the Yanomamö Indians', in J. Haas (ed.) *The Anthropology of War*, Cambridge: Cambridge University Press.

Descola, P. (1993) 'Les affinités sélectives : alliance, guerre et prédation dans l'ensemble Jivaro', *L'Homme XXXIII* 2–3: 171–90.

Dupuy, J.-P., and Varela, F. (1992) 'Understanding origins: an introduction', in F. Varela and J.-P. Dupuy (eds) *Understanding Origins. Contemporary Views on the Origin of Life, Mind and Society*. Dortrecht, Boston, London: Kluwer.

Durbin, M. (1977) A Survey of the Carib language family. *Anthropological Papers of the University of Arizona* 28: 23–38.

Ferguson, R.B. (1990) 'Blood on the Leviathan: western contact and warfare in Amazonia', *American Ethnologist* 17(2): 237–57.

—— (1995) *Yanomami Warfare: A Political History*, Santa Fe: School of American Research Press.

Godelier, M., Trautmann, T. R. and Tjon Sie Fat, F. E. (eds) (1998) *Transformations of Kinship*, Washington, London: Smithsonian Institution Press.

Gusinde, M. (1955) 'Meine forschungsreise zu den Yupa-Indianern im westlichen Venezuela', *Anthropos* 50: 418–27.

Guss, D. M. (1991) ''All things made': myths of the Origins of Artefacts', in M. H. Preuss (ed.) *Past, Present, and Future. Selected Papers on Latin American Indian Literatures*, Culver City, California: Labyrinthos.

Halbmayer, E. (1998) *Kannibalistische Sonne, Schwiegervater Mond und die Yukpa*, Frankfurt/Main: Brandes & Apsel.

—— (2000) 'Principles of social organization, sexual relations and cosmology among the Yukpa of north-western Venezuela', unpublished manuscript, Paris.

Harris, M. (1984) 'A cultural materialist theory of band and village warfare: the Yanomamö test', in B. Ferguson (ed.) *Warfare, Culture and Environment*, Orlando: Academic Press.

Henley, P. (1996) 'South Indian models in the Amazonian lowlands', *Manchester Papers in Social Anthropology* 1: 1–80.

Lévi-Strauss, C. (1943) 'Guerre et commerce chez les Indiens de l'Amérique du Sud', *Renaissance* 1(1–2): 122–39.

Lhermillier, A. (1980) 'La société Yu´pa-Macoita de la Sierra de Perijá au Venezuela: résistance et transformations des structures traditionnelles, Vol. 1', unpublished Dissertation, École des Hautes Études en Sciences Sociales.

Lhermillier, N. (1980) 'La Société Yu´pa-Macoita de la Sierra de Perijá au Venezuela: vie économique et sociale de la communauté de Samamo, Vol. 2', unpublished dissertation, École des Hautes Études en Sciences Sociales.

Lizot, J. (1989) 'A propos de la Guerre: Une réponse à N. Chagnon', *Journal de Société des Américanistes* 75: 91–113.

—— (1994) 'On Warfare: An Answer to N. A. Chagnon', *American Ethnologist* 21: 845–62.

Lizzaralde, M. (1988) *Índice y Mapa de Grupos Etnolingüísticos Autóctonos de América del Sur*, Caracas: Instituto Caribe de Antropología y Sociología, Fundación La Salle de Ciencias Naturales.

Menget, P. (1985) 'Guerre, Sociétés et vision du monde dans le basses terres de L'Amérique du Sud: jalons pour une étude comparative', *Journal de la Société des Américanistes* 71: 129–41.

OCEI (1993) *Censo Indígena de Venezuela 1992*, Caracas: Oficina Central de Estadística e Informática.

Oquendo, L. (1998) 'Is Japreria a Yukpa dialect?', unpublished paper presented at the Annual Meeting of the Linguistic Society of America, New York.

Paolisso, M.J. (1985) 'Subsistence and coffee cultivation among the Irapa-Yukpa of Venezuela: a cultural ecological investigation', unpublished Dissertation, University of California, Los Angeles.

Paolisso, M.J. and Sackett, R. (1985) 'Traditional meat procurement strategies among the Irapa-Yukpa of the Venezuela–Colombia border area', *Research in Economic Anthropology* 7: 177–99.

Reichel-Dolmatoff, G. (1945) 'Los Indios Motilones', *Revista del Instituto Etnológico Nacional* 2: 15–115.

—— (1960) 'Contribuciones al Conocimiento de las Tribus de la Región de Perijá', *Revista Colombiana de Antropologia* 9: 159–98.

Reichel-Dolmatoff, G. and Clark, A.L. (1950) 'Parentesco, parentela y

Agresión entre los Iroka', *Journal de la Société des Américanistes* 39: 97–109.
Riches, D. (1986) 'The Phenomenon of Violence', in D. Riches (ed.) *The Anthropology of Violence*, Oxford: Basil Blackwell.
Rival, L. (1996) *Hijos del Sol, Padres del Jaguar: Los Huaorani de Ayer y Hoy*, Quito: Abya Yala.
Rivet, P. and Armellada, F. C. de (1950) 'Les Indiens Motilones', *Journal de la Société des Américanistes* 39: 15–57.
Ruddle, K. (1970) 'The hunting technology of the Maracá Indians,' *Anthropológica* 25: 21–63.
—— (1971) 'Notes on the Nomenclature and Distribution of the Yukpa-Yuko Tribe', *Antropológica* 30: 18–28.
—— (1974) *The Yukpa Cultivation System: A Study of Shifting Cultivation in Colombia and Venezuela*, Berkeley, Los Angeles and London: University of California Press.
Ruddle, K. and Wilbert, J. (1983) 'Los Yukpa', in R. Lizzaralde and H. Seijas (eds) *Etnología Contemporanea I: Los Aborigenes de Venezuela* (General Editor: Walter Coppens) Caracas: Fundación La Salle de Ciencias Naturales, Instituto Caribe de Antropología y Sociología.
Sahlins, M. (1972) *Stone Age Economics*, London: Tavistock Publications.
Spencer Brown, G. (1973) *Laws of Form*, New York: Bentam Books.
Vegamian, F.M. de (1978) *Diccionario Ilustrado Yupa-Español, Español Yukpa*, Caracas: Formateca.
Viveiros de Castro, E.B. (1993) 'Alguns Aspectos da afinidade no Dravidianato Amazônico', in M. M. Carneiro da Cunha and E. B. Viveiros de Castro (eds) *Amazônia: Etnologia e Historia Indígena*, São Paulo: Universidade de São Paulo, Núcleo de História Indígena.
Wavrin, M. de (1948) *Les Indiens sauvages de l'Amérique du Sud*, Paris: Payot.
—— (1953) *Chez les Indiens de Colombie*, Paris: Plon.
Wilbert, J. (1960) 'Zur Kenntnis der Parirí', *Archiv für Völkerkunde* 15: 80–153.
—— (1962) 'Erzählgut der Yupa-Indianer', *Anthropos* 57: 861–88.
—— (1974) *Yukpa Folktales*, Los Angeles: University of California Press.

Chapter 4

The interpretation of violent worldviews

Cannibalism and other violent images of the Caribbean

Bettina E. Schmidt

Introduction

In December 1998 the New York Times reported that a Vodou priest in New Jersey was indicted on charges of conspiring to kill a woman at a religious ceremony. While the incident itself still remains controversial – if the woman was burned by the priest or set herself ablaze by bumping into a candle – the case attracted considerable attention. Even today Vodou still conjures up images of human sacrifice and cannibalism. It was easy to make people believe in an attempted murder, even when the police failed to find any motive (*New York Times*, 12 December 1998, p. B1). The woman was indeed injured during the ceremony, but this does not provide sufficient grounds simplistically to reduce the religious system of Vodou to one aspect, viz. violence.

Cannibalism has inspired the European imagination for centuries. Rather than being regarded as culturally constructed acts of violence, cannibal images have been instrumentalized by Europeans in the Caribbean (and elsewhere) for establishing a faultline between 'civilization' and 'savagery'.

In studying cannibalism, we have to keep in mind what David Riches states about violence in general: the concept of violence implies a form of behaviour that in some sense is illegitimate or unacceptable, but must be considered legitimate by the performer (1986: 1). Even if the cannibal act is unacceptable in our cultural system, in other cultures there may be reasons for accepting it. Joanna Overing, for example, describes cannibalism among the – normally very peaceful – Piaroa, where it can order relationships between groups 'and in doing so is a discourse forthcoming from a particular metaphysics about the nature of social life itself' (1986: 100). The same can be suggested for Caribbean cannibalism, where cannibal acts have, nearly always, fulfilled a social function for the community.

The way cannibal acts are perceived is as important as the act itself for the understanding of anthropophagy. Therefore, cannibalism should be approached from a dialectical perspective, as an act of physical hurt as well as a violent imaginary used in the construction of the Other. By comparing the attitudes toward Caribbean cannibalism and African-American slave religions, in particular Haitian Vodou, this chapter will demonstrate how the stereotypical perception of violent acts has continued to influence our view of Caribbean cultural concepts and still shapes intergroup confrontations.

The appearance of Caribbean cannibals

On 23 November 1492 Christopher Columbus wrote in his journal that the island he was approaching was, according to the Indians

> very extensive and that in it were people who had one eye in the forehead, and others whom they called 'cannibals'. Of these last, they showed great fear, and when they saw that this course was being taken, they were speechless, he says, because these people ate them and because they are very warlike.
>
> (quoted in Hulme 1986: 16–17)

In this report a group of indigenous people called 'cannibals' made their first appearance in a European text, and a new term was coined. Even though Columbus did not actually meet the Indians with 'one eye in the forehead', he did not question the existence of the 'cannibals'. The image of people eating their own kind was not invented in the Caribbean, of course. Even Herodotus described man-eating as a 'way of life', as customary among the Massagetae and the Androphagae.

But the label 'cannibal' was born from this first encounter between Caribbeans and Europeans. It is used to this day as a synonym for wild, uncivilised men, whom the colonizers saw 'behind each landmark set in place by the march of European culture' (Bartra 1997: 1).

It is difficult to tell myth from reality, especially in a violent, but also fascinating context such as this. The consumption of one's own kind seems to capture our imagination in a unique way and guides our thoughts in only one direction: to condemn cannibalism as 'barbarous' and non-human behaviour. As Donald Tuzin and Paula Brown note, 'the idea of people eating their own kind has a long, if not precisely honorable, history in the intellectual and folk traditions of the West' (1983: 1).

In spite of early descriptions of cannibalism as customary behaviour, as an important part of some cultures, by Ewald Volhard (1968, original 1939) for example, the scientific community often takes a limited view of anthropophagy. Marvin Harris (1977) in a materialistic argument reduces cannibalism to its nutritional value, while in Eli Sagan's words, cannibalism was 'the elementary form of institutionalised aggression' (1974: 132). Instead of regarding cannibalism as one important element of a cultural system, a view like Sagan's, which has been held dear by the European colonial imagination from the earliest times, reduces the whole religious system of the Caribbean Indians to one single aspect, that of violence.

The Brazilian anthropologist Eduardo Viveiros de Castro demonstrates in his ethnography of the Araweté, a Tupi-Guarani group of the eastern Amazon Basin, a different way of looking at cannibalism. He shows that it can have meaning beyond the violent act and even beyond metaphor. As described in his book *From the Enemy's Point of View* cannibalism plays a central role in the cosmologies of Amazon societies. After comparing different attitudes toward cannibalism in this area, he concludes:

> The Tupinamba's anthropological cannibalism, the Araweté's divine cannibalism, and the anticannibal religion of the Guarani are all transformations of the same theme: the instability of Culture between Nature and Supernature. Thus, we can recuperate the meaning of cannibalism as a sacrificial structure without resorting to the notion of communion with the ancestors.
>
> (Viveiros de Castro 1992: 301)

Through cannibal consumption, the community incorporates the Other, and therefore transforms itself into the enemy, as Viveiros de Castro concludes. Finally, 'the victory over death was achieved through cannibalism from everyone's point of view: the one who killed, the one who dies, the one who ate' (1992: 303).

Because of the extinction of the indigenous population it is impossible to conduct this kind of ethnographic fieldwork in the

Caribbean. We have to rely on descriptions of cannibal ceremonies by hostile outsiders, by colonisers and missionaries who witnessed cannibal customs in strange ceremonies without understanding the meaning of the rituals. Even more often, their notion of cannibalism was extracted from stories that were told by the (potential) cannibals' enemies. On these grounds alone, the reliability of these sources must be questioned, as we will see later. Based on the discourse on cannibalism in the Caribbean two different types of intergroup conflict can be distinguished from which stories of cannibalism were generated: between two different Caribbean people and between Europeans and Caribbeans. The problems in understanding anthropophagy in the Caribbean result from the Eurocentric perspective that misunderstood, used and sometimes even denied the existence of cannibalism.

Archaeological studies suggest that Caribbean cannibalism did actually exist as 'a limited, ritual act associated with victory in battle and funerary customs' (Whitehead 1984: 81). Based on Spanish and non-Spanish sources, Neil Whitehead concludes that the taking of human trophies as well as ritual cannibalism of war captives were customary among the Caribs and other indigenous groups such as the Arawak and Tupinamba in South America (1984: 69). Regarding the Caribbean he states that:

> There are examples of Spanish reports [. . .], which attempt to account for Carib cannibalism in its social context [. . .]. In these accounts the notion that the Caribs ate human flesh as a means of subsistence is firmly rejected, while the prevalence of endocannibalistic funerary rites and the exocannibalism of war captives, or *itotos*, is shown to be common among other Amerindian groups, not just the Caribs.
>
> (Whitehead 1984: 76–7)

But despite Whitehead's research, the discussion about the existence of cannibalism continues. Our knowledge about the former population of the Caribbean islands is remarkably scanty as compared to their historical significance. And now it is too late to ask the Caribs themselves. Today it seems impossible, as Peter Mason states, to 'make a distinction between image and reality' in regard to cannibalism (1990: 54).

In this chapter, I will not once again dwell on rumours, but focus on the patterns of interaction between Europeans and

Caribbeans. Their conflict can be seen as an example of the clash of different cultural systems. I am no longer concerned with the phenomenon of cannibalism, but with its construction. And at this point deconstruction begins.

The denial of cannibalism

When we consider the triangle of violence – perpetrator, victim and witnesses – it is evident that barely an outside eyewitness of cannibalism has ever existed but a lot of second-hand observations. The interpretation of cannibalism depends on the reliability of the sources, as William Arens has shown in his classic book *The Man-eating Myth*, where he demystifies cannibalism as an ideological construct of Western imperialism. Dismissing all reports not derived directly from eyewitnesses as unreliable, and those first-hand reports (e.g. by Hans Staden) as dubious because the witness had survived, Arens doubts that cannibalism ever existed.[1]

The colonial construction of cannibalism as a boundary between 'civilisation' and 'savagery' persists today not only in our imagination but also in our scientific discourse. The focus on violent aspects of 'exotic' religions was (and still is) an integral element of the Eurocentric suppression not only of violence, but also of cultures who celebrate violence.

Today, the negative image of anthropophagy once created by colonialism has been replaced with the denial that cannibalism ever existed. Any discussion of this custom as an element in a cultural context is reprimanded as discriminatory of the culture referred to. What was once branded as savage has now become a lie. The literary historian Peter Hulme defines cannibalism as: 'the image of ferocious consumption of human flesh frequently used to mark the boundary between one community and its others, a term that has gained its entire meaning from within the discourse of European colonialism' (Hulme 1986: 86). Through the analysis of colonial reports, Hulme demonstrates how cannibalism was used as an excuse for the destruction of indigenous cultures: in the eyes of the conquerors those Indians were cannibals who resisted European domination. In the colonial discourse cannibalism became inextricably linked to resistance against European colonisation.

When we regard all sources on cannibalism – especially the reports of the conquerors and the colonists – as part of a colonial discourse and, therefore, all stories about cannibals as stereotypical colonial fiction, it seems difficult to accept the existence of cannibalism. Because the cannibal imaginary was used by the colonisers to legitimise the extinction of the indigenous population, it has been argued, it can only be a European invention. In this discussion the results of ethnographic research among other cannibals, especially in the Amazon basin,[2] tends to be ignored. Yet the acknowledgement of the existence of cannibal rituals in other contexts than the Caribbean could also establish the Caribbean cannibalism as a historical fact. Even archaeological evidence of cannibal acts can be found in the Caribbean. As Philip Boucher asks: 'What about the fractured human bones found at some Carib archaeological sites'? (1992: 7). The critics of the existence of cannibalism fail to consider the consequences their view of cannibalism as colonial stereotype entail: to regard cannibalism purely as a colonial invention inevitably leads to the negative stereotyping of a culture that includes (or formerly included) cannibalism as a central aspect of their symbolic universe. In the end, the indigenous culture is once again subject to discrimination, once again marginalised on the basis of colonial stereotypes. This will be demonstrated by the following discussion of Caribbean cannibalism in the context of colonial discourse.

Caribbean cannibalism and colonial discourse

In order to situate the problematic concepts of Caribbean cannibalism in colonial discourse I will begin by outlining some central topics of this discourse. Peter Hulme describes his concept of colonial discourse in the introduction to his well-known book *Colonial Encounters* as:

> [. . .] an ensemble of linguistically-based practices unified by their common deployment in the management of colonial relationships, an ensemble that could combine the most formulaic and bureaucratic of official documents [. . .] with the most non-functional and unprepossessing of romantic novels [. . .]. Underlying the idea of colonial discourse [. . .] is the presumption that during the colonial period large parts of the non-European world were *produced* for Europe through a discourse that implicated sets of questions and assumptions, methods of procedure and analysis, and kinds of writing and imagery, normally separated out into the discrete areas of

> military strategy, political order, social reform, imaginative literature, personal memoirs and so on.
>
> (Hulme 1986: 2)

Hulme's concept is based exclusively on sources written by Europeans and excludes any other kinds of sources, from Mestizo writings to oral tradition. All criticisms aside, colonial discourse has become a metaphor for the construction of the Other in speaking about him (Wehrheim-Peuker 1998: 10–11).

While Hulme focuses on the relationship between Europe and America, other colonial theorists like Homi Bhabha expand the concept of colonial discourse to stand as a global category of the nineteenth century. His definition of colonial discourse includes the aspect of race: 'The objective of colonial discourse is to construe the colonized as a population of degenerate types on the basis of racial origin, in order to justify conquest and to establish systems of administration and instruction' (Bhabha 1986: 154). Bhabha's definition of colonial discourse can be extended to other colonial periods. The concept of colonial discourse as construed originally for the American context can no longer be limited either geographically or historically. From this viewpoint, Wehrheim-Peuker defines colonial discourse as a systematic term that allows the investigation of specific discursive patterns, centred around the representation of the Other (1998: 13). In her book *The Defeated Conquest* she connects, for example, the colonial with the mysogynous discourse. From a feminist perspective she compares American cannibals to European (female) witches, both of whom appear as symbols of the unknown, jeopardising the European (and male) position of power.[3] By virtue of their very existence (be it real or imagined), witches as well as cannibals have threatened the very structure of European society. Thus, the aggressors eventually present themselves as potential victims. In both discourses historical reality is ignored.

It is important to remember that the figure of the native Caribbean as portrayed in the discourse of European colonialism is not identical to the historical Caribbean. Cannibalism has influenced our understanding of the Caribbean more as part of the colonial discourse than as an historical phenomenon. Instead of being regarded as a cultural phenomenon, cannibalism became 'the creator of an ethnic stereotype' (Whitehead 1984: 69), a factor in the establishment of an ethnic boundary. Since Columbus's time two different kinds of indigenous groups have been distinguished in the Caribbean, 'Arawaks' and 'Caribs'. While the first group is described as calm and peaceful, the second was transformed into violent cannibals. It is cannibalism that separates the 'Arawaks' from the 'Caribs'.

The dichotomy between Arawaks and Caribs as based on cannibalism served to justify different colonial attitudes. Rumours of deposits of gold on one island were closely followed by rumours of cannibalism, leading to the enslavement and, usually, the extinction of the inhabitants. This construed contrast between the Noble Savage and the Wild Savage even found its way into the anthropological discourse, into the *Handbook of South American Indians* for example, where the Arawak are described as calm, 'noble' Indians in contrast to the aggressive Caribs (Rouse 1948: 495–6). In the view of Peter Hulme, the ethnic map of the Caribbean was created by the colonial presence which established the dichotomy between two ethnically identical groups.

This argument recalls Drummond's analysis. Based on material from Guayana, Lee Drummond views the dichotomy between Arawaks and Caribs as a 'pair of polarised stereotypes':

> The European experience in the Caribbean and the Guianas was . . . with one of two kinds of Indians, as different in the colonists' eyes as night and day: the Arawak and the Carib. The Carib were distinguishable as a people by their warlike nature; they, or their ancestors, had pillaged and cannibalized throughout the Lesser Antilles and along the 'Wild Coast' of the Guianas. The Arawak, in contrast, were notable for their 'pacific disposition' . . . They submitted to extermination with admirable grace and, where a few survived, settled down peacefully in villages near colonial settlements.
>
> (Drummond 1977: 78)

Following Drummond's lead, Hulme notes that after having been established the stereotypes became something like a 'self-fulfilling prophecy': peaceful behaviour leads to the identification as Arawaks and hostile behaviour to the identification as Caribs (1986: 65–7), without any real dialogue with the foreign culture ever taking place.

Hulme stresses that the dichotomy of stereotypes did not originate from ethnographic reality but from European tradition. He identifies two European discourses at the base of the divergent perception of indigenous societies. On one hand, he sees the discourse on Oriental civilisation dating back to the voyages of Marco Polo, which includes keywords like 'gold' and the 'Grand Khan' and was always considered as good and noble. On the other, he notes a discourse on savagery based on Herodotus which includes keywords like 'monstrosity', 'anthropophagy' and again 'gold' (Hulme 1986: 20–2). While the first discourse ultimately motivated the voyages of Columbus, even in the first weeks of his voyage the two began to mix. Later, arguments taken from the second discourse were used in vindicating his lack of success. Cannibalism as a constitutive boundary between two ethnic groups in the Caribbean became a crucial factor in the cultural conflict between Europeans and Caribbeans.

As important as this aspect is, it contains a pitfall, and not only for anthropologists. By being denied their own cultural context of cannibalism, the Caribbean Indians have once again become the victims of an uneven exchange. Both Drummond and Hulme have inspired us to think more seriously about our own European traditions. Yet by this very literary turn, they obstruct our view on what the ethnographic reality of non-European cultures may have been like.

In a way, this literary turn continues the colonial tradition. Columbus, as described by Hulme, had to return with tales of man-eating because he came back from outside of civilisation (1986: 85). Hulme himself has to come back from his excursions into the sources on anthropophagy with tales of colonialism, because he comes back from inside our civilisation. The indigenous cultures are marginalised within both concepts, whether they have included cannibalism or not. The unconscious horror toward cannibal acts triggered two different reactions that were based on the same misunderstanding of a strange violent practice.

What can be extracted from Hulme's study is not the existence or non-existence of cannibalism, but the European system of ideas at the margin of our own community. It is within this framework, but without the possibility of any real dialogue between Europe and the Caribbean, that the Indians' behaviour has been interpreted, first by Columbus and now by Hulme. There never existed – and there still does not exist – any real interest in understanding the Caribbean cultures beyond their relevance as an argument in our own discourse.

For Columbus as well as for Peter Hulme, trying to understand cannibalism from within is out of the question. In the eyes of

Columbus, an invention of the Devil could not be part of a religion. And for Hulme, an invention of the Europeans could not be part of an indigenous non-Western culture.

Before I expand my argument by looking at the Afro-Caribbean context, I will briefly summarise the steps taken so far. I started with the controversial discussion on the 'evidence' of cannibalism in anthropology and literary history. While (many) anthropologists believe in the existence of cannibalism as based on various sources of evidence, literary historians often deny its existence because of the way cannibalism was abused in the colonial discourse. The argument of cannibalism was employed by the colonists to justify violence against the indigenous population. Because eating one's own kind was regarded as inhuman, the colonists felt themselves justified in killing the savage Indians. This same colonial strategy, which finally led to the extinction of the Caribbean natives, nowadays leads scholars to deny the very existence of cannibalism.

I argue that we cannot dispute the existence of a cultural trait just because it has been abused in colonial discourse. The idea of colonial invention and the scholarly denial of cannibalism on theoretical grounds both dissociate cannibal acts from their religious context and (more or less unconsciously) reduce in one sweep the Caribbean religion to a single minor aspect, the trait of cannibalism. The different reasonings behind both attitudes aside, they are based on the stereotypical representation of violent practices. The image of cannibalism creates such horror that an objective discussion of the sources becomes impossible, even in the academic arena.

Obeah, Vodou and other images of African slaves

The encounter between European colonisers and African slaves in the Caribbean was in many respects different from the previous encounter between the Europeans and the indigenous population, but demonstrated a similar attitude. Stereotypes from colonial discourse structured the European behaviour toward African slaves in the same way as they did the behaviour toward native Caribbeans. Acquiescent slaves were considered good slaves and those who resisted bad slaves, who were therefore portrayed as savages and ultimately even as cannibals, as is amply demonstrated by examples from Jamaican and Haitian history.

Slavery held an imminent danger. While every slave forced to work against his or her will was considered potentially dangerous, in the case of African slaves, the danger was even greater, because they epitomised the 'wild man' *par excellence*, the dangerous Other.

African slaves – like Caribbean Indians – were regarded as material property and not as human beings. Every kind of resistance was taken as a sign of a 'non-human' character.[4] In both cases, resistance was viewed as rooted in religion, since only savage (that is, non-Christian) minds were thought to harbour aggression against European civilisation. This is demonstrated by the example of the Jamaican Obeahmen.

During colonial times Obeah[5] was considered sorcery where human body parts were used in magical rituals (Götz 1995: 117). The (mostly male) priests, the Obeahmen, were often viewed by English colonists as dangerous rabble-rousers who led (peaceful) slaves to revolt. Because of their strange supernatural powers, slave-owners suspected them of being able to manipulate their slaves at will. Consequently, soon after the great slave rebellion in Jamaica in 1760, the first anti-Obeah Law was passed (Götz 1995: 142).

The Obeahmen's ability to communicate with the African gods was interpreted as worship of the devil and other evil spirits. Every unexplained death and even accidents were suspected to be the work of an Obeahman. They became the scapegoats on which the white masters could project their fears and shortcomings (Götz 1995: 163). When the Maroons won their independence from the British Crown, the Obeahmen were subjected to more and more restrictive regulation. Only a short time before emancipation the British Crown passed a law against vagrancy which explicitly referred – without any explanation – to Obeah in the preamble. Obeah has become synonymous with a 'heathen' culture that threatened the European civilisation in the Caribbean. The oppressors were transformed into victims, the rebellious slaves turning into performers of black magic.[6]

The same attitude prevails with respect to the Haitian Vodou. Alfred Métraux begins his book *Le vaudou haitien* (1958) with these sentences: 'Some exotic words are loaded with great conjuring power. "Vodou" is one of them. It creates mostly visions of mysterious death, secret rites or saturnalia celebrated by the blacks "enraptured by blood, sex and God"' (Métraux 1998: 11). Métraux's intention is to portray the Haitian religion as an empirical reality. However, even he does not escape the exoticisation of Vodou.

More than any other African-American religion, Vodou has suffered from stigmatisation by outsiders. Its origin exhibits the same pattern as any other African-American religion. During the slave trade, members of different cultures were mixed on the slave ships and later in the slave barracks on the plantations. In the Americas, they built new traditions out of an amalgamation of traits from their old religions. Particularly the religious and medical traditions were of importance for survival in the barracks. Under the cover of various Christian traditions emerged new syncretic religions. The Christian cover was important in order to prevent persecution by the Church and the colonial law, which banned all forms of 'heathen' worship. In this process, various syncretic religions were created in almost every colony, such as Santería in Cuba, Candomblé in Brazil or Vodou in Haiti.

All of these religions have taken on their recent appearance only after emancipation, when the former slaves were allowed to establish their own temples or churches in accordance with the Christian tradition of the colony. During the time of enslavement, the African slaves had not been regarded as human beings and were denied any pastoral care or even a religion at all. Every gathering of slaves was considered rebellious and dangerous for the colonial order. While in the Spanish and Portuguese colonies the Catholic Church had allowed the slaves to organise processions in honour of a saint, the slave-owners looked upon every meeting of their African slaves with horror – especially when the drums were beaten: to them, the drums meant Africa, mysterious power, black magic and ultimately, rebellion.

Obviously, this 'chain of evidence' is nothing but a myth, as for example Léon-François Hoffmann demonstrates in his analysis of the Bois-Caïman ceremony. Still, it is generally believed today that the general uprising of the slaves in Saint-Dominigue in 1791, which finally led to Haitian independence, was prepared during a Vodou ceremony one week before the rebellion took place. This story is taught in schools and constitutes an important founding myth of Haitian identity (Hoffmann 1996: 35).

The earliest description of the Bois-Caïman ceremony was published by Antoine Dalmas in his *Histoire de la révolution de Saint-Domingue* (Paris, 1814). According to this book, a black pig was sacrificed during the ceremony and its blood drunk by the rebellious slaves. Dalmas describes the African slaves and their religion in a way both absurd and violent. His information was in fact derived from the interrogation of prisoners after the revolt. He never took part in a Vodou ritual himself, let alone in the famous Bois-Caïman ceremony.

Although he does not use the term Vodou, Dalmas identifies the religion not only as 'absurd and sanguinary', but as one which contains 'the most frightful crimes'. Later, Vodou became increasingly associated with 'superstition and black magic, where human sacrifices [were] routinely offered to the African deities' (Hoffmann 1996: 37). Even without any base in eyewitness accounts, the story of the ceremony was elaborated in increasingly colourful terms through the years, taking on even more horrible aspects for the European slave-owners in the other colonies.

At some later date, another terrifying aspect was included in the form of an old woman, who seemed to inspire even more horror than the other slaves. Soon after the first description of the Bois-Caïman ceremony, a virgin priestess was introduced into the story that later became transformed into an old woman offering the sacrifice.[7]

After gaining independence through the successful slave uprising, Haiti posed a particular threat to European colonial power. Since then, Europeans have viewed Afro-Caribbean religious traditions as the main focus of resistance against slavery. Any religious or even medical aspects of Vodou were disputed. Vodou was reduced to the single aspect of black magic. In the eyes of Europeans, not only every unexplained death or accident was attributed to Vodou rituals, but also every act of resistance against the colonisers. Ironically, European observers thus may have believed more in the supernatural power of the Vodou priests than their slaves did. Sulikowski notes:

> Out of the physical terror, where torture acted as part of the mode of production of slavery, the colonial mind extracted an imagery of the slaves as other than human, wielding a kind of monopoly on magic power as a mysterious weapon to strike at the oppressors.
>
> (Sulikowski 1996: 80)

Afro-Caribbean cannibalism

The same kind of colonial discourse that created cannibalism has also generated the image of Vodou. In both cases, images were construed that served the ends of the colonial discourse rather than the portrayal of real religious practices. Once again the victims were transformed into the aggressors, the slaves became the masters of supernatural power.

Even the image of cannibalism surfaces again at this point in time. In 1884 Spenser St John, a former British consul in Haiti, published his view of Haiti and Vodou in his book *Hayti or the Black Republic*. When the first edition appeared, it was heavily criticised for its negative attitude toward Haitians and especially for its description of Vodou. In the second edition, published only a few years later, St John even extended the two chapters on Vodou, where he described cannibal rites as a central element of Vodou ceremonialism:

> There is no subject of which it is more difficult to treat than Vaudoux-worship and the cannibalism which too often accompanies its rites. Few living out of the Black Republic are aware of the extent to which it is carried, and if I insist at length upon the subject, it is in order to endeavour to fix attention on this frightful blot, and thus induce enlightened Haytians to take measures for its extirpation, if that be possible.
> (St John 1971: 187)

After these introductory sentences, St John relates various cannibal incidents, all of which are supposed to have taken place after Haiti became independent. While most parts of *Hayti or the Black Republic* – even the description of Vodou ceremonies – are based on the French book *Description topographique* [. . .] *de la partie française de l'île de Saint-Domingue* by Moreau de St Méry (1797), the cannibal component was added by St John. He himself acknowledges that the main difference between St Méry's and his own account lies in his emphasis on cannibalism: 'In studying this account, freely taken from Moreau de St Méry, I have been struck how little change, except for the worse, has taken place during the last century' (1971: 199). The 'worse' for him means cannibalism.

The source mentioned for the story about cannibalism in Vodou ceremonies is a French priest whose story was told to St John by Monseigneur Guilloux, Archbishop of Port-au-Prince. While the first part of the ceremony in St John's book is more or less identical with St Méry's description, the story changes dramatically after an animal sacrifice has taken place:

> Presently an athletic young negro came and knelt before the priestess, and said, 'Oh Maman, I have a favour to ask.' 'What is it, my son?' 'Give us to complete the sacrifice the goat without horns.' She gave a sign of assent; the crowd in the shed separated, and there on the floor was a child sitting with its feet bound. In an instant a rope, already passed through a block, was tightened, the child's feet flew up towards the roof, and the Papaloi approached it with a knife. The loud shriek given by the victim aroused the curé to the truth of what was going on. He shouted, 'Oh, spare the child!' and would have darted forward, but he was seized by his friends around him and literally carried away. There was a short pursuit, but the French priest got safely back to the town. He tried to rouse the police to hasten to the spot, but they would do nothing. In the morning they accompanied him to the scene of the sacrifice, where they found the remains of the feast, and near the shed the boiled skull of the child.
>
> (St John 1971: 201)

This dramatic description of a presumed act of cannibalism is only one of many examples. St John never questions the reliability of his sources because, as he writes, 'what could be more direct than the testimony of this curé' (1971: 202). The inconsistency of a French priest being allowed to witness an illegal ceremony during which a child would be sacrificed and even 'cooked', never occurs to him. Nor does he mention any evidence beyond his personal memory. He even added descriptions of several cannibal ceremonies for the second edition of his book. The only sources he gives are rumours that were passed on to him after his arrival in Haiti and various newspaper articles. Logically, most of the ceremonies described in the second edition could be expected to have taken place after the first edition was published – and thus after he had left Haiti.

Nevertheless, St John's fabrications made his book a success. It influenced the perception of Vodou for decades.[8] Owing to his imaginative narrative, Vodou continues to be identified with cannibalism in the popular mind. Based on *Hayti or the Black Republic,* cannibal Vodou ceremonies have been included in most of the writings about Vodou up to the middle of the twentieth century. Even more influential than St John became the artist William Seabrook some decades later, who repeated the stories about human sacrifice, sorcery and necromancy in his book *The Magic*

Island (1929). His portrayal of Vodou influenced most of the popular 'Zombie' movies at the time.

Today, Vodou has been transformed into a general myth of horror, a durable image of evil. Despite substantial scholarly research on Vodou, which fails to substantiate any of St John's claims, and without a single reliable eyewitness account or any archaeological evidence, the image of Vodou still remains tied to the image of cannibalism. As in the case of Caribbean cannibalism, it has become seemingly impossible to distinguish between the construed image of Vodou and the real religion.

The reasons for the inclusion of cannibalism in the image of Vodou are various. First of all, Vodou does indeed contain elements that seem violent to the outside observer, especially the sacrifice of animals which forms an important part of the worship of the *lwas*, as the supernatural beings in Vodou are called. Despite the fact that blood sacrifice rituals are common in many religions, to non-believers they seem violent and hard to accept. It may seem like a small step to replace animals with humans. And because the animals sacrificed are eaten after the ritual, it did not seen far-fetched to assume that sacrificed humans would also have been consumed as part of the ceremony.

And yet not every religion that practises animal sacrifice is charged with cannibalism. Vodou seems to have touched upon another secret fear in the mind of European colonists. As the comparison with Caribbean cannibalism indicates, the early perception of Vodou, especially of the Bois-Caïman ceremony, identifies the religion with acts of rebellion by African slaves. The drums as a symbol for Africa, the rites of possession during all-night ceremonies as a symbol of heathen worship, and the fact that Haiti's independence was won by a slave rebellion, all of these aspects taken together laid the foundation for a negative image of Vodou which ultimately led to the assumption that even humans were commonly sacrificed to the *lwas*.

The historical subjects that performed these assumed acts of violence have been ignored in this concept. Neither St John nor Seabrook were interested in communicating directly with practitioners of Vodou. Even today, when numerous scholarly publications on Vodou are easily accessible, the community's internal perspective on the ritual still tends to be neglected. It seems that only those studies that focus on one narrow aspect of Vodou, for example the medical anthropological interpretation of the Haitian

Vodou as 'creole medicine' by Johannes Sommerfeld (1994), are able to evade the imaginary horror constructed in the colonial discourse. However, this involves once again the narrowing of a complex religious reality down to one minor aspect.

Conclusion

No other phenomenon in the colonisation of the Americas has charged debates and misconceptions to the extent that cannibalism has. The violent image of cannibalism was used as a boundary marker between ethnic groups and as a key element in the legitimising discourse of colonial domination. Thus, it became an important resource in the cultural conflict between Europeans and Caribbeans. Yet, cannibalism was indeed a ritual of violence and not a mere image, even if it has inspired the colonial imagination to a much greater extent as an image than as a practice.

By comparing Caribbean cannibalism to alleged Vodou cannibalism I have tried to show how the notion of 'cannibalism' became an important element of the encounter between different cultural systems, the native Caribbean as well as the Afro-Caribbean on one side and the European on the other. Although the European cultural system was the one that dominated the political reality in the Caribbean, the other two were discursively construed not as victims, but as perpetrators of violence. Cannibalism became the key symbol in the representation of 'other' cultures as violent and savage, thus demanding their oppression, even their extermination. Without any real knowledge of these 'others', the European colonisers throughout history have built their image of them around one major aspect: the – real or imagined – practice of cannibalism.

The relationship between worldviews and violence can be viewed from another perspective. Not only did Caribbean cultural systems (of the Caribbean Indians as well as of the African slaves) contain elements that were (and are) in fact violent, such as blood sacrifice, but it was the European reaction to these other cultures that created an atmosphere of extreme violence: in the colonial discourse, all non-Christian ideas and practices were interpreted as non-human, therefore requiring elimination.

From the beginning of the colonial encounter, the negative image connected with cannibalism has been reproduced over and over. While some Afro-Caribbean belief systems succeeded in being accepted as religions after independence, cannibalism as well as

Vodou continue to be haunted to the present by the images of violent 'othering' established in colonial discourse.

The two examples of cannibalism in the Caribbean I have discussed, one a violent practice and the other a violent image, demonstrate the different perspectives on this topic. In recent years, the discussion was dominated by literary studies, especially by Peter Hulme. While these literary studies have helped us to understand the European discourse, they have paid little attention to ethnographic reality, the domain of the anthropologist, who seem to have very little to say in this discussion. This silence may be explained, on the one hand, by the impossibility of conducting ethnographic research among Caribbean cannibals, since they have long disappeared. The comparison with other American cannibal culture can only provide some clues, because almost nothing at all is known about the culture of the Caribbean Indians. Based on various linguistic and cultural similarities between the Caribbean Indians and ethnic groups in the Amazon basin, we can assume some correspondences in the cannibal concepts. This careful comparison makes it possible to suggest that the cannibal act in the Caribbean – as in the Amazon – was part of religion.

As the example of Vodou shows, the acceptance of a foreign religion remains problematic today, especially if the belief system includes ritual customs that seem strange and revolting to the observer. While the cannibal elements of Vodou have obviously been invented by outsiders and have nothing to do with the religion itself, Vodou does include some violent aspects, which have encouraged the cultural misunderstanding to some degree. Horrified by images of blood sacrifice, European colonists inevitably had to misunderstand Vodou from their viewpoint. Their own cultural system was by itself highly violent towards 'others' – even if they did not eat them.

Notes

1 Cf. also Barker/Hulme/Iversen (eds) 1998.

2 Cf. Clastres 1972: 309–46 on Guayakí cannibalism; Lizot 1985: 3 on the Yanomami concept of cannibalism, or Maranhão 1998 for a postmodern interpretation of cannibalism in the Amazon basin. See also Sanday 1989 for a interpretation of cannibalism as a cultural system.

3 'The Christian-man can only control himself if he dominates the other, therefore a constant of the (colonial and mysogynous) othering dis-

course is to portray the other in his otherness as a danger to the self' (Wehrheim-Peuker 1998: 188, translated by B. E. S.).

4 Resistance against slavery and runaway slave identity remain focal points in the construction of diasporic black identification to this day.

5 Cf. Olmos and Paravisini-Gebert 1997 and Hedrick *et al.* (1984) for the religious concepts of Obeah.

6 Obeah continues to be viewed with suspicion by Jamaican intellectuals who draw a clear distinction between the 'balm yard' healers on one side and Obeah as black magic on the other.

7 This is one of the earliest traces of the notion – which has become much more elaborate since – that Afro-Caribbean religions are dominated by women.

8 Cf. Bremer 1996.

Bibliography

Arens, W. (1979) *The Man-eating Myth: Anthropology and Anthropophagy*, New York: Oxford University Press.

Barker, F., Hulme, P. and Iversen, M. (eds) (1998) *Cannibalism and the Colonial World*, Cambridge, New York and Melbourne: Cambridge University Press.

Bartra, R. (1997) *The Artificial Savage: Modern Myths of the Wild Man*, Ann Arbor: University of Michigan Press.

Bhabha, H. K. (1986) 'The other question: difference, discrimination and the discourse of colonialism', in F. Barker, P. Hulme, M. Iversen and D. Loxley (eds) *Literature, Politics and Theory: Papers from the Essex Conference 1976–84*, London and New York: Methuen.

Boucher, P. P. (1992) *Cannibal Encounters: Europeans and Island Caribs, 1492–1763*, Baltimore and London: Johns Hopkins University Press.

Bremer, T. (1996) 'Zur Frühgeschichte der Selbst- und Fremdwahrnehmung schwarzer Kulturformen in der Karibik: Spenser St. Johns Darstellung des haitianischen Vaudou (1884/89)', in M. Kremser (ed.) *Ay BoBo – afro-karibische Religionen, Zweite Internationale Tagung der Gesellschaft für Karibikforschung Wien 1990, Teil 2: Voodoo*, Wien: WUV-Universitaets-Verlag.

Clastres, Pierre (1972) *Chronique des Indiens Guayaki, ce que Savent les Aché Chasseurs Nomades du Paraguay*, Paris: Plon.

Dalmas, A. (1814) *Histoire de la révolution de Saint-Dominigue*, Paris: Mame Frères.

Drummond, L. (1977) 'On being Carib', in E. Basso (ed.) *Carib-speaking Indians: Culture, Society and Language*, Tuscon: University of Arizona Press.

Götz, N. (1995) *Obeah – Hexerei in der Karibik – zwischen Macht und Ohnmacht*, Frankfurt am Main: Peter Lang.

Harris, M. (1977) *Cannibals and Kings: the Origins of Cultures,* New York: Random House.

Hedrick, B. C., Stephens, J. E., Yawney, C. D. and Manning, F. E. (1984) *Anthropological Investigations in the Caribbean, selected Papers,* Greeley, Colorado: University of Northern Colorado.

Hoffmann, L.-F. (1996) 'Myth, history and literature: the Bois-Caïman ceremony', in M. Kremser (ed.) *Ay BoBo – afro-karibische Religionen, Zweite Internationale Tagung der Gesellschaft für Karibikforschung Wien 1990, Teil 2: Voodoo,* Wien: WUV-Universitaets-Verlag.

Hulme, P. (1986) *Colonial Encounters: Europe and the Native Caribbean, 1492–1797,* London and New York: Methuen.

Lizot, J. (1985) [1976] *Tales of the Yanomami. Daily Life in the Venezuelan Forest,* Cambridge and London: Cambridge University Press.

Maranhão, T. (1998) 'The Adventures of ontology in the Amazon forest', *Paideuma* 44: 155–68.

Mason, P. (1990) *Deconstructing America: Representations of the Other,* London and New York: Routledge.

Métraux, A. (1998) [1958] *Le Vaudou Haïtien,* Paris: Gallimard.

Moreau de Saint-Méry, L.-E. (1797) [1784] *Description topographique, physique, civile, politique et histoire de la partie française de l'île de Saint-Domingue,* Philadelphia.

Olmos, M. F. and Paravisini-Gebert, L. (eds) (1997) *Sacred Possessions: Vodou, Santería, Obeah, and the Caribbean,* New Brunswick, N.J: Rutgers University Press.

Overing, J. (1986) 'Images of cannibalism, death and domination in a 'non-violent' society', in D. Riches (ed.) *The Anthropology of Violence,* Oxford and New York: Basil Blackwell.

Riches, D. (1986) 'The phenomenon of violence', in D. Riches (ed.) *The Anthropology of Violence,* Oxford and New York: Basil Blackwell.

Rouse, I. (1948) 'The West Indies', in J. Steward (ed.) *Handbook of South American Indians, Vol.4: The Circum-Caribbean Tribes,* New York: Smithsonian Institute, Bureau of American Ethnology.

Sagan, E. (1974) *Cannibalism: Human Aggression and Cultural Form,* New York: Harper Torchbooks.

Sanday, P. G. (1989) [1986] *Divine Hunger: Cannibalism as a Cultural System,* Cambridge: Cambridge University Press.

Seabrook, W. B. (1929) *The Magic Island,* London and Sydney: The literary guild of America.

Sommerfeld, J. (1994) *Körper, Krise und Vodou: eine Studie zur Kreolmedizin und Gesundheitsversorgung in Haiti,* Münster and Hamburg: Lit.

St John, S. (1971) [1884/1889] *Hayti or The Black Republic,* London: Frank Cass & Co.

Sulikowski, U. (1996) 'Hollywoodzombie: Vodou and the Caribbean in mainstream cinema', in M. Kremser (ed.) *Ay BoBo – afro-karibische*

Religionen, Zweite Internationale Tagung der Gesellschaft für Karibikforschung Wien 1990, Teil 2: Voodoo, Wien: WUV-Universitaets-Verlag.

Tuzin, D. and Brown, P. (1983) 'Editor's Preface', in P. Brown and D. Tuzin (eds) *The Ethnography of Cannibalism,* Washington: Society of Psychology and Anthropology.

Viveiros de Castro, E. (1992) *From the Enemy's Point of View: Humanity and Divinity in an Amazonian Society,* Chicago and London: University of Chicago Press.

Volhard, E. (1968) [1939] *Kannibalismus,* New York and London: Johnson Reprint Corporation.

Wehrheim-Peuker, M. (1998) *Die gescheiterte Eroberung: eine diskursanalytische Betrachtung früher Französischer Amerikatexte,* Tübingen: Gunter Narr Verlag.

Whitehead, N. L. (1984) 'Carib Cannibalism, the Historical Evidence', *Journal de la Société des Américanistes* 70: 69–88.

Chapter 5

The enactment of 'tradition'

Albanian constructions of identity, violence and power in times of crisis

Stephanie Schwandner-Sievers

This essay attempts to describe local strategies and rationales of coping with crises. These crises are characterised through situations of a vacuum of state power in different local Albanian settings at different periods during the 1990s. In these crises, 'tradition' became a resource for information on alternative local social order shaped by indigenous perceptions of diverse pre-communist and communist histories.[1] In some settings, such 'tradition' is effectively used to justify, excuse and direct violence. In others, local 'traditionalisation' may not provide arguments for violence, as though violent acts may nevertheless happen – without reference to local 'tradition'. While, in this essay, local socio-political processes will be set into context with central ones, the main objective is to show that Albanian actors have reason and rationale to revitalise 'tradition', and that this is strategically adapted to circumstances. 'Tradition' proves a particularly useful ideological resource in negotiating control of scarce economic resources, such as land, and in determining social inclusion and exclusion. The use of violence in these processes can provide an effective means to an end. Recourse to violence is particularly powerful, because not morally contestable, where local constructions of identity and history explain it as legitimate in terms of 'tradition'. It will therefore be argued that the 'enactment of tradition' constitutes an effective strategy for establishing power in different local contexts. With such politics 'traditionalist' actors not only promote themselves, they may also create public and social coercion in an attempt to install local (and group-internal) peace and order, while – with more or less success – violence is fenced in and directed according to a re-invented 'traditional' logic.

The focus on politics and variation in the context of time and space in Albania aims to contradict any assumptions that Albanians are helplessly shackled by traditions of violence. Examples are taken from research in the Albanian North (the city of Shkodra and the mountainous Dukagjin area) and the South (the cities of Saranda and Korca and the mountainous Kurvelesh area). Lastly, in the light of these findings, parallels in the developments in Kosovo before and after the Kosovo War of 1999 will briefly be addressed.

Albanian transitions

The Albanian history of 'post-communist transition' was marked by the withdrawal of the totalitarian state presence in the farthest corners of the country, and by repeated processes of complete state disintegration. *Nuk ka shteti*, 'there is no state', became a phrase used throughout the country.

Albanians were found to differentiate between, first, the *Chaos* of 1992, which occurred as a result of the first changes of the political system. 'Chaos' was characterised by enormous waves of emigration as well as by the destruction of public property throughout the country. The former one-party regime was replaced by party pluralism, and free elections eventually lifted the so-called Democratic Party under President Sali Berisha, who originates from Northern Albania, into power.

Second, the Albanian *War* of 1997 occurred after this ruling party lost legitimacy in 1996 because of fraudulent elections. After a time lag of a few months, the economic disintegration of the country followed. When the so-called pyramid schemes collapsed in early 1997 most of the savings of the entire population, many profits from years of working abroad, dissolved overnight. Outraged people looted the county's numerous army depots and armed themselves. The south, where the Socialist opposition had its base, de facto suspended loyalty to the central government and some former communist military leaders took charge. Following the arming of the entire population, a number of casualties were caused by accidents due to irresponsible use of weapons, such as the arbitrary shooting in the air for joy or demonstrations of power. However, most cases of violence at this time, such as homicides, were interpreted to be caused by rivalries of local, newly developing gangs in different parts of Albania. The majority of the weapons remained in private ownership, unless sold through secret channels to Kosovo and elsewhere. Even prominent members of the interim 'reconciliation government' were said to have engaged in contraband activities. An international peace force was called into the country, and elections took place under protective supervision of the Organisation for Security and Cooperation in Europe (OSCE) and international troops.

The Albanian situation could comprehensively be described in the words Katherine Verdery used to define state-building processes in Balkan history: 'various groups establish and fight over symbolic conventions, strive for legitimacy, and fix intergroup relations and the distributions associated with them' (Verdery 1994: 45). Also Michael Hechter's thoughts concerning counter-productive group solidarity in state-building processes apply. According to him, 'predatory groups . . . impose negative externalities on members of other [state-constructive] groups by appropriating their resources.' While they have to rely on specific modes of internal cohesion, and their solidarity becomes a value of high relevance, it contradicts state integration and overarching modes of solidarity (Hechter 1995: 61).

The last major internal Albanian *Crisis* occurred when the opposition leader Azem Hajdari, a former leader of the student protests, which eventually led to the breakdown of the one-party regime, and a loyal follower to Sali Berisha, was killed in September 1998. The assassination was related to the North Albanian 'tradition' of customary revenge killing as well as to contraband activities in the Northern border area from which Hajdari and his personal enemy Gafur Mazreku, a member of parliament of the ruling 'Socialist Party', came (Krasztev 1999: 3). This particular region became infamous for its customary 'traditions' of feuding which were terminated during Communism.[2] Subsequently, the so-called 'Democratic Party' boycotted parliament accusing the ruling party of endangering Albanian civilisation and integrity, thereby reproducing a disastrous political fragmentation in Albanian politics. Paradoxically, it was the 1999 Kosovo War with approximately half a million of Kosovar-Albanian refugees fleeing into Albania which finally led to integrated governmental politics.

The times of political crises were particularly felt outside the relatively secure geographical triangle of the capital Tirana and the cities Kavaja and Durres in central Albania. Up to the time of writing of this article, lack of security was internally and internationally perceived as the major obstacle to investment and to the development of the country. Tribalist gang-wars, banditry and corruption are often cited as factors opposing private investment in Albania. In the spring and summer of 1999, a number of refugees from Kosovo as well as a few OSCE monitors were robbed in the northern part of the country. Eventually, facing damage to the national image, the government employed specially-trained police forces in the region, particularly in the city of Bajram Curri.[3] Government officials now claim some success in suppressing local banditry. However, other hot-spots in the country are still waiting for a similar intervention against violent gangs engaged in smuggling refugees, women for prostitution, arms, cars, drugs, cheese, and similar commodities. The term 'Mafia' has been employed to describe these globally linked criminal network activities (cf. Sisti 1999),[4] however, there have been warnings of a form of Orientalism in the application of this term (Sampson 1998). Recent fieldwork evidence suggests that Albanian contraband to a large extent, composes part of local and family subsistence economies securing survival where facing a lack of alternatives.[5]

Northern *kanun* re-invented[6]

In early 1992 Berit Backer, a Norwegian anthropologist, portrayed in a documentary film life in Rrogam and Thethi, villages of the so-called north Albanian Alps (Backer 1992). The locals were desperately waiting for party officials to come and regulate their conflicts resulting from new legislation concerning the privatisation and redistribution of formerly collectivised agricultural land. Land commissions were supposed to be set up and organise distribution according to a *per capita* rule allocating equal amounts of land to every single former labourer of the local co-operative. This rule was in favour of those families who had settled in the area during communism, of the former landless as well as of those families of former communist officials. However, the *per capita* rule opposed the interests of other families who saw better chances in acquiring more land through claiming rights of descent and inheritance referring to the pre-communist status. In Backer's film, lurking conflicts were just avoided when, in fact, eventually the state official arrived, and for the moment managed to enforce state prescriptions.

With political changes in the capital, the presence and authority of the former party officials soon vanished completely. From then on mountain farmers waited in vain for the intervention of a third party to solve their village conflicts. In large parts of the region, a massive population increase due to communist population policies had increased the pressures on land, and this soon led to violent conflicts, even within families (De Waal 1996). Disputes and conflict over land and former boundaries were seen as the main reason for re-emerging feuds. When, only two years later, in 1993, we conducted fieldwork in an area very near the one Backer had visited, we found pre-communist rituals had been revitalised and traditionalist discourses were omnipresent; both were locally subsumed under the Ottoman term for local customary self-governance, '*kanun*'.

In northern Albania reference to *kanun* varies by specific names given to it, which are derived from mythical medieval tribal rulers and forefathers who are believed to be the founders or codifiers of *kanun* seen as ancient customary law. There is the so-called '*kanun* of the mountains', or the '*kanun* of Skanderbeg' or the '*kanun* of Lekë Dukagjin' which people proudly claim composes a part of their identity and oral tradition. Past and present *kanun* rhetoric and ritual employ a dualistic symbolism, mainly the colours black and white. In *kanun* rituals of incorporation this appears in movements from left to right and west to east. In rituals of marriage, hospitality or reconciliation, former outsiders like the bride, the guest, the former enemy in feuding, are ritually transformed into a category of persons called *mik*, 'friend' (from Latin *amicus*). The security of these new affiliates is ideally guaranteed through a special concept called *besa*. This derives etymologically from *be, beja*, 'the oath'. *Besa* is usually translated as 'honour of the house', 'hospitality', 'the given word', 'protection guarantee', also 'reconciliation', 'alliance', etc. Past and present rhetoric on having *besa*, being a *besnik*, in contrast to the opposite (*pabese*, 'non-faithful' and 'non-trustworthy'), highlight the ideal values of internal cohesion, peace and solidarity of kin and constructed 'friend' networks, and declare any 'others' who have not been successfully integrated, as potential *pabese*, i.e. as dangerous (cf. Schwandner-Sievers 1999). Around the turn of the century it was described how in robbery, violence was honourably channelled according to prescription of the *kanun* proverb: 'the wolf licks his own flesh, but eats that of others' (Mjedia 1901: 357–8; Gjeçov 1989: 122, 158–9). Edith Durham confirms that in pre-communist times 'robbery from another tribe with which no *besa* exists [was] rather a virtue than a crime' (Durham 1985: 204). On the other hand, somebody who did not pay the appropriate respect to a *mik*, possibly even dared to steal from him, or broke a *besa* in any other way, was regarded as dishonoured. Such a 'traitor' of the *besa* bond was considered to be *faqe e zezë*, 'black faced' [i.e. 'dishonoured'] by *kanun*. 'Everything must be given with the left hand and passed under the knee until he avenges his guest', and he was excluded from taking part in the village men's assemblies if his *mik* had come to death while under *besa* protection guarantee (cf. Gjeçov 1989: 126, 136).

In summary, *kanun* symbolism reveals a dichotomous worldview categorising people into the trustworthy 'us' who need to be protected, and the unfaithful, dangerous or treacherous 'others' who may be assaulted or expelled. Such an 'othering' can, as was shown, take place within the group of reference. This happens if one of the group's members does not conform or obey the norms explicitly set on stage, or phrased, for example in village narratives on 'honour'. Therefore, a traditionalist rhetoric that emphasises *kanun* black and white categorisations can serve, and effectively be mobilised, in local politics of exclusion and inclusion such as in contemporary redistribution processes of land. In *kanun* revitalisation processes the old local patrilinear descent groups tend to favour themselves. According to *kanun*, they are the only legitimate holders of land in the northern Albanian mountains. Yet, how and to what extent was pre-communist *kanun* re-established in the region in post-communist transition times?

The most prominent early printed collection of north Albanian local proverbs was published in 1933 by the Franciscan Seminary of the northern town Shkodra (Skutari). These had been collected by one of the patriotic missionaries, Padre Shtjefen Gjeçov. He arranged the proverbs in paragraphs and articles, creating the image of a fixed codification. However, variations always existed through time, space and person, differing in details of interpretation as to how to behave properly in feuding, and in respect of the guidelines of how to save, restore or prove 'honour', social status and pride.[7] In the mountains, single copies of Gjeçov's printed *kanun* were hidden from the communist authorities. Today, a second, inexpensive edition has been published by the re-established Franciscan Seminary of Shkodra, and between 1993 and 1996 it was available in many book kiosks. A more expensive version, including a parallel English translation, was published in 1993 in the US American diaspora.[8] The Franciscans also published, for the first time, a collection of the '*kanun* of Skanderbeg' in 1993 which ethnographically covers an area slightly further south (Kruja, Mati) than the '*kanun* of Lekë Dukagjin'.

Of course, these printed sources could have had a fundamental impact on the revitalisation of *kanun* ritual such as feuding. Opinions vary on who bears responsibilities. Was a *kanun* logic re-invented through the publishing activities of the conservative American diaspora or the local Franciscans? Or were pre-communist feuds simply revived by local families who waited to take their revenge until they could act without risking collective conviction under totalitarian legislation in this post-communist vacuum of power?

Field experience in 1992 and 1993 showed that the printed *kanun* was not necessarily referred to, but that local community elders and descendants of pre-communist influential families claimed to know the 'old *kanun*' and how to properly enact it, while the younger generation had a rather ambiguous attitude towards its revitalisation. Yet, *kanun* memory of the elders appeared to have been shattered, or was actually completely reinvented because:

> the Partisans murdered close to a third of the territory's adult male population in the autumn of 1944. These were the élite of the clans and tribes . . . In a word everyone was lost who could have passed on knowledge of the law, their own history, the workings of self government, and the people's religion, if there was in fact such a thing.
>
> (Krasztev 1999: 10)

This presumably fundamental caesura in tradition (in the sense of customs and beliefs transmitted through the generations) also becomes evident in the fact that the elders sometimes hold inaccurate information, or that they themselves appear senile.

This was seen when a ritual blood peace-making ceremony, which related to a single case of attempted homicide and was conducted under the guidance of a community elder, failed. Some participants later explained that this failure was partially a result of the fact that the old expert had 'forgotten' that the *kanun* rule 'blood for blood' implies that no reconciliation can be required unless the parties involved feel that there has been a fair 'balance of blood'. This means that a minimum of one similar attack in revenge must have taken place before negotiations may start. In this case, *kanun* became relevant as a tool to solve a situation of latent threat, however, it was reinvented in vain because of contradicting interpretations.[9] It seems therefore that *kanun* and the elders become an important device for the younger generation only in times of immediate need.

If they ever had, the villagers elders lost their ultimate power of enforcing *kanun* rules in the villages which pre-communist *kanun* allocated to them, and even more so outside village boundaries. The local Franciscan priest, Ernesto Troshani, who had led the failed ritual, recounts the opposite attitude of the victim, a man around thirty, who had denied the offender forgiveness. It is this age-class 'that does not respect the elders, especially if they left the mountains and their people because of poverty. In the villages, in contrast, there are never problems conducting blood peace successfully. This is because the elders, by their authority, guarantee the obedience of *kanun* and assure peace in the community.' This statement seems quite idealistic. Nevertheless, it is this age group in the northern villages which is apt to emphasise the *kanun's* value as a collective moral authority. According to Ernesto Troshani, another reason for the decline of effectiveness in *kanun* practices can be seen in twenty-five years of state-imposed atheism (since 1967) which destroyed the recognition of the sacral components of *kanun* formerly guaranteeing respect.[10] In an oral interview conducted in 1996, the Albanian customary law expert Ismet Elezi stressed that: 'it is these forty- and fifty-year-olds [brought up in these rigorous times] who know very little of *kanun*. They heard it as a word, but they don't know it and they don't respect it.' However, it seems that many of this middle generation are apparently taking part in the new *kanun* rituals. They may have difficulties constructing 'tradition', since the rituals were not practised and therefore not sustained since the 1950s, yet, in case of emergency, they still hope for its suggestive power.

Quite often, these new threatening situations seem to be created by adolescent males and young men. Contesting status – hardly achievable by alternative options in disadvantaged contemporary Albanian society – they display aggressive male behaviour and easily over-react to anything considered an insult. Elezi confirmed that also in regard to the last pre-communist cases, the elders 'were the most powerful supporters, but the actual killing in feud was pushed by young men aiming to be less looked down to' (Elezi 1983:

204).[11] Comparing today's logic of banditry of young-men gangs with robbery as documented in history (see above, and Gjeçov 1989: 158–9), arguably this generation re-invents *kanun*-tradition in a less explicit but yet even more genuine way than the elder generation.[12]

In 1993 we witnessed the first attempts of re-vitalising *kanun* rituals in mountain villages. For example, a first post-communist meeting called *kuvend* (from Latin conventio, 'council'), in accordance with *kanun* language the council of tribal leaders, took place at the village cemetery of Abate. This village, incidentally, was visited and described by Edith Durham in 1909. More than 90 years later, it cannot be ruled out that in this case we anthropologists became, unwillingly, also culprits of revitalisation, which may possibly have been 'performed' in reaction to our curious questions about *kanun*. Young men at the outer circle of the meeting in a barely hidden manner ridiculed the event and questioned its genuine significance. Among other revitalised rituals which we observed, was a ceremonial mourning for a recently deceased elderly 'honourable man' of a neighbouring village. The performative aspect of the ritual became evident when my colleague Robert Pichler and I realised that the villagers had been waiting until we arrived to start this impressive ceremony. They explained that genuine performance of this 'archaic' and 'autochthonous' ritual had been prohibited during communism.[13]

It seems that knowledge of these 'traditions' and rituals could partly have been transmitted through Albanian folklore politics, which attempted to 'domesticate' them. 'Tradition', in national communist ideology, had to be situated in the pre-communist past, which was claimed to have been overcome through communist modernity. On the one hand, northern Albania was seen as the cradle of the nation, and its local rituals and values as 'ancient', so as proof of a 'pure' national Albanian culture. Elements of *kanun* ritual were celebrated on stage at national folklore festivals, and *besa* entered the literature as a national 'virtue'. On the other hand, enactment of 'tradition' as an integral part of village live was prohibited. The paraphernalia of such performances were safely housed in the national Museum and the act itself, 'domesticated' and transformed into standard folklore on official stages. Therefore, Northern Albanians conceive of themselves as the only true, pure and 'autochthonous' Albanians while, at the same time, they find themselves excluded from national processes of development in the present.

Nevertheless, *kanun* and *besa* traditions have repeatedly and effectively been mobilised in order to build internal peace on national or regional levels. *Kanun* tradition showed a capacity for wide internal appeasement in face of an overwhelmingly threatening 'other'. In 1997, when Albania completely disintegrated and everyone, anticipating the need for self-defence, armed himself, north Albanians expressed pride in the fact that there were, temporarily, no cases of homicide in their area, and that feuding was suspended for the time of the so-called 'war'. In other words, the area proved to be most peaceful under conditions of outside chaos. *Besa* in history repeatedly worked to ensure internal cohesion when there was an outside threat.[14] In 1990, Kosovo Albanians postponed internal conflicts and feuds when Serbian hegemony pressures were increasing. Under the guidance of the Kosovo-Albanian ethnographer Anton Cetta, mass reconciliation rituals of *bese-lidhje* (*besa*-binding) took place in a deliberate attempt to use *kanun* and its peace-building capacities. In 1999 young Albanian men swore allegiance to the Kosovo Liberation Army by giving their *besa*. These rituals were reinvented originally by radical Diaspora nationalists (Judah 2000: 99). As mentioned previously, *kanun* ritual also serves to settle much more localised conflicts such as questions on the borderlines of pastures. In 1994 we documented how elders like Ded Noja from Thethi, the same village in which Backer filmed, instructed their co-villagers about the 'proper' *kanun* ritual to settle land disputes and to confirm boundaries. After negotiations, a stone is thrown to mark the border while swearing 'by the mind [or 'flesh'] and spirit of my ancestors', an agreement supposed to be so holy that doubt about it would entail the spilling of blood (Bock and Schwandner 1994).

However, it is not only internal peace and conflict solution, which can be achieved through employment of *kanun* tradition. As will be shown below, where 'we' and 'the other' are defined locally in northern Albania, *kanun* revitalisation contributed to the escalation of feuds, led to the expulsion of former community members, and re-produced pre-communist forms of marriage arrangements without unexpected 'modern' consequences.

In the contemporary context, reference to *kanun* still seems to emerge whenever a particular group needs to both define and ensure its internal coherence, and to direct violence against group outsiders. Thus, young men can acquire prestige through directing violence against village outsiders, whereas prestige of the elders is constructed in the context of appeasement and authority exercised inside the villages. Codes of honour exist with any Albanian brigands as they do with youth gangs all over the world, but for northern Albanians who choose recourse to violence along lines of group inclusion or exclusion, *kanun* rhetoric confers an advantage. If necessary, violent acts can be glorified, or excused, by local 'tradition'. Those classified as outsiders do not only exist outside the village. The northern Albanian 'dialectics of honour', by defining social hierarchies inside the village, analogously determine the insiders and outsiders of the community. People, who in the public opinion are considered 'dishonoured', can, with reference to *kanun*, become open targets for public mockery or assaults.[15] Incidentally, performances of public ostracism were common on television in communist times and continued during transition when criminals were regularly shown on screen. Using notions of public shame on a local as well as on a national level may serve as a deterrent for transgressing social norms. However, these practices can become highly effective locally, as means of expulsion and exclusion in a situation of scarcity.

Margaret Hasluck wrote in 1954 that:

> a man slow to kill his enemy was thought 'disgraced' and was described as 'low class' and 'bad'. Among the Highlanders he risked finding that other men had contemptuously come to sleep with his wife, his daughter could not marry into a 'good' family and his son must marry a 'bad' girl. . . . [Further South] he paid visits at his peril; his coffee cup was only half-filled, and before being handed to him it was passed under the host's left arm, or even his left leg to remind him of his disgrace. He was often mocked openly.
>
> (Hasluck 1967: 391)

Restrictions on marriage chances can again be assumed for girls whose families are not valued for their protective capacities. Also, recent reports claim that, again, local marriage plans are badly restricted in cases of families fearing to become victim of a feud (cf. Kikia 1999).

Apparently, the revitalised custom of arranged marriages with reference to 'proper' *kanun*, is repeatedly exploited. While fathers assumed they were giving their daughter to a prestigious 'big man with connections abroad', or these young women assumed they had found an escape route from isolated northern lands, they soon learnt that they were the victims of deception. Today, many girls from the north are said to have ended up as prostitutes in Italy; some, through such utilisation of 'tradition', others through being kidnapped (which some have interpreted as the re-occurrence of customs of bride robbery), other families seem to have deliberately sacrificed a girl because of poverty. Consequently, these women find themselves 'trapped in traditions of honour'. Interviewees in Italy said that their fathers would kill them if they returned home.[16] This evokes an association with a well-known old *kanun* saying: 'the bride with a cartridge on her back' (Hasluck 1954: 213). If the bride committed adultery, her husband was permitted to shoot her with this bullet provided by her father. This symbolism ensured that the problem of liability was solved and the act would not entail 'blood', i.e. feud, between the in-laws. A case of adultery occurred while we were doing fieldwork in Dukagjin in 1993. Bride and lover were both shot by her husband. The village agreed that this was right and in accordance with *kanun* – although there was, nevertheless, a fear of the re-emergence of an old feud with the young woman's village. There was no trust and reliance that the others would obey the same interpretation of *kanun* symbolism.

In short, the politics of prestige and social status, control of economic resources, and the use, as well as the fear, of violence are effectively inter-related in a *kanun* system of meaning. Proving high status means to acquire social capital ('honour'), which guarantees access to various resources such as advantageous arranged marriages or power in village politics that are denied to people of low status, and violence is accepted as a legitimate tool for these ends (cf. Schneider 1971). In 1993 in the Dukagjin region, we were told about symbols of low status: a dishonoured family was said to be required to cover their bowed heads on their way to church. This open display of lost honour forces the victims to attempt a status inversion, because 'by his successful crime the murderer had proved himself the better man, and the victim could not endure this inferiority and was bound to strike back in kind' (Hasluck 1967: 392).

There are two options in *kanun* discourse used to invert a low status into a new reputation after a murder. The first is to ritually forgive, 'if you see fit', which usually can only be done if some time has past after the last murder or if it has been recognised that the guilt was partly shared by the victim. Forgiving must imply the opportunity for the victim's family to compensate their status ('honour' or integrity) deficit by the demonstration of extreme generosity, provided in a ritual play with time and the ritual humiliation of the original offender in order to equalise status. Historically, these demands were met in all reconciliation ritual variation, which, for example, forced the guilty petitioner to kneel down for hours with a heavy rifle on his neck (Hahn 1854: 177; Hasluck 1967: 404ff.; cf. Bourdieu 1976: 11–47). Yet, in the failed reconciliation ritual mentioned previously, the priests ignored this symbolism when asking the victim (instead of the original perpetrator) to humbly kneel down while swearing vengeance on a Christian bible and cross. As observed in 1994 in Thethi, after a successful reconciliation, *kanun* promoters seek to confirm this by pushing the former opponents to form a blood brotherhood thereby indicating equalised status and community integrity, as in pre-communist times.

The second option leaves no doubt that the original victim has 'washed his blackened face' as it is commonly expressed in *kanun* language. The old *kanun* proverb gives the formula of how to clean a face, that is, according to persisting perceptions, 'blackened': 'the soap of a man is the gun-powder' (cf. Cozzi 1910: 664). Homicide in feuding is, therefore, the safest way to prove manliness, strength and integrity of a family without any state guarantees of individual respect and collective security. It serves as a legitimate sanction with a long-term option in feuding as well as an immediate reaction in private responsibility which may result in new feuds. Actually, the people of Miredita distinguished, in 1992, between feud cases 'with memory' and those 'without memory,' that is the 'obligation to take blood' for disputes of the grandfathers in pre-communist times, and newly emerged cases resulting from new conflicts, for example, in the land reprivatisation processes, or about village authority.

It can be stated that in northern Albania, with reference to *kanun*, former tribal leaders and their descendants could emerge as an active interest group in village politics in opposition to central state politics. In communist Albania it had been a top priority to fight the 'traditional patriarchal family' (cf. Alia 1989). Thus, these families had been among the most persecuted, condemned to poverty and humiliated. With political liberation, these people, not compromised through being former communists, realised that the best opportunities in village struggles for power were through a retraditionalisation. They successfully took their chance to invert power relations (cf. Pichler 1995), to renew their prestige and to reclaim back inherited private property rights by referring to a past social order.

In 1995, international consultants soon noticed that it was in the northern mountain villages where the egalitarian precepts of the land distribution reform of 1991 were not accepted and often caused new conflicts. They understood that:

> the force of beliefs about the sanctity of private property are very strong, so that in some villages people who were excluded from the land distribution process because their families had no claim to land from before collectivisation often accepted their fate without complaint, since they believed they had no legitimate claim and consequently, they emigrated.
>
> (Stanfield and Kukeli 1995: 3)

We can assume that there were incidents of forceful expulsion in many cases rather than voluntary emigration. Many families may have left the area accepting that the revitalised system of traditionalist reference as well as the scarcity of resources did not leave them any immediate alternative.

The refocusing on *kanun* in Northern Albania proved to be two-sided: it may create social order and fence in violence for those included through identifying and identified with 'tradition', and it directs violence against, and economically excludes by the same token, those defined as 'outsiders'. However, competing systems of reference or different interpretations of 'tradition' have led to new feuds. Meanwhile, the new-old village elders organised prestigious mediation, reconciliation and pacification ceremonies based on the same *kanun* value principles which are supposed to direct feuding. Among their fellow Albanians in Kosovo or central and southern Albanian settings, young men from northern Albania are held responsible for most crimes. They are known as 'hooligans' or 'Chechnians', who rightly or wrongly become easily suspected of their readiness to disturb local peace when arriving somewhere outside their place of origin. Yet, *kanun* is challenged by influences such as television and the return of state power in the area. It seems doomed considering the fact that it does not provide anymore an unambiguous and predictable alternative rule of law as, arguably, it did in Ottoman times.

Southern recourses to patriarchy?

When, in 1995, I first started fieldwork in the southeastern Albanian city of Korca, I used what I had learnt to be the polite and appropriate words of first acquaintance: 'I am very honoured to be a guest of this house. . . .', and immediately evoked gales of laughter from my hosts. Very quickly I lost my well-trained northern Albanian *kanun* language and understood that various attitudes towards 'tradition' are at work in different Albanian settings. In fact, it was claimed that in the southwest Albanian mountainous region of Labëria, a *kanun* of *papa zhuli* or of *idriz sulli* was actively referred to until the mid-1950s (Godin 1956: 184).[17] However, fieldwork in the village of Fterre in this region failed to provide any evidence of reference to a new *kanun* discourse. Except, that is, when scoffing at northern 'backwardness.'

In those southern villages and cities I visited, the pre-eminent self-definition is that of 'progressive' and 'modern'. The Albanian partisan movement originated in the south, and many of the elders look back on their history as partisans. Almost 10 per cent of these fighters were women, and new emancipatory ideas of love matches, rather than arranged marriages as part of the village men's politics, were realised in those early times of communism.[18] The elder generation looks back on a history of actively participating in the state-building process and of transforming patriarchal 'tradition' into a more homogenous, 'modern communist society'. Many express pride in this history although there is also frustration with the failure of the former regime. Others, formerly belonging to the wealthy and, consequently, persecuted during communism, still share high ideals of 'education' for their children, and of 'modernity', with these former partisans.

In this atmosphere the constitutional land reform of 1991 that ordered land and cattle redistribution on egalitarian terms was first successfully implemented. Land redistribution commissions were set up and worked according to the legal prescriptions. However, fieldwork and interviews in 1998 in rural southwest Albania showed that these arrangements lasted only until the disintegration of Albania in 1997. In the process of a general uproar against Berisha's government, estate registries and files were destroyed. In the village Fterre, those who were able to claim land through inheritance nevertheless took it back in cases where it did not evoke opposition immediately. This was possible because most former occupants had left the villages for Greece or Italy. Migration in this area generally releases pressure on land and subsistence economy. However, patterns of ownership are increasingly developing and seem to resemble pre-communist status in southern Albania as well. Territorial property claimed through descent is again assigned a sentimental value, and those claims become increasingly acknowledged in this village though not always with whole-hearted consent. The former landless, such as shepherds, withdraw from land first assigned to them, even if they have worked for the local agricultural co-operative, and work with livestock on communal pastures just as before. Land is scarce and can secure the bare survival only for a minority of villagers.

As a preliminary summary – the rural situation in the south resembles increasingly the northern situation. However, in the south, conflict regulation in land issues developed with a six years' time lag. This was when the vacuum of state power forced the locals effectively to rely on modes of self-regulation in these areas as well.

Additionally, southern 'retraditionalisation' seems to be an involuntary effect of the disastrous security situation and embodied in what appears to be new patriarchal gender relations. The latent possibility of violence led to the establishment of Ottoman-style self-defence organisations of young men in the village or city quarter. At the same time, young women are kept at home and are thereby denied equal chances in education. In attempting culturally to 'translate' their reasons for keeping the girls at home, village fathers explained the situation to us by arguing that there was a 'tradition of fundamentalism'. However, the girls themselves know why they are forced to stay at home: 'head-hunters' from the other side of the mountains could suddenly pass through the village square and search for 'female commodity' to sell as prostitutes to Italy. They keep themselves entertained by watching satellite TV. Consequently, in interviews, some girls expressed their pity for our societies which, as they had learnt from international TV, were ruled by violence, sex and crime.

Agricultural subsistence economy in the village, as in many others, is to a large extent based on growing marijuana. This is not consumed in the village, but the young men of the village engage in collecting, pressing and transporting the dried crop to the near harbour cities (Vlora or Saranda), or to the Greek border, or beyond, or into Athens. Earnings depend on how far a man pursues this risky endeavour. There seems to be a clear division of labour between those young men who still remain in the village and those who have settled in the nearby harbour town, between inside and outside of the village borders. Consumption and contraband activities take place only outside the village, and form part of the everyday life business of those who have left its borders. Inside the village, growing crops and effective protection of the village and its inhabitants are the more dominant tasks for young men to acquire prestige. However, the 'good boys' of this village might be, at other times, the predators on the highway on the other side of the mountain.

New 'markets of violence' (cf. Elwert 1997) situated in west and south Albanian cities at a harbour, a border or a main transport road, as well as in trading centres abroad (Italy, Greece, Germany, Switzerland), compete in the non-regulated informal sector with unpredictable and, apparently, sometimes brutalised forms of violence. It seems that 'modernised' forms of *kanun* have developed in these 'dislocated' settings outside any village or family control, employing military high-mortality technology and developing globalised links while depending on ideas of internal solidarity and personal networks, such as kin, neighbour or age-class groups. Similarities to *kanun* concepts of friend and foe, loyalty and treachery, group integrity and the legitimisation of violence against outsiders or the treacherous, are evident.[19]

Until now, local political big men, representatives of the 1997 upheaval, have established so-called 'security committees', and many police officers in southern Albania are hard to tell apart from the leaders of these violent gangs. In 1998 it was still the police that many feared when they came to visit the village, where they were considered to be the most dangerous bandits. For example, while we were working in Fterre in 1998, a shoot-out between groups of former and of new police officers took place in Saranda. The locals related this to the 'police-gangs' competition to control revenues of protection money taken from other people's profits in the drug trafficking business to Greece. *Besa* might not necessarily be named as such in southern Albania where 'traditionalist' discourses are not put on the stage. However, as a concept it seems to be present. *Besa* is transformed into a commodity when community and gang outsiders are forced to purchase protection (cf. Nicholson 1998). Violent gangs employ a system of prestige meant to ensure internal group cohesion. In this, violence has to be directed against the outsider, those who transgress the group's norms, and those who legitimately fall prey to the predators. Prestige (or '*ndera*', honour) therefore, is judged according to ideas of loyalty and treachery, and according to a man's capacity to accumulate and distribute new wealth.

Reconsidering Kosovo

When on 12 June 1999 the Serbian forces left Kosovo and NATO troops entered, a chronicle of post-war violence was opened. Already by mid-August some journalists and policy makers were convinced that 'now mafia wages war in Kosovo' (Beaumont 1999). Over the summer, some Albanian writers critically pointed to local racism expressed in violent attacks at the expense of Serbs and other non-Albanians such as the Slavic-speaking Gorani or Roma. The most prominent of these writers is Veton Surroj, editor of the daily *Koha Ditore*, who himself became the subject of massive threats. At the same time, OSCE crime statistics reported for the first four post-war months in Kosovo, 348 murders, 116 kidnappings, 1,070 lootings and 1,106 cases of arson. This breakdown in precise figures is considered not certain, however, and other sources mention an average of thirty people being killed every week in Kosovo – a number which resembles the situation during the airstrikes. However, today this violence hits only non-Albanians, whereas during the airstrikes, this number included Albanians and non-Albanians alike. Several hundred thousand non-Albanians have been driven out of the area since Kosovo became 'appeased' under NATO protectorate (Dauti 1999).

Opinions vary as to what extent a 'new Kosovo mafia', Albanian criminal gangs who are trespassing the border, frustrated Albanian individuals, or systematically organised former members of the guerrilla 'Kosovo Liberation Army', are to blame for these acts of violent expulsion. Fieldwork in the spring of 2000 in a number of urban and rural sites of Kosovo showed that those Albanians currently investing into rebuilding their houses explicitly distance themselves from traditionalist logic, and many pointed to the need for juridical justice as the only route to solve local conflict. However, there are reasons to assume that there are still active interest groups which employ the same 'traditionalist logic' described above. When in 1996 the Kosovo Liberation Army first acquired some reputation in the international press, this related to the killing of Albanians who continued to trade with or had friendship relations with Serbian citizens of Kosovo. Homicide was justified according to the previously described notions of loyalty and treachery in terms of an ethnicist group definition. It was traditionalist Albanians such as the Jashari family (which, in 1998, was systematically and entirely extinguished by a Serb paramilitary raid) in a joint endeavour with organised nationalist diaspora radicals that gave momentum to the violent escalation of the Kosovo conflict.[20] Unfortunately, those who use a traditionalist nationalist rhetoric in which violence and heroism are glorified are often louder than their national counterparts who seek peace.

Concluding remarks

The effects of a vacuum of state power in different Albanian settings in the north and south became effective at different times of the so-called transition. It has been shown how, in the north, the use of violence was justified through traditionalist discourses at a very early stage. Violence and 'tradition' were analysed as strategic tools for defining exclusion and inclusion in the access to new resources such as land, which became accessible after the breakdown of earlier Albanian isolationism. In looking at the intentions and profits of the violent actor in terms of 'power, prestige and commodity transactions', an idea taken from Elwert's interpretation of 'markets of violence' (Elwert 1997: 3), the instrumental value of a retraditionalisation became evident. It was also shown how revitalising 'tradition' relates to aspirations in status struggles of different generations following a 'traditionalist' logic. Violence was shown to be a powerful tool in local distribution processes, particularly where 'tradition' served to justify it. Traditionalist logic effectively determines inclusion and exclusion in rights to scarce land or territory (Kosovo), and ultimately, who will experience expulsion, or rather who has first to decide to go.

The north/south differentiation described attempted to go beyond common and simplified media explanations of Albanian disintegration arguing that differences lay in northern tribal structures as opposed to southern Mediterranean social structures. A north/south difference emerged in terms of a time lag. The particular period when villagers retreated to local modes of self-regulation was explained in relation to central processes. Differences were shown to be based on the factor of when state administration began to neglect the particular area. Another variation seems to be based on local self-images which either explicitly express preference for 'traditionalist', or, respectively, for 'modernist' discourses. Also, the local availability of (mythologised) pools of pre-communist knowledge, i.e. 'tradition', was considered.

Since my last research in Albania was completed in 1998, the Albanian state has successfully started to reclaim the monopoly of power. However, as with Kosovo, it still must guarantee security and a fair resource allocation to those parts of the populations who do not enforce their claims with guns.

Notes

1 The aspect of different local histories and memories shaping orientation is elaborated in more detail in the article 'Times Past – References for the Construction of Local Order in Present-Day Albania' (Schwandner-Sievers, forthcoming 2001).

2 A recent article in an Albanian daily mentioned a figure of 2,300 families hiding because of feuds (cf. Kikia 1999). For a discussion of reasons why feuds were successfully suppressed during Communism, cf. Schwandner-Sievers 1999.

3 Considering that most Albanians have supported the refugees to an enormous extent, and 'the national tradition of hospitality' was celebrated in all national media, this local 'deviation' led to special efforts to re-appropriate the monopoly of force in the North (cf. lecture by former OSCE monitor Christopher Dwan: 'The security situation in Northern Albania during the Kosovo crisis', *Centre for South East European Studies, University College London, lunch-time seminar*, November 3, 1999).

4 Notably Kosovars in Albania and Albanians in Kosovo are understood to have formed these networks.

5 Cf. Kaser, Pichler and Schwandner-Sievers (2001). Joint fieldwork with students was conducted in Southern Albania in summer 1998.

6 Fieldwork was conducted in these areas in 1992 (Shkodra, Mirëdita) and 1993 (Dukagjin), further visits were undertaken irregularily. Major descriptive parts in this section are identical with either Schwandner-Sievers 1999, or Schwandner-Sievers (forthcoming). Other results of joint fieldwork were published earlier in Kaser and Eberhardt 1995.

7 Best collection of variations in Hasluck 1954.

8 The English translation of this edition does, unfortunately, not provide many of the 'colourful' metaphors used in the Albanian original, Gjeçov 1989 (translated by L. Fox).

9 6 December 1992 in a new slum-like suburb of the northern town of Shkodra where many young families settled who emigrated from the hard conditions in the mountains. Reasons for the failed reconciliation ritual were explained in a different way (see below) by the clerical ritual leader Ernest Troshani who later became the Catholic bishop of the area.

10 Troshani was interviewed the day after the failed reconciliation ritual December 1992. Obviously, there is a nostalgia for a 'pure' *kanun* by any priest in Gjeçov's tradition whose *kanun* also guaranteed respect for church representatives. It should also be stressed that the influence of television also accounts for new orientations among locals.

11 Unfortunately, Elezi distinguishes only between men more than fifty years old and less than fifty.

12 Notably, the *kanun* term *ndera*, usually translated as 'honour', can also be translated as: 'value', 'profit', 'use' as well as to 'social value', 'prestige' (cf. Buchholz 1977: 341–2).

13 I was always impressed by local knowledge of such terms as 'autochthony'.

14 For a list of such historical *besa* serving large-scale internal appeasement see Schwandner-Sievers 1999.

15 In Mirëdita we observed such an expression of public ostracism when young men threw stones in someone's windows. In post-war Kosovo, children sometimes throw stones against members of the disliked other ethnic group in the village.

16 Debbie Dejardin of University College London is currently conducting PhD research on these issues. I am grateful for her sharing some of these insights with me.

17 This author found striking similarities comparing Northern and Southern *kanun* variants.

18 Cf. Donnert 1999: 9 and Emadi 1993.

19 Robert Pichler collected empirical data when researching for the OSCE on the security situation in Southern Albania in 1997. In a lecture 'Contesting the state monopoly: law, order and authorities in times of a power vacuum' at the School of Slavonic and East European Studies, University of London, he presented some of his results (6 March 1998). From the south-west Albanian harbour city Vlora he reported incidents illustrative of an immediate preparedness to use violence, and the on-the-spot organisation of young-men gangs, affiliated along lines of kinship, neighbourhood and friendship.

20 These processes of escalation, as well as the use of traditionalist discourses in justification of violence in the pre-war Kosovo developments have recently been described in detail by Tim Judah (Judah 2000).

Bibliography

Alia, Z. (1989) *Die Familie und ihre Struktur in der SVR Albanien*, Tirana: 8 Nentori.

Backer, B. (1992) 'The Albanians of Rrogam' (documentary film), Series: *Disappearing World*, Granada Films.

Beaumont, P. (1999) 'Now mafia wages war in Kosovo', *The Observer*, 15 August 1999: 19.

Bock, C. and Schwandner, S. (1994) 'Der Kanun des Lek Dukagjin: Das nordalbanische Gewohnheitsrecht nach dem Kommunismus', *Vox TV, Magazine of Sueddeutsche Zeitung*, 18 October 1994 (20-minute TV transmission).

Bourdieu, P. (1976) *Entwurf einer Theorie der Praxis auf der Ethnologischen Grundlage der Kabylischen Gesellschaft*, Frankfurt: Suhrkamp Verlag.

Buchholz, O., Fiedler, W. and Uhlisch, G. (1977) *Wörterbuch Albanisch – Deutsch*, Leipzig: VEB Verlag Enzyklopaedie.

Cozzi, E. (1910) 'La vendetta del sangue nelle Montagne dell'Alta Albania', *Anthropos* 5: 654–87.

Dauti, D. (1999) 'The killings in Kosovo continue', Institute for War and Peace Reporting (*info@iwpr.net*), IWPR's Balkan Crisis Report, No. 91, 9 November 1999.

De Waal, C. (1996) 'Decollectivisation and total scarcity in high Albania', in R. Abrahams (ed.) *After Socialism: Land Reform and Social Change in Eastern Europe*, Providence and Oxford: Berghahn.

Donnert, C. (1999) *Trees of Blood and Trees of Milk: Customary Law and the Construction of Gender in Albania* (MA Gender Studies Dissertation, School of Slavonic and East European Studies, forthcoming on www.ssees.ac.uk), London: Centre for South East European Studies.

Durham, E. (1985) [1909] *High Albania*, Boston: Beacon.

Elezi, I. (1983) *E Drejta Zakonore Penale e Shqiptareve dhë Lufta për Zhdukjen e Mbeturinave të saj në Shqipëri* [The Customary Penal Law of the Albanians and the Fight for Eliminating its relicts in Albania], Tirana: 8 Nentori.

Elwert, G. (1997) 'Gewaltmärkte: Beobachtungen zur Zwecksrationalität der Gewalt', in T. v. Trotha (ed.) *Soziologie der Gewalt*, Opladen-Wiesbaden: Westdeutscher Verlag.

Emadi, H. (1993) 'Development Strategies and Women in Albania', *East European Quarterly* 27(1): 79–96.

Gjeçov, Sh. (1989) *Kanuni i Lekë Dukagjinit – The Code of Lekë Dukagjini* (with a translation and an introduction by Leonard Fox, original 1933), New York: Gjonlekaj

Godin, A. F. von (1956) 'Das albanische Gewohnheitsrecht, Kanun i Lek Dukagjjinit', *Zeitschrift für vergleichende Rechtswissenschaft* 58: 121–96.

Hahn, J. G. von (1854) *Albanesische Studien*, 3 Vol., Wien: k.-k. Hof- and Staatsdruckerei.

Hasluck, M. (1954) *The Unwritten Law of Albania*. London: Cambridge University Press.

—— (1967) 'The Albania blood feud', P. Bohannan (ed.) *Law and Warfare: Studies in the Anthropology of Conflict*, Garden City, New York: Natural History Press.

Hechter, M. (1995) 'Explaining nationalist violence', *Nations and Nationalism* 1(1): 53–68.

Judah, T. (2000) *Kosovo: War and Revenge*, New Haven and London: Yale University Press.

Kaser, K. and Eberhardt, H. (eds) (1995) *Albanien: Stammesgesellschaft zwischen Tradition und Moderne*, Wien and Köln: Boehlau.

Kaser, K., Pichler, R. and Schwandner-Sievers, S. (2001) *Die weite Welt und das Dorf. Albanische Emigrationen am Ende des 20. Jahrhunderts*, Vienna, Cologne, Weimer: Boehlau Verlag.

Kikia, M. (1999) 'Gjakmarrja, lufta mes shqiptareve qe nuk do the shuhet', *Koha Jone*, 10 October 1999.

Kraszev, P. (1999) 'The price of amnesia: interpretations of vendetta in Albania', draft submitted to Stephen Baister, M. Rady, S. Schwandner-Sievers (eds) (forthcoming) *Custom and Law in a Time of Transition: The Albanian Case* (proceedings of the Albanian Studies Day at SSEES, February 1999).

Mjedia, D. L. (1901) 'Das Recht der Stämme von Dukadschin', *Zeitschrift für Ethnologie* 1901: 353–8.

Nicholson, B. (1998) 'Down Among the Bandits: Fieldwork in South Albania May–June 1997', *network bsa* (Newsletter of the British Sociological Association) 69: 27–8.

Pichler, R. (1995) 'Macht der Gewohnheit: Die Dukagjin-Staemme und ihr Gewohnheitsrecht', in K. Kaser and H. Eberhardt (eds) *Albanien: Stammesgesellschaft zwischen Tradition und Moderne*, Wien and Köln: Boehlau.

—— (1998) 'Contesting the state monopoly: law, order and authorities in times of a power vacuum', lecture presented at the School of Slavonic and East European Studies, University of London, 6 March 1998.

Sampson, S. (1998) 'Exporting democracy, preventing mafia: the rebirth of 'Eastern Europe' in the era of *post*-post-communism', in B. Petersen *et al.* (eds) *Collective Identities in Eastern Europe*, Lund: Lund University Press.

Schneider, J. (1971) 'Of vigilance and virgins: honour, shame and access to resources in Mediterranean societies', *Ethnology* 9: 1–24.

Schwandner-Sievers, S. (1999) 'Humiliation and reconciliation in northern Albania: the logics of feuding in symbolic and diachronic perspectives', in G. Elwert, S. Feuchtwang and D. Neubert (eds) *Dynamics of Violence: Processes of Escalation and De-escalation in Violent Group Conflicts*, Berlin: Duncker and Humblot.

—— (forthcoming 2001) 'Times past – references for the construction of local order in present-day Albania', in M. Todorova (ed.) *National Memory in the Balkans.*

Sisti, L. (1999) 'Mafia e re shqiptare', *Klan*, 31 January 1999: 16–19.

Stanfield, D. and Kukeli, A. (1995) 'Consolidation of the Albanian agricultural land reform through a program for creating an immovable property registration system', draft paper prepared for the Central Europe Conference, Budapest, 12–16 June 1995.

Verdery, K. (1994) 'Ethnicity, nationalism, and state-making? Ethnic groups and boundaries, past and future', in H. Vermeulen and C. Govers (eds) *The Anthropology of Ethnicity: Beyond 'Ethnic Groups and Boundaries'*, Amsterdam: Het Spinhuis.

Violence and conflict

Chapter 6

Violence and culture

Anthropological and evolutionary-psychological reflections on inter-group conflict in southern Ethiopia

Jon Abbink

Introduction

This chapter is an anthropological reflection on inter-personal violence and its social and psychological roots in a small-scale African society. Anthropology by convention works from local-level empirical studies to explore the nature of diversity and similarity in human behaviour, usually on the assumptions that humans function on the basis of similar and comparable psycho-biological traits, and that socio-cultural conditions are decisive in determining how and to what extent these traits are expressed. The following discussion is based on my observation of a non-industrial, agro-pastoral society in southern Ethiopia, and on the conviction that not only social and historical conditions but also culture and psychology are important to understand constructions and practices of violence. The case to be discussed has no direct similarity to the many headline-making armed conflicts of a more political nature, as found in, e.g., Sierra Leone, Somalia, ex-Zaire, Angola, Indonesia or Burma. Similar, however, to other persistent situations of violence across the globe, the Suri[1] case underlines that an understanding of *cultural* backgrounds and commitments of the people who fight is essential. As Paul Richards has shown in his recent book on the Sierra Leone war (1996), we ignore the local cultural narratives and meanings that inform the participants at the peril of misunderstanding the nature and extent of violence. In this chapter, I will also claim that in itself the cultural perspective needs to be augmented with a theory of human behaviour and motivation. Asserting that violence is 'culturally constructed' only serves as explanation up to a certain point. The underlying rationality of violent performance, either seen in an instrumental or in a cognitive way (relating it to world views or cultural representations)[2] is also conditioned by the concern of humans with reproduction and social success.

As the experience of many anthropologists has shown, conflict and violence are a more and more common aspect of the social life of the communities that they study, and often defy easy explanation. I begin with a personal experience.

> One evening at around 9.00 p.m., some years ago when doing field-work in southern Ethiopia, I was called by two neighbours of mine, one of them the local chief of the Dizi people. They pleaded with me to come and go with them to look at four girls who had been shot in an ambush. On the scene, a forty minutes' walk, wailing women and men, relatives and neighbours, were gathered. It was obvious: three girls were dead, the fourth badly wounded, and not much could be done without specialised medical aid. A messenger was dispatched to a neighbouring village where some clinic workers and a group of soldiers were stationed. From the way the girls had been shot, it was also immediately clear who had carried it out: young men from the Suri, an ethnic group of cattle herders in the lowlands, about a four hours' walk from the Dizi area. The surviving girl, who escaped death because of keeping herself as if dead, told us later that it was an ambush whereby the three Suri boys, armed with Kalashnikov assault-rifles, had shot them while they had come back from the fields, carrying firewood. When the girls fell to the ground, the Suri youths came out, trembling and shouting, and stood over the girls to see whether they were dead. One man fired extra bullets at two girls whom he thought might still be alive. Then they quickly made off to their homesteads in the lowlands.

Seen in the global context or even in the regional context of violent encounters (in the Horn of Africa), this incident is perhaps nothing remarkable, neither in scale nor in nature. However, in view of the reported history (by local people) in the past century of largely peaceful relations between Suri and Dizi, the two ethnic groups in question, in fact it *was*. It was an indication of some of the changes in group relations and norms and values that had been occurring in this remote southern Ethiopian region for only a short period. The question is why the largely ritual forms of violence in this area, specifically among the agro-pastoral Suri, have been transformed into 'real', almost unrestrained, violence, subverting the rules both between and within the communities.

This particular incident also had a devastating impact on the local community of Dizi people (indigenous subsistence farmers, numbering about 25,000) because of the fact that the attack was unprovoked, seemed to have no material or other purpose,[3] and had targeted four young girls, from 18 to 20 years of age. Two of them were planning to be married soon.

During his commemorative speech at the grave-site, the local Dizi chief, next to lamenting the general crisis in Suri–Dizi relations, explicitly referred to these young girls dying before having reached maturity and having become mothers in the following words: 'These young women . . . imagine how many children they could have carried. . . . Now they die without children to make their parents rejoice and satisfied. Their names will be lost, and no sons and daughters will live to help the family or to invoke the name of their mother . . .'.

Evolutionary psychology, culture and violence

This reference to what we might call the 'lost reproductive chances' of the girls made me reflect on the underlying factors of conflict between ethnic groups in the Ethiopian Southwest, and on the possible goal-oriented, instrumental role of aggression and violence between these, in several respects, 'competing' groups. It is a known fact (Daly and Wilson 1988) that homicides are mostly perpetrated between unrelated people (although they are often not unacquainted), and usually *not* done blindly in a fit of rage. The three Suri killers, I propose, also knew exactly what they were doing: they purposely targeted four young Dizi girls, not Suri girls, and specifically of that age. They knew the cultivation sites of those girls and their activities from previous observation, and had gone there to lie in wait and shoot them. Despite appearances therefore, it was not a mad, random killing: there was a deliberate intimidation effect here in their striking at young nubile Dizi women. This aspect of 'goal-orientation' and its cultural referents has in general not been sufficiently explored in studies on violence, although cases like the one just presented may be widespread and warrant more systematic study.

The remark of the Dizi chief also brings into focus the question of the connection between violent aggression, kinship and reproductive, or what have been called 'inclusive fitness', chances: is there one, and if so, do people further such chances by violence[4] in inter-group contacts? In other words, does the aggression pay (in a reproductive sense?) It may be interesting to address such a general question with an eye to 'evolutionary psychology', one of the newer applications of neo-Darwinian theory in anthropology. This approach is not to be identified with behavioural ecology or sociobiology, which remain obsessed with genetics as a causal framework for social behaviour (and of course unpopular among most anthropologists). Robert Wright, in his recent thought-provoking survey of evolutionary psychology in his book *The Moral Animal* (1994), has demonstrated the potential of this approach for asking productive questions about humans and society. The evolutionary psychology approach in a way goes 'back to basics': to the evolved psychological mechanisms of humans underlying social behaviour in their strivings for survival, status, social capital and reproduction. Evolutionary psychology intends to rise above standard cultural descriptions and interpretations to move to a more deductive theory of motivation informing inter-personal actions. Key concepts used in this approach are: *selection, adaptation, problem-solving, and maximisation of personal and kin 'fitness'* (i.e. survival). Even if it may *not* necessarily have a more comprehensive or explanatory power, evolutionary psychology may at least generate new questions and hypotheses. Evolutionary psychology emphasises questions relating to competition, aggression, strife and violence, and the cogency of its assumptions and explanatory claims should be critically assessed.[5]

The above-mentioned guiding principles underlying the evolution of humanity that crystallised in the long period of small-scale hunter-gatherer existence (often called the EEA, the 'environment of evolutionary adaptation'[6]), have yielded various characteristics of human behaviour and psychological functioning, and have also influenced the human use of culture Humans have specific patterns of co-operation and conflict, partner selection and social investment, and show a pervasive concern with: (a) status and prestige,[7] (b) reciprocity, (c) alternating co-operation and competition in the light of own social advantage, (d) a tendency to nepotism, and (e) ideas of retaliation and revenge in situations of death or physical threat to survival or reproductive chances, including those of kin, and if there is a threat to lose public 'face'. Ultimately, evolutionary psychology deals with the fairly universal 'psychological mechanisms that come between theories of selection pressures on the one hand and fully realised socio-cultural behaviour on the other' (Cosmides *et al.* 1992: 6).[8] Among these mechanisms is also the aggressive drive – although aggression does not always mean 'violence'.

Without claiming here that social relations and cultural process can be explained in full by this new line of evolutionary psychology thought, it might be said that many anthropologists, due to a chiefly culturalist training, have missed the relevance of psycho-biological factors underlying social behaviour. For example, the seminal studies in the 1960s and 1970s by human biologists Williams, Hamilton (1964) and Trivers (1971) on the biological-natural bases of kin relations and kin selection, altruism, etc., were ignored in social studies, although they had a *direct* bearing on the understanding of reciprocity, kinship structures, demography and family life of people in most ethnographic settings. This has, in my view, led to awkward errors and to repeated reinventions of the wheel. Phenomena like kin-group solidarity, sibling rivalry and co-operation, generation conflict, gender antagonisms, or parental 'investment strategies' in offspring and each other, are *not only* social or cultural constructions depending on property rights, inheritance, religious values, etc., but are rooted in predictable psycho-biological propensities.[9]

This chapter is confined to a consideration of only some aspects of the relation between changing patterns of violence and reproductive/survival concerns in inter-ethnic relations (Suri and Dizi communities) in the southern Ethiopian context.

Relevance of the Suri case

The Suri are (an as yet 'unglobalised') society of cattle herders and cultivators in the marginal lowlands of southern Ethiopia, close to the border with Sudan, and number about 26,000 to 28,000 people. They are virtually a monolingual group, and still retain a fair amount of political and economic autonomy within the Ethiopian state. Contacts with other agro-pastoral and agricultural groups as well as villagers (traders, administrators, teachers, etc.) are limited, consisting of trade in livestock, tools, gold, ornaments, and occasionally food items in times of need. There is little intermarriage with other ethnic groups.

Like most cattle-herding people in East Africa, they are patrilineal and polygamous, with a subordinate position of women in political life and the management of the principal wealth, that is cattle herds. The Suri have no central leaders, but an authority structure based on a leading age-grade and religious mediators (see Abbink 1997a).[10]

In the last ten to fifteen years, the Suri have had to deal with far-reaching processes of socio-political change. Indeed, they can be seen as being in a phase of 'accelerated history',[11] which has in many respects led to a sense of crisis. These accelerations include the following: a succession of ecological problems such as drought, famine[12] and cattle disease; influx of a new arms technology (automatic weapons) which has replaced the old in a matter of one or two years; the expansion of the economic base (beyond the pastoral economy: illegal hunting and gold trading especially); the growing but unequal contacts with outside forces and their impact (including the state imposing a new authority structure); and finally, the emergence of serious internal dissent within the society.[13]

There is also an inexorable process of incorporation of this local society in another field of forces constituted by: (a) the regional disturbances in northern Kenya (conflict between the Turkana, Nyangatom and the state) leading to ethnic migrations (to the north); (b) the Sudanese civil war, leading to a substantial trade in arms and ammunition and also population movements; and (c) encroaching tourism and missionary influence. The impact of these latter two 'globalising' forces is growing, but we won't go into this here except to note that the encounter of Suri with tourists is highly problematic and occasionally violent (armed threats and robbery). For our purposes, it is important to note that the context and structure of Suri violence has been greatly transformed under the impact of these changes.

Accounting for inter-ethnic violence

The Suri, as an agro-pastoralist people in a precarious environment, have always lived in close contact with other, often hostile, groups. Violent encounters with the latter were frequent. Still, this violent contact with non-Suri in the pre-state context was largely *ritualised*. This recalls the human condition of the 'ancestral environment' (or the EEA, see note 6), where ritualisation was developed as a specific cultural trait, an evolved inhibition or adaptation which humans share with many primates and with the ancestral hominids (cf. Fox 1994a: 78–9), and which was expressed in cultural representations.

Among the Suri, the culturally encoded ritual violence could be seen as an implicit goal-oriented phenomenon. This aspect was evident, for instance, (a) in raiding: the enhancing of survival by defence or attack, permitting competition for access to vital resources (pasture, water holes), (b) in stick-duelling: the making of claims to sexual access and a reproductive career, and (c) in the relations between clans, kin and household groups: observing balanced reciprocity in social life. To give examples: killing enemies or losing your own people during a cattle raid was not seen as disastrous; inflicting bloody wounds and breaking bones during ceremonial stick-duelling was not 'controversial'; a revenge killing was in no way frowned upon if compensation payment had not been forthcoming after a (previous) homicide. In short, violence was seen as an inevitable aspect of life but was – with some exceptions – culturally under control. Hence, if one could in any way speak of a 'culture of violence' (a difficult term[14]), it was a ritualised one, based on cultural metaphors and practices showing an 'uncontested' exercise of force (cf. Riches 1991, cited in note 2).

At this juncture in their history, however (the late 1990s), the Suri show the abandonment of 'ritual violence', i.e. the ordered management of uncontested aggression, both inter- and intragroup. Empirically, we see a conversion of ritual violence into 'real violence', i.e. unsanctioned, arbitrary, unmanageable, cruel (to local standards), and with unpredictable consequences (cf. Abbink 1998b). The 'agent' of this conversion is the social stratum of young men (of one age-grade).

If, as is now the case among the Suri, the ritual-cultural bounds are broken, this is exceptional in view of the 'natural tendency' toward ritualisation and restraint (cf. Fox 1994b: 88–90) among humans. Also, the Suri idea of sociality does not assume that humans are 'inherently or naturally violent'.[15] They think that humans are 'human' – i.e. not like animals – because of their always and automatically being social and organised: living in kin groups and in networks of friendship or affinal alliance and committed to their long-term survival interests. (Only if this sociality is manifestly taken advantage of or purposely betrayed by the others, is a legitimate resort to aggressive force is made to restore the balance.)

The present crisis is due to rapid social changes, and reinforced by new options made available by these changes. We look at the breakdown of this ritual containment in two fields: raiding and trading.

First: raiding and counter-raiding between Suri and their agro-pastoral neighbours (Nyangatom and Toposa people, together about 73,000 people) has for them been a fact of life 'since time immemorial'. It had a (perhaps surprising) number of underlying rules (giving warnings before the actual raid, no burning of pasture, no poisoning of wells, no killing of cattle, no raping and killing of women). The material interests of both groups were the same, and competition was obvious. However, in this situation, violence was not only mutually accepted, but also seen as a way to create distinction, to affirm boundaries. In addition, it was seen as 'exciting' and was done for its own sake (this is an underestimated but real dimension of violent action). But there was no attempt – and no possibility – to 'root out the opponents' or conquer all of their territory. There were bond-friendships between the groups, and people visited each other in their villages in the periods of peace when no raids were going on.

At the present time, all these things have changed: Suri did not regain parity with the Nyangatom, did not evict them from territory conquered or occupied by them, and they did not take up former bond-friendships. Most importantly, in major cattle raids where Nyangatom took away large numbers of their cattle, the Suri defenders have occasionally opened fire on the animals, rather than letting them fall into the hands of the enemy. This act to shoot their beloved cattle was unprecedented, and needless to say not authorised by the reigning age-grade of elders. This is one instance where we may see the decline of the 'ritual language of violence', with 'real' violence, i.e. contested and socially destructive, taking its place.

Second: trading and exchanging. On their eastern flanks, the Suri are bordered by a highland cultivator people, the Dizi. From them, no cattle was raided (they didn't have much in the first place). They entertained peaceful trading relations and some intermarriage.[16] The Suri recognised the Dizi as the original inhabitants and lords of the land. At the end of the nineteenth century (in a period of drought and famine from 1889 to 1894), the Suri moved more toward the Dizi highlands (and came into closer contact with them). At this time an agreement was made up under which the Suri (who live in lowland areas with precarious rainfall) recognised the rain-making powers of the Dizi chiefs and could call upon their help (food and sacrificial rites for rain). In this context, a special ritual procedure was designed. Implicitly it also meant that the Dizi permitted the Suri to move into areas nominally theirs (for cattle-herding and hunting-gathering).[17] A myth relating the common descent of the chiefly families of the Dizi and the Suri leading clan (from the same mother) was also created at this juncture. Although other elements in the oral tradition of both groups suggest that this was a purely 'fictional' connection, the important point was that in the myth the two groups were declared kin.[18]

Nevertheless, one can see underlying problems in this alliance of Suri and Dizi: it was a treaty, recently concluded and in certain circumstances; there was a hierarchical element involved, contrasting with Suri egalitarianism;[19] and there was a discrepancy in the long-term material interests and in the socio-economic systems of the two groups.[20]

Under the impact of ecological crises, the arms influx, and the involuntary population movements, the Dizi–Suri relationship broke down. One reason is the continued imbalance with the Nyangatom, who now had the support of the more than 60,000-strong Toposa people encroaching on the Suri eco-niche from the west, due to the pressures of the Sudanese civil war. This meant that the Suri could never regain their erstwhile parity and could not return to areas and pastures from which they had been evicted in the mid-1980s. The only option was to slowly expand towards the Dizi highlands, which is what they did. This expansion was carried out with violent means: not only taking over cultivation sites, bee-hives, alluvial gold-panning areas and hunting grounds, but also stealing livestock, attacking villages, killing travellers and elders, and abducting or shooting Dizi girls. When occasionally a Dizi killed a Suri, the retaliatory response (a life for a life) of the Suri as a whole was often excessive. For example, in one instance in 1991, a Dizi village was razed to the ground, forty-three people killed with rifle-fire and machetes and the cattle taken away after one Suri was killed in a brawl. These actions were meant as a campaign of intimidation and the pattern perhaps reveals a Suri obsession with competition over resources and fertility. This exercise of violence was also fuelled by motives internal to Suri society, to which we come in the next section.

Accounting for intra-ethnic violence

Perhaps most surprising is the quick breakdown of ritual violence *within* Suri society. If external relations deteriorated one might expect more internal solidarity against enemy groups posing a survival threat. But instead we have seen the development of more individual battles, family strife and lineage antagonism, sometimes leading to feuding without end. Why? With recourse to the evolutionary psychology perspective, focusing on the recurring psychological concerns of people, one could identity several factors.

Underlying Suri social life and violent practice was a strong perception (culturally embedded in metaphors, stories and ritual contexts) of social relations as a balancing act, a zero-sum game, a perpetual and jealously guarded play of reciprocity. (This could be substantiated by a closer institutional analysis of Suri society which I will not give here; compare also Abbink 1998b.) Equality and reciprocity were indeed seen as 'natural' and specifically human, but its breach was resented strongly. Violent redress was a concomitant, an ever-present option, and in itself uncontested. This applied to individuals, villages and territorial groups.

A complicating factor of intra-ethnic violence was the crisis in the age-grade system, specifically that of the loss of authority of the reigning age-grade of elders over the youngsters (Abbink 1998a). The Suri age-grade system has four grades, and the two lower ones are normatively subservient to the two higher ones. The core relationship was between the grade of the unmarried young men, the so-called 'warriors' (*tègay*, i.e. uninitiated) and the junior elders, called *rórà*. Due to the new power-position of the young men (through gold and guns), they could ward off claims of the elders, stall their own initiation – because it would have meant a responsibility they did not yet want – and extend their period of 'youthful exuberance'. It effectively meant that the usual mechanism of 'imitating-the-high-in-status' (Barkow 1994: 130) was failing.

If we look at the relationship among the Suri (in so far as possible in the time-span of a few years) between 'aggressive behaviour' as a raider, a dueller or a family tyrant on the one hand and economic or 'reproductive success' on the other (i.e. having more cattle, more women and more children) we do not see a *direct* positive correlation.[21] There was indeed a correlation between the achievement of social *prestige* – and then not only in duelling and raiding, but also in public speaking at political debates, in forging alliances or in successful trading – with reproductive chances. However, the social sanctioning (and conversion) of prestige was made possible only after the ritual entrance of a male in the third age-grade of the 'real adults', called *rórà*. Most males took a second or third wife (after their first one when still a *tègay*) after entering the *rórà* ('junior elder') grade. But we saw that the initiation – done approximately every twenty to twenty-five years – was purposely delayed by youngsters and elders. It is significant that in this period, the youngsters did not stress the value of marriage and having children (no reproductive motives) but that of liaisons with different girls, without commitment.

We pursue this point of alleged reproductive concerns in briefly discussing two traditional Suri institutions.

First: ceremonial duelling. This is a form of 'ritualised violence' acted out in a public arena with thousands of people watching, prominent among them large numbers of unmarried teenage girls. For the Suri duelling is like a sport, done in the name of a social/territorial unit of which the duellers were a member. There are rules, such as never kill an opponent, participation only of males of a certain age-grade, supervision by referees, and limited time of a bout. When an opponent is accidentally killed, all duelling is immediately cancelled, and people go home. It is easy to see why: instead of a meeting- and training-ground, the duelling arena has then become a lethal battleground. When such 'real violence' occurs, the ritual frame is broken and the whole procedure should be stopped. Although it is violent in the sense that serious flesh wounds and broken bones are common, duelling combat is meant to be ceremonial: for showing off as much as for being 'successful' (i.e. winning). Participating and showing courage in the fight is stated to be more important than to win. Also, while there are some overall successful fighters, not all contests are won by the same people. Wounds and scars are shown with pride not with shame.

The duels are obviously different from fights and battles with non-Suri enemy groups because they have no rewards except male prestige-building and display in front of girls. As such, the duels are a variation of the universal theme which evolutionary psychologists have called the 'young male syndrome': a pattern of show-off peer violence of a social group on the margins of society (see Daly and Wilson 1985 on male youths in Detroit). The duelling institution also shows an unmistakable connection with what evolutionary psychologists call 'strategies of mating or partner choice', and reproduction. This aspect is explicitly recognised by nubile Suri teenage girls coming to the duelling ground. Also interesting is that at the end of the day, the winner of the contest is carried to the girls on a platform. In this way, duelling provides an inevitable forum of male–female contacts, whereby girls among themselves make a first choice as to whom their partners might be for various kinds of contacts. Although it is not important that one always choose a winner, a girl does not choose someone who never participated. My inquiries on present and past 'duelling heroes' did not reveal that they had significantly more chances to marry more wives or to get more children (or had actual reproductive success attributed to their status as top duellers).

Ceremonial duelling has, however, undergone a transformation since the influx of modern weapons, because of the fact that the young men have a new power position because of their fire-power and their newly acquired money from gold sales. Also in this context, real violence has broken through the ritual bounds. Referees have great trouble in keeping order, the frequency and length of duelling has increased enormously, losing parties use Kalashnikovs to vent their anger, and there is a tendency to settle real scores – i.e. conflicts which have nothing to do with the duelling – in and around the duelling arena, which has become an unsafe place to be in.

Second: another institution in flux is that of the homicide-compensation procedures. After a homicide, people are less patient to sit out the traditional compensation talks which can take months, even a year or more (to settle the amount of cattle to be transferred and which girl to be handed over to the family of the victim). This has led to short-term violent action on the part of the victim's family if they can get away with it. This depends on the strength of the kin group. All this again leads to feuding, which was not so common in the recent past. (Such feuding conflicts have also affected the family of the three ritual leaders, the *komoru*. In one family, there has been a long line of killings between two lineages since one of their two *komoru*s was accidentally shot and killed in 1990. Suri themselves say that this is unprecedented and that they do not know what to do.) Thus, the idea of revenge and retaliation has become an end in itself, and has a counter-productive effect from the point of view of group selection and inclusive fitness.

The disruption created by internal violence was more deeply regretted by, especially, elder Suri than that of external violence. Perhaps they now realised for the first time that there never had been internal peace, that their society had always been ridden by latent tension and strife between groups claiming structural equality. The system had worked when the authority and role of the leading age-grade was still respected. But as this feature of social organisation of the Suri was eroded due to the new economic wealth and the unforeseen aggressive power of youngsters of the *tègay* grade, it crumbled. Thus, as in their external relations, there was also an erosion of customary rules and norms of ritual violence management in their internal relations.

These new forms of real (i.e. unmediated, direct) violence within Suri society may have short-term advantages for the perpetrators: they can gain resources and prestige among peers in a situation of relative impunity, because the age-grade system does not work properly and there is no restraining of structure authority. Some youngsters plainly told me that they had made an 'investment' in rifles and ammunition, and that they had to use them to reap the 'benefits'. However, the long-term effects are not assured: feuding is more persistent, more agnates are killed, more children are fatherless and poor, dependent on relatives and shocked by the experience. Social co-operation is undermined, and all in all the inclusive fitness of families and lineages is reduced. In such circumstances, it appears that aggression 'does not pay'. The society has not found a cultural answer yet to the management of extreme firepower and sudden youth power on the basis of automatic weapons that were 'abused'. We see here, in the setting of a materially simple society of agro-pastoralists, that a technological factor – combined with social contradictions – undermines the evolutionary tendency in human socio-cultural life toward restraint and ritualisation.

Suri violence and 'adaptation'

Summarising the recent history of violence among the Suri, we see the first break with the past in the period when their agro-pastoralist neighbours (the Nyangatom) got hold of automatic rifles (in the late 1970s) and changed the relationship between themselves and Suri from one of a 'balance of deterrence' into one of prey and hunter (cf. Fox 1994b: 92–3). Such a situation usually leads to extreme violence. Hundreds of Suri at this time fell victim to Nyangatom violence.

The Suri's turn came around 1987 when new loads of weapons reached them as well. This was the second breakpoint: it allowed the Suri partly to retaliate, and to acquire more cattle (which means chances for marriage alliance and thus fertility) from other sources. They could also keep other potential competitors under control, and find new occasions for violent performance to build up male peer-group prestige (in raids and ambushes on Dizi and other highlanders). In this situation of crisis, the Suri, by using more unrestrained violence towards outsiders, also made a statement that – even when in deep trouble – they do not want to give up their independence, group identity, and freedom of action.[22]

They took the same course of violent engagement against army units of the new Ethiopian government which came to their area in 1991–2. However, this eventually led to a battle in 1994 in which hundreds of Suri (manly women and children) died in two days of fighting. This was perhaps the best proof that, as an 'adaptive system' Suri society, endangering its own women and children due to excessive violence of the one age-grade of men, did not perform well in new circumstances.

Overseeing the process of accelerated social change, the response of the Suri to use short-term violence was perhaps understandable. But as a long-term strategy for either reproductive or survival purposes it proved contradictory. In times of famine crisis and enemy warfare (the early 1980s), the tendency 'to make up for human and material losses' with any means had a certain logic. The violence against the Dizi is 'understandable' (not morally) from the perspective of competition, and the clear aim of targeting women and cattle as prey illustrates their aims to not only gain easy access to peer status (through violent performance impossible to act out against their traditional Nyangatom enemies) but also to pre-empt the growth and fertility of the Dizi people in the adjoining and partly shared territory.

But when violent competition and 'deculturalisation' work against peaceful inter-ethnic contacts and exchange relations in the long run, and against co-operation and alliance on the level of Suri lineages and even households, Suri society as a whole, as a separate unit, is endangered.[23] This indicates that in terms of selection and long-term group fitness, the course taken by the Suri (especially the young armed group of the *tègay*) is not a certain way to enhancing their own advantages and reproductive success.

Concluding remarks

Suri culture always showed the presence and expression of aggression and violence – although often uncontested: it was part of their way of life (e.g. in their rituals, in duelling, and reflected in oral traditions of clans and leaders, and in personal praise songs, recalling the deeds of the singer). Violence was perhaps 'inevitable' in a cattle-herding society in an insecure environment, in competition, and with precarious mediation mechanisms. In this respect, 'violence' was not a problem but just a fact of life. In the words of R. Fox (1989: 143–4) the Suri had a society with a 'high-keyed arousal system'. Violence was a way to prestige and distinction, a way to stake culturally sanctioned claims, and also an affirmation of difference and of identity, both among competing Suri territorial units (herding units) and of Suri vis-à-vis other ethnic groups.

The de-ritualisation of Suri violent behaviour has primarily been a reflection of the flux of external and internal conditions in the wider regional (and global) context, such as recurring ecological crisis, the arrival of automatic rifles revolutionising the use of armed combat and raiding, state-political pressure, and the growing sense of inequality between groups. These posed new challenges for their adaptive strategy. Some traditional domains in which this violence was expressed were reciprocity and exchange relations, male–female relations, reproduction strategies and the symbolism of fertility. The incident mentioned at the beginning of this chapter was a conscious Suri blow to the idea of Dizi survival and reproduction.

It was more evidence of the subversion of traditional concerns of equality and balanced reciprocity, and of a decline of altruistic, co-operative behaviour both in- and outside the Suri group (recall also the cancelling of the Dizi–Suri rain-agreement, the break-off of bond-friendships, the efforts to duck out of homicide compensations). Prestige competition was deflected from the framework of the age-grade system – with its formerly authoritative 'reigning' age-set – towards those of the peer group, seeing itself in a false position of autonomy. As we saw, this led to a predictable effort to delay the initiation of the new age-set[24] – a protest against becoming adult, because it would mean a loss of leverage and freedom of action (sexual play, mobility, robbery, killing).

Among the group of young males, the purely instrumental use of violence – due mainly to the external factor of sudden availability of effective and intimidating fire-power – has gained a momentum of its own. It has obviated the need for ritual mechanisms of conflict control with Suri society. In large part, the new technology of violence itself transformed ritual violence into real violence due to the decline of the role of what Robin Fox has called 'circuit breakers': factors inhibiting the build-up towards a real outburst (Fox 1994b: 90): the quick-firing automatic weapons can be used faster and more efficiently – without a moment's reflection – than a knife in the sheath, a wooden pole, or a spear. It has also been substantiated in other research that when people have a choice of arms in a conflict situation they always reach for the most powerful one.

In the instances of the breakthrough of 'real' violence in ritual contexts we see the resurfacing of the immediate concerns of Suri personal and group survival: not primarily because in every human there is an aggressive impulse waiting to come out, but because of critical socio-political conditions which limit options, curtail balanced reciprocity, impose hierarchy and dominance, and threaten the 'group fitness' of a community. But the Suri instance also shows that 'real violence' as a strategy is ultimately counter-adaptive.[25] Historically speaking, it may also be an exceptional pattern of behaviour (part of an oscillating movement over time between ritual and real violence), generated by rapid upheavals in a society undergoing a difficult confrontation with 'modernity', and confined largely to the stratum of young males who have not yet made it in society. In any case, we see that the 'young male syndrome', as identified by Daly and Wilson some years ago in the city of Detroit (1985), is not confined to modern industrial urban societies. Although such a '(sub-)culture of violence' is transitional and emerges at points of social crisis, it can develop anywhere as a temporary formation. It is, however, unlikely to be durable. Violent 'overdetermination' of a society, endangering 'inclusive fitness' (i.e. social success and reproduction) of the kin group (and possibly the own ethnic group), eventually produces counter-images and practices of renewal and restoration, especially in a relatively close-knit, small-scale society like the Suri. This process may lead them to re-emphasise cultural norms and representations (e.g. as expressed by the elders and ritual leaders) that 'contest' the violent acts that have encroached upon their own society but have no cultural or other legitimacy.[26]

Acknowledgements

I acknowledge with gratitude support for fieldwork in Ethiopia (1991–4) received from the Royal Netherlands Academy of Science (KNAW), the Netherlands Organisation for Scientific Research in the Tropics (WOTRO 52–610), and the African Studies Centre, Leiden. I thank the Institute of Ethiopian Studies (Addis Ababa University) for institutional support, local officials and inhabitants of the Maji and Adikiaz areas, especially Ato Addiburji Adikyaz, and

Mr John Haspels, resident field representative of the EECMY and LWF in Tulgit, Maji Zone, for information and assistance. I am most indebted to the Chai-Suri people of Makara.

Notes

1 The Suri in the area under discussion comprise two sub-groups: Chai and Tirma. The Suri are also called Surma by their neighbours.
2 These aspects were explored in more detail in Abbink 1998b.
3 The girls had *not* been raped or robbed beforehand.
4 Defined as the use of symbols and acts of intimidation and/or physical force against humans or other living beings to gain or maintain power or to pre-empt or kill them. That is, it must have the 'contestable' aspect, which D. Riches (1991: 295) saw as essential. His concise definition: violence is '. . . contestably rendering physical hurt'. See also Riches 1986: 11–12.
5 In several social science domains, evolutionary psychology has already made essential contributions. See Symons 1979; Draper and Harpending 1982; also Daly and Wilson 1988 (up to a certain point).
6 The environment of evolutionary adaptation covers about 99 per cent of human/hominoid history. The decisive evolutionary period for humans (*Homo sapiens*) was of course the Upper-Palaeolithic.
7 The concern with status and prestige is a human universal. It was already the central theme in the great epics of Homer. See the excellent study by Van Wees 1992.
8 The theory does *not* depend on sociobiological concepts like 'fitness maximisation' and 'genetic selfishness', which represent a worldview rather than an empirical theory.
9 The disadvantages of evolutionary psychology as it is now are, however, the following: the lack of interesting *cultural* accounts, the neo-functionalist slant of its explanatory models, the tendency toward scientistic language and thinking, the crusading tone of many of its writings, and the production of crude humbug revealing an impoverished worldview of 'might is right' (e.g. the work of D. Buss on 'mate preference mechanisms' in Barkow *et al.* 1992).
10 The Suri saw themselves and were seen by others as a specific cultural unit as well: they had different socio-cultural arrangements, rituals and religious customs, and were self-conscious and defensive about their way of life. They were small-scale and close-knit, despising non-Suri agricultural people for their (what they see as a kind of) 'pathetic' way of life.
11 Compare Hann 1994.
12 These factors have contributed to insecurity, destitution and death among the Suri in the last two decades. The last serious drought was in 1993, and before that in 1984–5, when about one-tenth of the population perished.

13 I have dealt with this topic in various other articles on which I partly draw here: 1994, 1997b, 1998a and b.

14 The concept 'culture of violence' is of course ambiguous: can a culture be said to contain ideas and behavioural templates that define, stimulate or condone violent behaviour, and if so does that explain its occurence? This may also be a problem of the outside observer whose idea of violence does not necessarily coincide with that of the people in question. More important is to look at the way in which violent behaviour, in the sense of rendering destructive harm to others, might become institutionalised in the way of life of a group, possibly forming a basis for new social or political identities. The expression of the psycho-biological traits of human behaviour is decisively influenced by the evolution of culture as a corpus of symbolic representations and as an *internalised* rule system (cf. Knauft 1991: 417), also in a cognitive sense. Bourdieu's habitus theory does not exclude the notion that violent behaviour as part of a socio-cultural environment is similarly internalised and embodied, affecting the construction and expression of culture. But such 'cultures of violence' are *not* timeless and invariant units and cannot be durable either.

15 Like the closely related Mursi, they have no 'Hobbesian' image of man (see the same argument by Turton 1994: 170–1), or of violence existing 'closely under the surface of civilisation' (Compare Duclos 1998 for an essential study of this pernicious idea in American society).

16 Dizi girls going to Suri, never vice versa (due to the Suri bridewealth system: giving cattle to the agnatic relatives of the girl).

17 It should be noted that with their Nyangatom agro-pastoral neighbours the Suri never felt the need to make such a 'pact'.

18 Again, nothing like this ever happened between the socio-culturally much more closely related Nyangatom and Suri.

19 Dizi and Suri societies were also predicated upon very different models of political authority (see Abbink 1994, 1997a; Haberland 1993).

20 Remarkable is that apparently with the Dizi (who are in physical type, culture, mentality and way of life different from Suri), sociality had to be sanctioned in an agreement, and that with the Nyangatom (also agro-pastoral lowlanders) it was taken for granted and needed no codification.

21 See Abbink 1997b.

22 In this context, they have also refused any agricultural settlement scheme proposed to them by government agencies and missionaries. They are still in a position to refuse them.

23 Violence as a short-term 'problem-solving' strategy has also imprinted itself on the minds of the very youngest generation, who see their parents and relatives falling away and their households crippled by the loss of labour power and social support. Chisholm (1993) has pointed out the negative impact of such life-history experiences for long-term reproductive strategies.

24 See Abbink 1998a for more on this initiation ceremony of the Chai subsection, amongst whom fieldwork was done. The second Suri subsection (Tirma) still had not performed its initiation as of early 1998.

25 Compare also J. Moore (1990) on violence among the Cheyenne.

26 For example, there are occasional signs of Suri recovery, the most important one being the organisation of the long-awaited age-grade initiation ceremony almost three years ago (after a ten-year delay, see Abbink 1998a). Hereby the *tègay* (youngster) age-grade finally gave in to the pressure of the elders to accept initiation. This has indeed led to a decline of violent incidents, although not to a total halt (Among the Suri group who have not yet done this initiation ceremony – the Tirma subgroup – violence is indeed still more prevalent.) Hence 'culture', as a resource and as a framework of valuation and prestige vis-à-vis external forces generating crisis, may be able to reassert itself.

Bibliography

Abbink, J. (1994) 'Changing patterns of 'ethnic' violence: peasant – pastoralist confrontation in southern Ethiopia and its implications for a theory of violence', *Sociologus* 44(1): 66–78.

—— (1997a) 'Authority and chieftaincy in Surma society (Ethiopia)', *Africa* (Roma) 52(3): 317–42.

—— (1997b) 'Violence, ritual and reproduction: Surma ceremonial duelling as a construction of sociality and sexuality', in K. Fukui, E. Kurimoto and M. Shigeta (eds) *Ethiopia in Broader Perspective*, vol. 2. Kyoto: Shokado.

—— (1998a) 'Violence and political discourse among the Chai Suri', in G.J. Dimmendaal and M. Last (eds) *Surmic Languages and Cultures*, Cologne: R. Köppe.

—— (1998b) 'Ritual and political forms of violent practice among the Suri of Southern Ethiopia', *Cahiers d'Etudes Africaines* XXXVIII (2–4): 150–2, 271–96.

Barkow, J. H. (1994) 'Evolutionary psychological anthropology', in Ph. K. Bock (ed.) *Handbook of Psychological Anthropology*, Westport and London: Greenwood Press.

Barkow, J. H., Cosmides, L. and Tooby, J. (eds) (1992) *The Adapted Mind. Evolutionary Psychology and the Generation of Culture*, New York and Oxford: Oxford University Press.

Chisholm, J. S. (1993) 'Death, hope and sex. Life-history theory and the development of reproductive strategies', *Current Anthropology* 34(1): 1–24.

Cosmides, L., Tooby, J. and Barkow, J. H. (1992) 'Introduction: evolutionary psychology and conceptual integration', in J. H. Barkow, L. Cosmides and J. Tooby (eds) *The Adapted Mind, Evolutionary*

Psychology and the Generation of Culture, New York and Oxford: Oxford University Press.

Daly, M. and Wilson, M. (1985) 'Competitiveness, risk taking and violence: the young male syndrome', *Ethology and Sociobiology* 6: 59–73.

—— (1988) *Homicide*, Chicago: Aldine and De Gruyter.

Draper, P. and Harpending, H. (1982) 'Father absence and reproductive strategy: an evolutionary perspective', *Journal of Anthropological Research* 38(3): 255–73.

Duclos, D. (1998) *The Werewolf Complex. America's Fascination with Violence*, Oxford and New York: Berg.

Fox, R. (1989) 'The violent imagination', in R. Fox (ed.) *The Search for Society*, New Brunswick and London: Transaction Publishers.

—— (1994a) 'Aggression then and now', in R. Fox (ed.) *The Challenge of Anthropology*, New Brunswick and London: Transaction Publishers.

—— (1994b) 'The human nature of violence', in R. Fox (ed.) *The Challenge of Anthropology*, New Brunswick and London: Transaction Publishers.

Haberland, E. (1993) *Hierarchie und Kaste. Zur Geschichte und politischen Struktur der Dizi in Südwest-Äthiopien*, Wiesbaden: F. Steiner.

Hamilton, W. D. (1964) 'The genetical evolution of social behaviour', *Journal of Theoretical Biology* 7: 1–52.

Hann, C. M. (ed.) (1994) *When History Accelerates: Essays on Rapid Social Change, Complexity and Creativity*. London: Athlone Press.

Knauft, B. M. (1991) 'Violence and sociality in human evolution', *Current Anthropology* 32(4): 391–428.

Moore, J. N. (1990) 'The reproductive success of Cheyenne war chiefs: a contrary case to Chagnon's Yanomamö', *Current Anthropology* 31(3): 322–30.

Richards, P. (1996) *Fighting for the Rainforest. War, Youth and Resources in Sierra Leone*, Oxford: James Currey.

Riches, D. (1991) 'Aggression, war, violence: space/time and paradigm', *Man* (n.s.) 26(2): 281–98.

—— (ed.) *The Anthropology of Violence*, Oxford: Basil Blackwell.

Symons, D. L. (1979) *The Evolution of Human Sexuality*, New York: Oxford University Press.

Trivers, R. (1971) 'The evolution of reciprocal altruism', *Quarterly Review of Biology* 46: 35–56.

Turton, D. (1994) 'We must teach them to be peaceful: Mursi views on being human and being Murs', in T. Tvedt (ed.) *Conflicts in the Horn of Africa: Human and Ecological Consequences of Warfare*, Uppsala: EPOS and Department of Social and Economic Geography, Uppsala University.

Van Wees, H. (1992) *Status Warriors. War, Violence and Society in Homer and History*. Amsterdam: J. C. Gieben.

Wright, R. (1994) *The Moral Animal. Why We Are The Way We Are: The New Science of Evolutionary Psychology*, New York: Pantheon Books (Random House).

Chapter 7

Violent events in the Western Apache past

Ethnohistory and ethno-ethnohistory

Ingo W. Schröder

Introduction

Similar to historically situated social praxis in general, war must be understood as being simultaneously shaped by the structural constraints of a given historical context and by the cultural mediation of this context through the actors' social ideology. While war results from conflicts caused by the objective structures of social reality, these conflicts are perceived through a specific cultural lens by any local collectivity. Reactions (ranging from violence to accommodation or avoidance) are not automatically enforced by the structural parameters, but are contingent on cultural models of decision-making in conflict situations. Moreover, these cultural models initially shape the representation of violence in a social arena, thus giving meaning to the actual conflict by situating it in a framework of appropriate reactions under comparable conditions in the past.[1]

To the analyst, war presents itself on two different levels: first, as action in response to concrete, observable structural factors (such as scarcity of resources, population movements, vertical and horizontal competition for power), that leaves behind material remains and whose impact on populations and environments can be evaluated; second, as discourse about violence in general or about specific confrontations in particular, situated in three very different communicative spaces: those of winners, losers and observers. These groups not only represent divergent interests and levels of involvement, but very often also different cultural backgrounds. Since historical instances of violence have only rarely been directly observed by anthropologists, there is no alternative available to dealing with this heterogeneous, often contradictory set of sources.

Anthropology usually tends to rearrange the evidence into the dichotomy of narratives by members of the culture studied (what has been termed 'ethno-ethnohistory' by Fogelson[2]), and all other kinds of data collected by the researcher ('ethnohistory'). This approach may not be especially well suited to analyse specific wars as multilateral events, but it serves well to highlight one society's cultural image of war.

The society in this case is the Western Apache.[3] Due to their long involvement in colonial frontier warfare the Apache, in general, are reputed to have an especially violent culture. Warfare did, indeed, occupy a prominent place in nineteenth-century Western Apache political economy and ideology (which are fairly well documented – considerably less is known about Apache culture during the earlier colonial period).[4] To analyse the Western Apaches' cultural model of war in a systematic manner, I pose four basic questions:

1 How are enemy images construed, perpetuated, or changed?
2 How is the use of violence against other groups legitimised in general?
3 Which are the concrete reasons for the use and targeting of external violence on specific occasions?
4 Which (individual or collective) goals are pursued and which results accomplished by the use of external violence?

The cultural construction of war

The highly fragmented nature of Apache socio-political organisation precluded anything resembling a unified set of external relations for the Western Apache. The decision-making power concerning war or peace lay in the hands of bands and clans pursuing local interests. However, in the long run, common patterns and historical trajectories emerge. Before this background it seems justified to speak of an overarching Western Apache concept of war.

During the pre-reservation period in the nineteenth century, Western Apache bands sustained hostile relations with three types of enemies: two categories of colonisers (which were distinguished terminologically), the Mexicans (*nakaiyé*, 'travellers')[5] and the Americans (*indaa*, 'enemies'), and various neighbouring Indian groups (mainly Pima/Papago, Navajo, and Yavapai).

A classical statement on Apache warfare from this period, by an Anglo-American observer, comes from Cremony:

> There is nothing which an Apache holds in greater detestation than labor or work of any kind. All occupations unconnected with war or plunder are esteemed altogether beneath his dignity and attention. He will patiently and industriously manufacture his bow and quiver full of arrows, his spear and other arms; but he disdains all other kinds of employment. He will suffer the pangs of hunger before engaging in the chase, and absolutely refuses to cultivate the ground, even at the cost of simply sowing the seed; but he is ever ready to take the war-path, and will undergo indescribable sufferings and hardships for the hope of a little plunder. Herein lies his credit and fame as a warrior; upon his success in such undertakings rests his whole celebrity and standing among the squaws whom he affects to treat with indifference, but whose smiles and favors are, after all, the greatest incentives to his acts.
>
> (Cremony 1868: 215–16)

A typical example of an Apache's way of remembering war reads quite differently:

> This is how it happened. This side of Phoenix the war party went. My father was along too. He had a spear and later fought with it there. When the party got near the Pimas' home that night, a chief with them called *Tlanagude* made a drum right there from cowhide, and got it all ready for the time when they would start the fight in the morning. When it got early morning he threw a rock up in the air and kept on doing this every so often, till he could see it all right. Then he knew it was time to start the attack, because it would also be light enough to see arrows and dodge them. 'Now let's go', he said, 'but first let's sing once more, and then we will go into the fight, as we may get killed.' So they sang one more song and then started for the Pima village. They set fire to the Pima tipis. *Tlanagude* started to beat his drum, and kept on hitting it while the men went into the fight. They killed lots of Pima men, and only one Pima man got away. He saved his life by fleeing to the top of a high sharp point down towards Phoenix, and I saw it one time when I was in the scouts over that way. Well, they got all the Pima women and girls in one bunch and then killed all the older ones, just saving the good, younger ones to take back with them. Captives that they brought home

> and let live were called *yodaschin*, which means 'born outside' (not in the Apache country). There are lots of them at Cibicue.
>
> (Nosey, quoted in Basso 1971: 285–6)

These two statements (which, although not contemporaneous, refer to the same time period) hardly seem comparable at all.

According to Goodwin, the Western Apache distinguished between two kinds of warfare: raiding (translated by him as 'to search out enemy property') and revenge (called 'warfare' by him and translated as 'to take death from an enemy'). Raids were undertaken with the explicit goal of acquiring material goods, especially food, in times of resource scarcity. Revenge parties set out to take revenge on one specific enemy group for the death of a clan relative. This conceptual distinction is ever present in narratives about war expeditions: on the one hand, they are described matter of factly as food acquisition forays – a motive which was always likely to take precedence over others, even on officially designated revenge parties.

> This time there were eleven of us, but two of the men came back home as soon as they had captured some stock. We used to do this quite often also; when some of the party had taken some stock, they would turn back and go home because they would be satisfied. But the others who had taken no stock would keep on till they had captured some horses and cattle.
>
> (Palmer Valor, quoted in Basso 1971: 47)

> I have been many times to Mexico this way when I was a young man. It is almost as if [I] had grown up in Mexico. From Mexico we always used to bring back lots of horses and cattle, burros and mules.
>
> (Palmer Valor, quoted in Basso 1971: 63)

Revenge parties, on the other hand, illustrate much more clearly the cultural ramifications of war in Apache society.

> This fall when we all went there a certain woman whose son had been killed by the White people about a year ago went to the chief there and spoke to him. She said, 'You have a bow and arrows. You know what happened to my son, so why don't you go to the White people and make war on them?' On

> account of this they decided to hold a war dance there, and then start out to fight the White people.
>
> (Joseph Hoffman, quoted in Basso 1971: 75)[6]

The basic plot of these narratives remains essentially unchanged: about a year after an Apache's death at the hands of an enemy, his clan relatives call for revenge, local headmen support the undertaking,[7] individuals from various bands (mainly members of the affected clan) meet at a prearranged time and place to prepare for war in a ritual manner. This ritual, the 'war dance', contains all the important elements in the cultural construction of war. Moreover, it was one of two occasions (along with the girls' puberty ceremony) for the clan to act as a unit, transcending the everyday solidarity to the band. It consisted of four phases:

1 Dance of participating clans
2 Women's dance to celebrate the expected booty
3 Social dance of men and women
4 A farewell ritual on the following morning: the twelve most respected warriors are called upon to sing about their past deeds and dramatically enact a raid to show how they intend to lead this one to success. The songs and the leader's speeches made on this occasion (and repeated on the road) convey the cultural values considered necessary for success in war.

> Don't run off. Stay here and fight. Don't go and leave the other poor men to do all the fighting. If you do this your name will not be good, and there will be bad stories going around about you back home.
>
> (Palmer Valor, quoted in Basso 1971: 68)

Other highly regarded qualities of the warrior were cleverness and endurance.

> Now it was seven nights and days since we had had a real sleep, and that's the way we used to do when we were on the warpath or on a raid. A man had to be mean and smart so that he would never be caught by the enemy.
>
> (Palmer Valor, quoted in Basso 1971: 51)

This also illustrates the Apache concept of bravery. The idea of being unafraid of danger always implied keeping one's cool in battle and, more importantly, to rely on the support of superhuman power (*diyih*). No Apache would have exposed himself to the dangers of war without the aid of a specific kind of power for war, whose origin was traced back directly to the culture hero *Nayinezgane* ('Slayer of Monsters'). No Apache war party could aspire to success without the leader's ability to command strong power of this kind.[8]

Not all the questions posed at the start of the chapter can be satisfactorily answered from the available data. There are few explicit statements on enemy images to be found in the narratives. 'Typical' enemies (like the Pima, in this case) are likely to be subject to derogatory ethnic stereotyping.

> I have heard that these people were like coyotes and that they wouldn't fight like men, but always came at night and hit us on the head with their clubs. They used no bow or gun, just a club to hit you on the head with. When they heard a gun go off, it made them sort of back up. They were scared of guns. They used to attack mostly in the summertime right in the middle of the night when everyone would be asleep.
>
> (Goodwin 1942: 87)

An important characteristic of the Apache worldview was the idea of being surrounded by a hostile world full of strangers (that is, people to whom no relations by blood or marriage existed) who were always likely to cause harm. War was regarded as a permanent state of either preventive or retaliatory aggression. 'Did not any people with enemies have the right to raid and kill them?' asks one of Goodwin's informants (1942: 94). As all neighbouring groups were considered potential enemies, the decision of which one to target by a raid was often based on contingency.[9]

The sources are, for the most part, not very specific about the cultural legitimation of violence either. Whereas the introduction of violence into the world is narrated in Western Apache mythology (through the killing of monsters by *Nayinezgane*; cf. Goodwin 1939: 3–12), this genre is completely silent about the organized use of violence among humans (i.e. war).

The only aspect of war that points beyond the practical reasonings outlined above can be found in its role in male initiation. Just as girls were identified with Changing Woman, the most important female mythical figure, during their puberty ceremony, boys as impersonators of the Slayer of Monsters, were expected to prove their ability in the most prestigious male activity, war. The participation in four war expeditions (under very strict ritual regulations) was considered necessary to achieve adult status. The male and female initiation rituals were explicitly identified as congruent with one another, by Apache informants, who were thereby according organised external violence as important a cultural role as female activities of resource procurement and housekeeping, that are enacted during *na'ii'ees* (the girls' puberty ceremony).

Much has already been said on the occasions for the use of violence. The Apaches' idea of a hostile outside world was actualized in concrete events that provided the occasions for revenge expeditions. Yet, just as likely (or even more so), expeditions could be initiated by the simple fact of food shortage.

Two types of outcome of war must be distinguished: collective and individual. On the collective side, there are the obvious tangible results, and there are the culturally defined goals and accomplishments of war: taking revenge on the hostile outside world, which has become manifest in one specific case; fulfilling social responsibilities toward relatives; and aspiring to fill the role of an 'ideal' Apache man, in whose life war played an important part. On the side of individual subjectivity, the narratives bear testimony of the joy and excitement involved in the adventure of war, which was remembered as something like a rough male sport; beyond that, success in war meant material well-being, wealth, and social prestige to the individual. The booty was redistributed and thus transformed into symbolic capital at the victory dance. The war dance (mentioned above) meant one of the very few occasions in Apache society for men to present themselves and be honoured in front of a large gathering of people.

To the Apache then, war was, on the one hand, a very practical pursuit of material benefits that required little bravery but much stealth, cleverness, strategising and cost-benefit calculation. Yet on the other, it was a ritual practice charged with religious meaning, which meant enacting moral values in the pursuit of culturally defined goals irreducible to the acquisition of material benefits, like revenge and courage in battle. This extremely flexible attitude toward the social objectives and targets of violence is expressed even more succinctly in two other contexts: feuding and scouting.[10] Western Apache stories, as well as the historical record, are full of references to the categorical switching between friends/allies and enemies. Members of different bands regularly fought against each other as allies of the US military (as they had done before as allies of the Spanish) if called upon.

In order to understand the cultural ideology behind this practice, one has to consider the Apaches' social imaginary (and, as its opposite, the 'hostile imaginary') as closely tied to everyday social experience. Apache ideas of community were expressed through cross-cutting loyalties enforced by relationship by blood (and, to a significantly lesser extent, by marriage) and by ties to a territory, or more specifically, to localities within this territory. Several extended families (*gotah*) co-operated in the exploitation of this territory, forming a band which was named after its territory. Since relatives were spread throughout this band, these collectivities of economic co-operation were, to a large extent, congruent with family ties. The non-localized nature of Western Apache clans made it possible to locate relatives in most of the bands that made up one of the five large divisions (and occasionally even in other divisions), so the concept of *ndee* ('people', the total social imaginary) could theoretically be extended to all White Mountain Apache, for example. Since actual interaction or co-operation between members of different bands was confined to a few occasions, however (revenge parties being one of them), this feeling of supralocal unity only rarely became relevant in everyday life. The Apache individual was aware that only relatives could be counted on in case of need, and were in turn, entitled to support by a strict moral code. Relations to everyone outside of this tightly circumscribed community were not governed by loyalty, but by the experience of more or less social distance and by a strategy of tactical mutualism (that is, co-operation if feasible, but confrontation as soon as other interests took precedence). A close look at Western Apache extra-band relations clearly shows that this pattern was followed with respect to any group outside of the concrete social imaginary, from non-related clans to other Apache bands, other Indian neighbours, and to the various colonial settlements in Mexico and the USA. The use of violence against any of these 'others' was a normal part of Apache cultural ideology, just as the 'others' were always expected to be ready and willing to use violence against the Apache – a threat that had been realised numerous times throughout the remembered past and the experienced present.[11]

Apache warfare and the historical record

The above remarks have made it clear that the indigenous and ethnohistorical perspectives cannot be kept completely distinct from one another. Historical evidence has been introduced to substantiate some statements about indigenous concepts. There are, in fact, several important parallels between the two perspectives: both *reconstruct* Apache warfare as events of the past. Although all Apache informants were, for the most part telling Goodwin about their own experiences, they were doing so from a distance of fifty to sixty years. Both Indians and anthropologists are thus making history, and since making history always means arranging past events in some retrospective order, this may represent Apache warfare as a much more structured endeavour than it actually was.

In addition to Apache narratives, the ethnohistorian relies on the historical record which contains numerous references to Apache warfare but also provides data on colonial structures and other parameters that are essential for the explanation of war.[12] Usually, neither of these sources intends to present a *complete* narrative of Apache warfare, but rather they focus on specific events which the narrator witnessed (either as participant or as observer) or heard about. In both cases, the events narrated were selected for their paradigmatic importance to some larger story – usually the narrator's life-story. This is where the problems for the ethnohistorian begin: only in very rare instances does the official record, the Euro-american and the Apache narratives, cover the same event, which makes the comparative analysis of sources a fairly complicated endeavour.

There is only one event for which contemporary evidence from both the Euroamerican and Apache sides exists – the Cibecue battle of 1881 (cf. Collins 1999; Davisson 1979; Goodwin and Kaut 1954; Kessel 1974, 1976; Thrapp 1967; official reports are compiled in National Archives Microfilm Publications, roll 36 (file 4327, AGO 1881)). The battle had nothing to do with an Apache war expedition but resulted from the Army's failed effort to arrest the leader of a nativistic movement who was reportly preaching the expulsion of Whites in his camp on Cibicue Creek in the White Mountains. A fight ensued during which some of the Apache scouts joined forces with the enemy, and the soldiers were forced to retreat with some casualties. Whereas the troops' actions have been reconstructed in minute detail, hardly anything is known about the Apaches' strategy, let alone their motivations and experience of this event. Even the reasons behind the scouts' defection – the only instance of its kind in the long history of Western Apache military service – remain shadowy and poorly understood, despite the fact that they were investigated in a court-martial, where three of them were sentenced to death for mutiny.

The consequences drawn by historians from the ambiguous and fragmentary record are usually to neglect the Indians' perspective and focus entirely on the military side of the event, relegating to the Apaches the time-honoured role of the anonymous enemy. This approach has received much criticism from Indian intellectuals, and rightly so. As the research by Davisson and Kessel shows, the lack of contemporary indigenous testimony can only partly be used as an excuse for failing to focus on Indians as historical actors. Oral traditions contain numerous details of social memory and background information. Even if these are lacking, much of the Indian perspective can be brought to life from a close reading of the colonisers' sources, if these are used with the intention of putting local action at the centre of the reconstruction.

Yet even if Indian and Euroamerican statements support each other in some ways with respect to the factual side of events, differences in perspective still remain. While both present stories that are meaningful within their specific contexts, these contexts are vastly different. When Apaches have talked about war, they were telling of acts and ideas of immense emotional importance to themselves, whereas the ethnohistorian views them from an analytical perspective, as something far removed from his everyday reality.

From the ethnohistorical point of view, the integration of Indian and Euroamerican sources into a common historical narrative adds several aspects to Apache warfare which are neglected by ethnoethnohistorical reconstructions.[13] These mainly concern the explanation of Western Apache external violence relative to structural conditions unrelated to cultural models.

1 Violence may have had an ecological dimension as a territorial strategy.
2 Possibly, Apache war patterns were even more flexible in practice than the cultural model suggests: the dichotomy of raid–revenge party cannot be reconstructed from Euroamerican

sources, which only account for differences in size and objectives of war expeditions.

3 The historical war complex developed in response to conditions set by Euroamerican colonialism, which entailed the comparatively easy access to resources, and at the same time, established a situation of permanent confrontation.

4 It seems plausible to see a developing prestige economy as one of the driving forces behind the accelerating rate of raids in the nineteenth century.[14]

All of these aspects make war look much more serious than the Apache remembered it.[15] They point toward the fact that war can very well be related to actual conflicts over imbalances of resources and power. Western Apache patterns of violent interaction oscillated between the triad of symbiosis, complementarity and confrontation. Although fixed in indigenous cultural theory, a band's external relations were, in practice, very flexible. Its interaction strategy was as much contingent on preconceived models as on the instrumentally rational evaluation of a specific historical situation.

In short, symbiotic relationships linked local groups in fairly stable relations, which occupied different positions in the production and redistribution of resources. Complementarity, while responding to the same basic pattern of resource availability, entailed a much more restricted form of interaction, which could mean balanced exchange (trade) on one occasion and negative exchange (raiding) on the next. Typically, complementary relations led to short-lived alliances against a common enemy, that could be broken as soon as other interests took precedence. Finally, confrontation meant that co-operative relations were absent over a long period of time, exchange taking place exclusively by force (raiding, territorial expansion) (cf. Albers 1993).

Viewed from this politico-economic perspective, war in Western Apache society can be described as an aspect of a 'moral economy' of external relations. It was embedded in a context of resource imbalances and economic interests, but these interests were expressed in terms of a moral code which affected everyday reality by structuring the rules of its experience. It is this moral code which speaks from the Apaches' narratives, while the structural conditions can only be reconstructed through other avenues of inquiry.

Conclusions: how to reconstruct war

War mobilises many different interests, in practice as well as in retrospective discourse. It produces divergent narratives that situate violent action in a meaningful context of the present, but these contexts, in turn, have to be located in the hierarchical space of winners and losers generated by these same wars. Moreover, the content and focus of these narratives shift with time.

Present-day Apaches tend to reconstruct war mainly in terms of the Apache–Euroamerican confrontation to a much larger extent than did Goodwin's informants in the 1930s, whose stories were much more individualised and included many references to inter-band and inter-tribal violence. The ethnohistorical reconstruction, on the other hand, has taken significant steps since then toward viewing Apache warfare as a complex, multicausal, multifunctional, and diachronically changing total social fact, thus deconstructing step by step the stereotype of the bloodthirsty savage (which, however, continues to be held dear in popular discourse). It may be added that this popular discourse also feeds back into the Apaches' view of their own history, although Apache élites tend to represent their own historical perspective as *per se* more authentic than anything that comes from the Euroamerican colonisers.

An understanding and explanation of colonial Apache warfare which aspires to more than representing the Indians as anonymous barbarians, can only be achieved by incorporating ethno-ethnohistorical views, written Euroamerican sources, and structural parameters of the historical situation into a holistic ethnohistorical approach. An analytical reconstruction of Western Apache warfare from this perspective may encompass the following subfields:

1 Structural context:
   - the political economy of conflict (local ecological conditions; population figures; economic gains and losses caused by war; intra-societal/local, horizontal/regional, and vertical/global power relations)
   - the historical development of warfare (how conflicts and institutionalised patterns of external violence have developed through time, and how actual violence is situated in the framework of experience).

2 Cultural context: the ideological construction of violence and war in a given society.

3 Practical context: the analysis of concrete events of violent interactions, utilising material remains, sources from participants, and sources from observers.
4 Representational context: the specific socio-historical conditions and political context within which war stories are told and analytical narratives about war are produced.

War as a total social fact can only be reconstructed by acknowledging its embeddedness in praxis *and* in culture. To reconstruct historical violence, one must avoid the pitfalls of either viewing war purely in terms of resource competition or other operational concepts or of reifying cultural discourse about past warfare. Even if not all the contradictions of these two perspectives can be integrated into one coherent history, the ethnohistorian must rely on all kinds of evidence. Quite probably, contradictions between reality and ideology are inherent in war just as in any other social phenomenon.

Notes

Most of the information for this chapter was collected during a Feodor Lynen Fellowship from the Alexander von Humboldt-Stiftung at the University of New Mexico, Albuquerque, 1997–99, and is part of an ongoing research project on Western Apache ethnohistory. This support is gratefully acknowledged. I would also like to thank Joseph C. Wilder and the staff at the Southwest Center, University of Arizona, Alan Ferg at the Arizona State Museum, the library staff at the Arizona Historical Society, and Louis H. Hieb at UNM, all of whom provided assistance and suggestions in various ways.

1 How, in other words, is the cultural model of war inculcated upon the individual warrior's mind? Two additional points are raised by this reasoning that I will not dwell upon in this chapter: (a) How much leeway for rational choice does remain? There is an ever-present danger of exoticising non-western cultures by attributing to them very little space for instrumentally rational cost-benefit evaluation, thus portraying them as slaves of cultural determinism that postulates a different rationality from our own; (b) Who represents the culturally appropriate course of action to the community, and how exactly is this accomplished? In hierarchical societies like states, wars are clearly 'made' by the ideologies of dominant élites, and even in small-scale, 'egalitarian' societies the legitimacy to represent a collective ethos is not evenly distributed among all of their members.

2 Defined as 'ethnohistory written from a native point of view' (Fogelson 1974: 106).

3 Following general anthropological practice, I designate by this term a number of linguistically closely related Apache bands living (since the mid-nineteenth century, at least) in east-central Arizona between Flagstaff and the Mogollon Rim to the north, Tucson to the south, the Arizona–New Mexico border to the east, and the Verde River to the west. Their main ethnographer, Grenville Goodwin, distinguishes between five groups for pre-reservation times (White Mountain, Cibecue, San Carlos, Southern and Northern Tonto), which, in turn, were subdivided into small local bands and extended family groups with little political cohesion.

4 The reconstruction of pre-reservation Western Apache culture relies – in addition to contemporary documents – primarily on Goodwin's ethnographic research in the 1930s (Goodwin 1942, n.d.; Basso 1971).

5 The spelling of Apache terms, except in the quotations, follows Bray's (1998) Western Apache Dictionary whenever possible.

6 A similar story could have been told about any other enemy group, not only about Euroamericans.

7 Since Western Apache clans were not localised, they could not organise a revenge party on their own without the support of the local headmen to whose bands the clan members belonged.

8 The Apache idea of *diyih* implies that all aspects of nature are imbued with special powers that may approach humans or be approached by them for support in any kind of undertaking. Numerous kinds of *diyih* of different strength and different fields of application were distinguished. Some individuals (*diyin*, 'medicine people') control more or stronger kinds of power than others and use them for social ends in the name of the community for healing or conducting ceremonies (or against the community, as witches) (cf. Basso 1969; Goodwin 1938).

9 The term employed for Americans by nineeenth-century Apaches clearly indicates that they were considered the enemies *par excellence* at that time. This, however, must be a recent application of the term *indaa*, since the Western Apaches had not come into contact with Americans prior to the 1850s.

10 A detailed study of Apache feuding has yet to be undertaken; it seems to have been a regular occurrence during the pre-reservation decades and became a serious disruptive force in the early years of reservation confinement. Western Apache (especially Cibecue and White Mountain) men were regularly employed as scouts against hostile bands since 1871. They continued to serve well into the twentieth century (cf. Mason 1970; Schröder 1998; Tate 1974).

11 Jastrzembski (1994) has described this attitude in detail for the Chiricahua.

12 Nineteenth-century historical sources may be divided into: (a) official Army and agency records; (b) contemporary observations by military men, government agents, and early settlers, on specific autobiographical events, on the Western Apache in general as a mixture of personal narrative and ethnography (exemplified by several Army surgeons writing in the 1860s and 1870s).

13 At the same time one must realise that other aspects of the Apaches' cultural construction of war cannot be linked at all to any evidence in the historical record.

14 This is suggested by Cole (1988) for the Chiricahua.

15 I have outlined the political economy of Western Apache warfare elsewhere (Schröder 1992).

Bibliography

Albers, P. (1993) 'Symbiosis, merger, and war: contrasting forms of intertribal relationships among historic Plains Indians', in J. H. Moore (ed.) *The Political Economy of North American Indians,* Norman: University of Oklahoma Press.

Basso, K. H. (1969) *Western Apache Witchcraft,* Anthropological Papers of the University of Arizona 15, Tucson: University of Arizona Press.

—— (1971) *Western Apache Raiding and Warfare. From the Notes of Grenville Goodwin,* Tucson: University of Arizona Press.

Bray, D. (ed.) (1998) *Western Apache–English Dictionary. A Community-Generated Bilingual Dictionary,* Tempe: Bilingual Press.

Cole, D. C. (1988) *The Chiricahua Apache, 1846–1876. From War to Reservation,* Albuquerque: University of New Mexico Press.

Collins, C. (1999) *Apache Nightmare. The Battle at Cibicue Creek,* Norman: University of Oklahoma Press.

Cremony, J. C. (1868) *Life Among the Apaches,* San Francisco: A. Roman & Co.

Davisson, L. (1979) 'New light on the Cibicue fight: untangling Apache identities', *Journal of Arizona History* 20: 423–44.

Fogelson, R. (1974) 'On the varieties of Indian history: Sequoyah and Traveller Bird', *Journal of Ethnic Studies* 2: 105–10.

Goodwin, G. (1938) 'White Mountain Apache Religion', *American Anthropologist* 40: 24–37.

—— (1939) *Myths and Tales of the White Mountain Apache,* Memoirs of the American Folklore Society 33, New York: American Folklore Society.

—— (1942) *The Social Organization of the Western Apache,* Chicago: University of Chicago Press.

—— (n.d.) *Goodwin Papers.* Fieldnotes on file with the Arizona State Museum Archives, Tucson.

Goodwin, G. and Kaut, C. (1954) 'A native religious movement among the White Mountain and Cibecue Apache', *Southwestern Journal of Anthropology* 10: 385–404.

Jastrzembski, J. C. (1994) *An Enemy's Ethnography. The 'Mexican' in Nineteenth Century Chiricahua Apache Ethnographic Practice,* unpublished Ph.D. dissertation, University of Chicago.

Kessel, W. B. (1974) 'The Battle of Cibicue and its aftermath. A White Mountain Apache's account', *Ethnohistory* 21: 123–34.

—— (1976) *White Mountain Apache Religious Cult Movements, A Study in Ethnohistory,* unpublished Ph.D. dissertation, University of Arizona, Tucson.

Mason, J. E. (1970) *The Use of Indian Scouts in the Apache Wars, 1870–1886,* unpublished Ph.D. dissertation, University of Indiana, Bloomington.

Schröder, I. W. (1992) *Krieg und Adaptation. Eine ökologische Analyse der Rolle aggressiven Verhaltens in Geschichte und Kultur der indianischen Gruppen des nordamerikanischen Südwestens,* Bonn: Holos.

— (1998) '"Apaches de Paz" to "Pershing's Pets": Historical patterns of Apache military cooperation with colonial powers (18th–20th Century)' in S. Dedenbach-Salazar Saenz, C. Arellano Hoffmann, E. König and H. Prümers (eds) *50 Years Americanist Studies at the University of Bonn,* Bonn Americanist Studies 30, Möckmühl: Saurwein.

Tate, M. L. (1974) *Apache Scouts, Police, and Judges as Agents of Acculturation, 1865–1920,* unpublished Ph.D. dissertation, University of Toledo.

Thrapp, D. L. (1967) *The Conquest of Apacheria,* Norman: University of Oklahoma Press.

Violence in war

Chapter 8

When silence makes history

Gender and memories of war violence from Somalia[1]

Francesca Declich

Introduction

This chapter explores some of the issues related to the way memories of war violence against men and women are reproduced and added to the symbolic capital of a group and the way in which more recent cases of war violence are interpreted in the light of past events. It tackles the essential gendered character of war violence in the experience of both men and women and the differential way such experience is 'filed' in the 'cultural archive' (James 1988) of a specific group. Part of the gendered process of compounding the experience of violence into memories seems to lie in the effects of internalisation, as opposed to externalisation, of different forms of violent acts and the eventual expression or non-expression of violent events in public arenas.

The fact that violent acts are perceived as being expressible and are expressed in public contexts strongly influences the way they are added to the symbolic capital of a group and marks the way individual people, male and female in different ways, will be able to resort to such capital to interpret the vicissitudes of their lives.

In a sense this chapter is an attempt at 'describing and analysing the tragic and the dreadful from an anthropological point of view', to join with Allen's aim (1990: 45), rather than as simply listing tragic events. Rather than participating in the process of 'commoditisation of despair' (Allen 1990: 46), now so central to aid enterprise, I shall attempt to analyse the dynamics underlying war violence in a specific group of people from Somalia.

War violence in southern Somalia: the data

During the war in Somalia atrocious violence occurred between groups of soldiers and even worse violence was perpetrated against civilians, men, women and children. The 'Somali Bantu'[2] living along the Juba River were forced to flee their farms as a result of violence and war-induced starvation.

The civil war in Somalia forced great numbers of migrants to take refuge in Kenya. It is estimated that in October 1992 more than 300,000 refugees in Kenya were Somalis, including registered and unregistered ones (Gallagher and Forbes Martin 1992: 16). Among those more than 11,000 were reported as being 'Bantu Somali' (UNHCR n.d. a, b and c), also an additional approximately 3,000 'Bantu Somali' had escaped to Tanzania.

An account of the scale and significant dimension of the violent acts perpetrated is not easy to describe. Mostly oral accounts of atrocities are reported individually by the victims, and specific surveys are needed to reveal a precise picture of the events. Therefore, this article only focuses on the dynamics of the formation of a social memory consequent to war violence.

Data for this paper have been gathered in a series of interviews and observations over several years. The initial two-year period of fieldwork and gathering of oral tradition sources among agriculturalists living along the Juba River was carried out between 1985 and 1988. Later, the civil war reached Mogadishu at the end of 1990 and it was no longer safe to carry out fieldwork in the country. Yet, visits to the refugee camps of Kenya, to the refugee settlement of Mkuiu in Tanzania and to scattered families of refugees settled in Dar Es Salaam were made from 1994 to 1998.

This analysis is, therefore based on an earlier collection of oral sources on the past and the cultural identity of the so-called Bantu Somali people of the Juba River, Zigula and Shanbara, as well as on data gathered subsequently in different phases up to 1998 on their integration into their countries of exile. Particularly fruitful were visits with exiles I had met before in Somalia, where a trusting relationship made it possible to receive confidential and intimate information if needed. In addition, the fact of meeting acquaintances initially in Kenya and later in Tanzania, facilitated observations on the different perspectives people were forming about exile, year by year.

Privileges of long-term acquaintance and reasons for talking about 'externalisation'

During a first visit to the refugee camps surrounding Daddab in Kenya, in March/April 1994, although some people had been in the refugee camps for almost two years, there were still arrivals from Kisimayu by car and on foot. My position of privileged observer was partly due to chance: I met Asho, a refugee woman whose family had been one of my best informants in southern Somalia six years before, and she accompanied me during the interviews. Also, when I arrived at a gathering of women, there were people who could remember me from Somalia. Both these factors created a climate in which the people (especially women) interviewed relied upon me and were willing to talk about their problems even without being asked.

I had gone to visit the refugees in Daddaab in order to know what their present situation was, the actual context and the reasons why they had decided to flee from Somalia. I was also concerned for the safety of many acquaintances. Obviously, bandits and military violence were the motive for their decision to flee, but I wanted to know more, and what they had to say about it.

During the interviews, my friend kept insisting that the women should speak of their rapes, arguing that I was a woman and that there was nothing to be ashamed of. At some point I asked her whether she herself had been raped. She denied that she had and recounted the following story: one night she had gone with other women in search of food into the cultivated fields. They had to go some twenty kilometres from home where, because of the war, sugarcanes had been left unattended on a state farm. It was night because during daylight it was too dangerous to be outside of one's home village. Male bandits and soldiers would try to mug you, take your property including clothes and shoes, threaten you with death and rape you if you did not give them all the possessions you presumably had hidden somewhere. The night was also a dangerous time to go out, although there was no other choice if the entire family was not to starve.

Thus, she said that all the women who accompanied her had been raped. She had been able to avoid rape, because she had a baby girl on her shoulder. She kept pinching the baby so that she would scream and cry to put off the rapists. I had the feeling that she might have made up what seemed to me an unlikely story. However, I did not express my suspicions as I thought she might avoid speaking further about the issue. And yet, whether or not she actually underwent rape is irrelevant if one looks at the effects the event of the general rape had had on her. Later, whenever I showed surprise or sorrow about the fact that a woman had been raped I was repeatedly scolded by her, as if I were too naive. Whenever a woman was looking for food outside or within the village, I was told, the probability of being raped was very high.

One year later, Asho had reached Dar Es Salaam. She had decided to move to her relatives in the Tanzanian town, for she no longer had a paid job in Daddaab, the Kenyan camp where she had stayed after escaping from Somalia. Being a single mother with five children, she thought she could do better in Tanzania by receiving food aid from the rural refugee settlement there, and also look for another job in Dar Es Salaam, where she had relatives. During the time I was there she singled out one problem in particular which had brought her from the rural refugee settlement to Dar Es Salaam. She claimed she had a strong chest pain which prevented her from doing agricultural work. She assumed this was due to a blow she had received when she was escaping from the attempted rape. She felt that she had caught tuberculosis and sought medical attention for it. Thus, she had obtained permission from the refugee settlement commandant to go to Dar Es Salaam for medical tests in the hospital. Her description of the flight from the rapists in Somalia this time included running away from them, falling on a root of a tree and hitting her thorax very hard. It is difficult to assess what really happened, but what is clear, is that this woman kept remembering that horrible night as something that had permanently damaged her health. Whenever she felt sick, she ascribed it to the day of the group rape which she had escaped. Medical tests and X-rays indicated that she was suffering from bronchitis.

Three years later, while discussing war violence again, Asho retold her story of group rape with some different details regarding the location of the event.

In previous years she had been willing to speak about those events, in fact, she could not stop herself from doing so. This time, however, she was talking about them as past 'stories of the war', the things she knew that I was interested in hearing. She mentioned again the series of events relating to the search for food in the sugarcane fields and that this was the only source of food available. Again she mentioned having pinched her baby daughter to escape being raped. When I expressed doubt about the effectiveness of this technique, she said that some women used other methods such as defecating and urinating to produce a bad body smell which would keep rapists at a distance. She mentioned these details only after my questions about the rape story. Asho was not willing to give details of what she considered to be an extreme, disgusting technique, even though an efficacious one.

In general, it was evident, especially during the first visits to the refugees, that there was an almost compulsive desire for refugee women and men to speak out about their traumatic experiences. For women this included rape and for men this included witnessing the rape of relatives. In later visits the effects of some such experiences became evident, yet other problems related to their daily life became more important to discuss with a foreigner. Traumatic experiences were described in a less anxious way, and some present events were interpreted as consequences of those dramatic experiences. Certainly, my long-term acquaintance with these people who had become refugees made it possible for them to express anxiety, and people hoped they could resolve some of their problems by speaking out to a foreigner who had proved friendly over a long period of time.

Reflecting on men's memories as compared to women's memories of war violence

The diachronic description of this painful event described by a woman compared with some of the men's stories about the violence they had suffered during the war offers an interesting insight into the divergent and gendered effects of the experience of war violence on the memories of people's lives.

In the same year of my first visit to Daddaab (1994), I also visited the refugee settlement of Mkuiu in northeast Tanzania. On my arrival, several people I had met in Somalia approached and invited me to tea, as is the custom in Somalia. One man explained to me that he could not plough his fields anymore, as he was suffering from a strong chest pain caused by repeated beatings and torture during the war. He told me his story. He lived in a village whose inhabitants had stayed neutral during the war. When some village men decided to join one party in the fight, rumours started circulating about stockpiles of firearms hidden in the neighbourhood. When the other faction gained a foothold in the village, my informant and other men were caught and tortured in order to obtain information about the whereabouts of the weapons. My informant was hung up by the knees on the branch of a tree and beaten on the shoulders, chest and legs. After realising he was unable to provide information, he was then released, partially incapacitated by his experience. He claimed that the strength had never returned to his arms. He asked me if I could help him to find a job that did not require physical work. He added that he was no longer young and was not strong enough for ploughing. The description of the event sounded convincing and I informed an officer in charge. Two years later I met him again. He had been appointed to an administrative job in the refugee settlement, possibly as a result of my mediation.

The focus here is on the way the two stories were told and the difference in emphasis. The man, who was also an old acquaintance of mine, was complaining about violence he had undergone during the war. There were no details about his intimate feelings. If they existed he seemed determined to hide them. He was simply describing the events in such a way as to touch my feelings and move me to act in order to meet his request for help. He was telling a true story and details of the incident were provided in a 'legitimate' fashion in order to claim benefits he urgently needed.

A detailed narrative implying a clear request for assistance like this did not emerge from the women's stories of war violence. They were unwilling to talk about their experiences of rape, the memory of which remained present but was not transformed into an heroic event. Perhaps the actual event of rape or the fear of it happening again persists in their minds. An illness of some kind may be attributed to the rape or near-rape. During the visit to Daddab only one ethnic Somali woman described her rape in detail in front of other women. She had undergone a serial rape in the town of Jilib while her husband was absent. This was a stain on her patrilineage. She was not a young, desirable woman, but was at least fifty years old.[3] She was first identified by her rapers as an enemy through requesting her Somali genealogy. An armed man was stationed at the front door as a guard and seven men entered the room in turn and raped her. The woman was evidently still suffering trauma from an event which probably had occurred two years before. She stressed the fact that she could not walk when the rapists left her – for her legs were trembling so badly. She now hated all members of that Somali patrilineage. If she only saw one, she said, she felt as though she wanted to disappear. Nevertheless, she could not help but live in a refugee camp side by side with numerous Somalis of that lineage.

In the future, when normal life has been restored, looking back on the war years, the man will probably tell the story of his torture to his children and grandchildren of both sexes. This torture may well be presented as his heroic past. The man, having become an elder, may be seen by the youth as a sort of hero who was able to overcome this atrocity and in public he may show pride for having survived.

On the other hand, the stories of sexual violence during the war, will be easily silenced. The woman who had been raped seven times in a matter of hours was in shock: one had the feeling that having an audience for such a story might save her sanity. She was trying to present her rape as an absurd situation so as to make the audience laugh at her plight. Most of the other women, however, kept their experience of being raped to themselves, assuming they could bear the weight of silence. In particular, they would not 'legitimately' claim to have been raped as if it were an heroic event; perhaps this missed claim to heroism prevents young women from becoming willing to identify with such kinds of heroism.

A step back in the past of the 'Somali Bantu': idioms to interpret the present

In the attempt to unravel the dynamics of memories of violence among the Zigula, it is worth analysing their already codified oral traditions about the past.

Memories of the Zigula's past are encompassed with signs of wars and cruel acts of war. The results of wars have always influenced the way in which the Zigula's past is remembered, possibly because the Zigula's freedom from slavery depended so much on their strength as warriors. Narratives of the Zigula's past are peppered with stories of abductions and kidnapping for slavery. Their concept of war, therefore, is very much shaped by the desire to keep members of their own group safe. It can be noticed that mention of abduction and child kidnapping is surrounded by considerable secrecy, as if reserved for listeners that could be trusted.[4] Those are all signs that remind us in some way of their past as persecuted former slaves, which they do not like to reveal.

In 1994, a Zigula man who had migrated to Dar Es Salaam before the war, interpreted the recent extreme violence of the Somalis against the Juba River Zigulas as revenge. At the end of the last century the Zigulas, after repeated attempts, had finally won against the Ogaden Somalis headed by Sheekh Cambuulo. This event is recounted as one of great violence. My informant reminded me that the Zigula's victory over the Somalis was celebrated by hanging Sheekh Cambuulo's head on a *mkui* tree close to the *Kamsuuma* village. It is said that during those days the Somalis asked for *abuur reeba,* namely 'please, leave at least some of us (literally *semen*)' for reproduction of children. The Zigula man in Dar Es Salaam used representations of previous wars as a cognitive tool in order to explain the present violence in terms of a reaction to the violence of that past.

It is common for most Zigula men to attempt to make sense of the recent violence they have suffered by comparing it with the violence described in the memory of the past wars. This is the kind of idiom one finds whenever asking for descriptions of the recent Somali war. It is only recently that more than one acquaintance of mine has shown disappointment that the scale of violence witnessed in the recent war was out of proportion to previous violence suffered.

Such an unusual amount of violence disappoints them, because they cannot find a satisfactory explanation for the present events by applying their traditional categories for understanding war. The explanatory scheme is that warlike actions should be in revenge of previous violent acts and, therefore, the recent atrocious events seem unjustified. According to the Zigulas, the strongest violent act that the Somali ethnic group could reasonably attempt to revenge is that depicted above; yet it seems not as violent as the present war.

On the other hand, the sexual violence experienced by women is not expressed openly by women in order to make some sense of past and future wars, nor does it seem to appear publicly in historic reconstruction of the past. Certainly, however, it is present in male and female gender consciousness. A strong motivation for fleeing from Somalia was to escape violence against women.

The sense of violation of one's intimate boundaries, of inevitability and vulnerability that such an experience conveys to the raped women seems not to be publicly expressed by women in heterosexual contexts but through denial or silence. This silence has influenced the construction of gender relationships and constitutes a sort of mute signal for the coming generations. A sense of limitation like this not only applies to women but also to the men who could not prevent their relatives from being raped.

It seems that violence against men and women is seen as an inevitable pain that Somali Bantu families have to share by gender in order to survive the war.

The following case helps to explain the gendered nature of war violence as it occurred in southern Somalia. Isha told me of events that created the greatest discomfort in her village. The bandits and soldiers used to raid villages and take all the available food and money hut by hut. For these reasons, many people had part of their money, food or milling machines hidden underground. Still the richest people in the villages became targets of armed threats. Some who refused to release their property were killed. For this reason, as in the case of Isha, many husbands travelled to Magadishu. Wives could then report to aggressors that only their husbands knew where the goods were hidden. However, in the case of Isha and many others, the aggressors did not believe her. Some women, she said, were raped because they were accused of 'not wanting to speak'. Some were raped in front of their relatives. As for herself, Isha said, they broke into her house 'and took everything they wanted without permission'. She never mentioned having been raped, yet the way she looked toward the horizon suggested that many women, if not herself, were raped in such a context.

As to my personal view, I will never understand why the husbands left the wives in such a dangerous situation knowing that they risked being raped. Possibly, there were no other choices or any other way of saving the husbands' lives and conserving the money needed to escape from Somalia to other East African countries (e.g. Kenya and Tanzania). When choosing between two forms of personal violence, one of which was death, the safety of the family was built on accepting the possibility that wives, daughters and other female relatives could be raped. In discussing this issue, informants said that men would be beaten, then forced to watch their daughters or wives being raped in front of them and, possibly, even killed. This may well be one reason why people were forced to choose the 'lesser' of two evils.

A history of gender and war violence embedded in the Goshas' narratives of the past

Collecting the oral historical record of events that had occurred among the Zigula since their settlement along the Juba in the nineteenth century gave me an insight into the gendered way the war and the current description of it were embedded in a Zigula historical narrative.

Rape and violence based on gender occurring during wars is not a new event and was not new for the Zigula. The freedom of the Zigula was built on the need to avoid the repetition of their history.

One should not forget that slave women were considered to be under the authority of their masters and were not in a position to easily refuse sexual intercourse with them. Although the Zigula claim they spent very little time as slaves (Cassanelli 1989; Declich 1986, 1992, 1995), this experience must have been known to them. Furthermore, the abduction of women for marriage was a common strategy of territorial occupation in the Somali lands in the nineteenth and early twentieth centuries (cf., for instance Cerulli 1934, 1957, 1959, 1964). The inter-ethnic exchange among Galla (Oromo), Somali and Bantu populations on the banks of the Juba River seems to have been largely based on this practice as well as on marriage exchanges for settling reparations after wars and alliances.

In other words, some sort of sexual violence toward women, defined as violation of their personal physical boundaries with sexual and procreational aims and for some social purpose, was part of the moral standard at least among people who lived on the Somali–Kenyan border at the turn of the twentieth century.

The Zigula men who fought to keep their freedom during the nineteenth century were engaged in a kind of crusade to protect, defend and maybe control the women of their group. Women, on the other hand, co-operated in this enterprise to protect themselves from slavery and from undesired sexual relations, as is shown by the following example.

The way memories of war violence became embedded in the 'cultural archive' and historical narratives of the Zigula is highlighted by several songs pertaining to the strictly feminine context of girls' initiations.

In 1987 a nearly-ninety-year-old woman described the meanings of the songs which were taught during initiation but which were also used in daily life in the first decades of the twentieth century to signal the arrival of enemies in a village. The woman talking to a group of informants I was meeting said that the songs were used by women staying in the village or in the fields to alert those who were in the vicinity of the approach of raiders. The group of women I was interviewing remembered that this happened at the end of the last century when Somalis came to kidnap children and abduct women in the fields for slavery. The songs were still used when enemies approached the area. In other words, they served as alarm songs as well as historic and didactic songs. The language of the song, incomprehensible to Somalis, hid the song's intention. While recalling those days, the old woman remembered foreign troops who had entered the village soon after she was married. These soldiers (either British, Italian or some other army) attempted to strip her of her clothes. She laughed, ashamed of her young age, and winked repeatedly to the other women present as if the event recalled details emerging from their past as well. However, she did not complete her story so it is not clear to me whether she was raped or not, nor was her story clear to me at the time of the interview, perhaps due to the way she told it. She remembered the fact without bearing a grudge, which seemed to be due to her old age and to the acceptance of the unchangeability of the past characteristic of old people looking back on their lives.

This acceptance of past events appears to represent a kind of moral standard, and the fact that none of those present showed disappointment or disbelief might also mark the way that younger women will interpret the abuses they have recently suffered.

However, the divergent and gendered way men and women recall events of sexual abuse in the past is significant. For instance, from the mid to the late nineteenth century, groups of slaves of different origin escaped from the Benaadir Somali's plantations and arrived at the Juba River. It is told that a group of them raided villages of the Bon hunters and gatherers, and coerced their women into marriage (cf. Declich 1986). This was reported privately to me by a male informant I had known for several months, with a sort of hilarious pride of a male descendant of that group. He used to ridicule the 'Bon' who were also considered to be uncivilised and primitive. Their women are said to be very free in their sexual habits. It is said that a guest of a 'Bon' couple may be offered access to the wife's sexual favours as a sign of hospitability.

Discussion of some data

Memories of war violence are deposited in a group's social memory even when they are not articulated. Although violence, and especially sexual violence toward women, is not mentioned directly in historical accounts of the past of the Zigula and the Gosha people of the Juba River, it still seems to be a rationale underlying the narrative of several historical events. Among the Zigula, many important territorial moves were made in order to avoid the sexual abuse of the group's women by foreigners, including sexual abuses in the form of abduction for marriage. Even recent events seem to follow this trend. Many of the Somali Bantu from the Juba decided to take refuge in Kenya because the situation was no longer tolerable from their viewpoint. Women and children left the country first, leaving men and boys behind. Looking for food as well as defending any means of survival meant risking death or rape. With all the young women of one's family at risk of being raped whenever troops came into a village, the situation became unbearable, and it is reported that this was the motivation for the move to refuge.

Conclusion

War violence is experienced in different ways and these are certainly gendered. In the Somali oral tradition these divergent experiences are reflected in the way history is told. Certain acts are silenced if they represent something to be hidden, or something shameful. Other acts are given great importance. Recently, at the panel on *Worldviews and Violence*, in Frankfurt, it was cleverly noted that in the Yemenite oral histories, acts of reconciliation are given much less importance in the narratives of past wars than warlike acts.[5] The Somali historical record appears to be similar in the case of sexual violence towards women as well as in the case of young boys and children's abduction for slavery. Several indications point to the fact that such abuses often occurred, but were never directly emphasised in historical narratives, despite the great concern about the issue in the group.

Historical narratives, on the contrary, are constructed by hiding things which need not to be said directly and emphasising those which can be said or are considered good to say. This is done according to a rationale understood by the members of a group of people. The results, however, are narratives characterised by gendered meanings that are perceived differently by men and women.[6] Such meanings, intertwined with related behaviour, form the 'cultural archive' to which people resort when they interpret expected and unexpected events in their lives.

Regardless of the reasons for either downplaying or emphasising certain events or actions, actors of historical narratives may become examples of behaviour, 'role models', for the listeners and especially the younger generations. Thus, different listeners, men and women, may perceive and interpret the Zigula history differently, especially the accounts of the Zigula warriors fighting Somalis.

Oral history involving amazing warlike actions by Zigula warriors could be considered as a kind of warning signal for other outside people who may want to attack the Zigulas. The meaning of this warning is: 'we know how to defend the women and children of our group'. Certainly women are not the heroes of these stories, as they are not the warriors. However, elder and adult women, especially very old women who have experienced sexual violence, may find a gendered meaning in the narrative, namely the silent or symbolised reference to their own safety and that of their children. Yet, in the past, women have also played their 'legitimate' public role in the defence of their group as is implied by the alarm songs described above. On the other hand, younger women may perceive the lack of female hero-models in such narratives as denying themselves a public role in society.

The perception of young females, however, may have become especially important in the context of rapid cultural change due to the present forced migration from Somalia to Tanzania.

These gendered meanings may be lost along with the loss of contact with their native Somali territory. For instance, Somali Zigula female elder leaders of women's rituals in Somalia could detect and were reminded of the gendered meanings when they recounted the narratives to me. However, such meanings, which silenced abuse of women and emphasised male deeds in war (with the exception of the history of the female *mganga Whanankhucha* who led the Zigula away from slavery[7]), may not make sense to younger Somali Zigula generations in exile in Tanzania, as they lose relevance to their real life. Such meanings that were connected with the historical narratives become difficult to uncover. What is left of such stories is that young men can identify with male deeds recounted in the Zigula's history, whereas young women do not find female actors in the historical narratives of their ancestors. It is ironic that the emphasis on the violence of masculine warlike action in historical narratives is no longer interpreted as a rhetorical form to also highlight the facts which have been silenced.

Notes

1 This paper was presented at the 4th EASA Conference in Frankfurt (4–7 September 1998) at the workshop on *Worldviews and Violence* and later at a seminar held at the Programme of African Studies of the Northwestern University where I was a Fulbright Research Scholar in the Summer/Autumn 1998. I am grateful for this opportunity granted by the Italian Fulbright Commission, which gave me the time

to think and write and for the good reception in Evanston at the Programme of African Studies where I could make the most of my time by working with the wonderful resources of the Africana collection in the library. Part of the fieldwork was carried out under financial support of the French Institute for Research in Africa in Nairobi and a post-doctoral grant of the Istituto Universitario Orientale di Napoli. My thanks for stimulating discussions on earlier versions of this paper go to Jane Guyer, William Murphy, Giulia Barrera, Akbar Virmani and the participants of the panel in Frankfurt. Personal names in the article are fictitious for ensuring privacy to people who have been kind in discussing very personal issues with me.

2 As regards this sort of recent ethnic categorization an in-depth discussion is in Declich 2000.

3 My emphasis on age here is not accidental. A fifty-year-old man explained to me that soldiers would especially rape young women, ignoring older ones. He related this to the fact that they would not rape his wives but only daughters and granddaughters. He mentioned this fact as one of the main reasons why he could not stay in his village any more. Cf. also Declich 2000.

4 Cf. also Declich 1997.

5 Personal communication.

6 For the gendered perception in a Zigula's audience cf. also Declich 1995.

7 For this tradition, cf. Cassanelli 1987; Grottanelli 1953; Menkhaus 1989; Declich 1995, 1996.

Bibliography

Allen, T. (1990) 'Violence and moral knowledge: observing social trauma in Sudan and Uganda', *Cambridge Anthropology* 13(2): 45–66.

Cassanelli, L. V. (1987) 'Social construction on the Somali frontier: Bantu former slave communities in the nineteenth century', in I. Kopytoff (ed.) *The African Frontier. The Reproduction for Traditional African Societies*, Bloomington: Indiana University Press.

Cerulli, E. (1934) 'Gruppi etnici negri nella Somalia', *Archivio per l'antropologia e l'etnologia* 64: 177–84.

—— (1957) *Somalia vol 1,* Roma: Istituto Poligrafico dello Stato.

—— (1959) *Somalia vol 2*, Roma: Istituto Poligrafico dello Stato.

—— (1964) *Somalia vol 3*, Roma: Istituto Poligrafico dello Stato.

Declich, F. (1986) 'I Goscia del Giuba: un gruppo etnico di origine bantu', *Africa* (Roma) 1986: 570–99.

—— (1992) 'Processo di formazione della identita culturale dei gruppi bautu della Somalia meridionale', Tesi di dottorato di ricerca (PhD), Istituto Universitario Orientale, Napoli.

—— (1995) ‘‘Gendered narratives’, history and identity: two centuries along the Juba River among the Zigula and Shanbara’, *History of Africa* 22: 93–122.

—— (1996) ‘Unraveling women’s history through comparative analysis: matriliny among the Zigula in Tanzania and Somalia’, unpublished paper presented to the Berkshire Conference on Women History, Chapel Hill, 7–9 June.

—— (1997) ‘The dynamics of integration, adoption and the desire for kin: a feature of southern Somali ‘Bantu’ identity’, unpublished paper given to the Conference on the Northwestern Indian Ocean as Cultural Corridor, Stockholm, 17–19 January.

—— (2000) ‘Fostering ethnic reinvention: gender impact of forced migration on Bantu Somali refugees in Kenya’, *Cahiers d’Etudes Africaines* 157(1): 25–53.

Epp, M. (1997) ‘Memory of Violence: Soviet and East European Mennonite refugees and rape in the Second World War’, *Journal of Women’s History* 9, 1: 58–87.

Gallagher, D. and Forbes Martin, S. (1992) *The Many Faces of the Somali Crisis: Humanitarian Issues in Somalia, Kenya and Ethiopia.* Washington: Refugee Policy Group.

Grottanelli, V. L. (1953) ‘I Bantu del Giuba nelle tradizioni del Watzegua’, *Geographica Helvetica* 8: 249–60.

James, W. (1988) *The Listening Ebony: Moral Knowledge, Religion and Power among the Uduk of Sudan*, Oxford: Clarendon Press.

Menkhaus, K. J. (1989) ‘Rural transformation and the roots of under-development in Somalia’s lower Jubba Valley’, PhD thesis, University of South Carolina.

UNHCR (n.d.) a *Dagahaley refugee camp.* Fact sheet.

—— (n.d.) b *Hagardeera refugee camp.* Fact sheet.

—— (n.d.) c *Ifo refugee camp.* Fact sheet.

Chapter 9

A turning point?

From civil struggle to civil war in Sri Lanka

Peter Kloos

'Violence' was one of the key words of the second half of the twentieth century, and for good reasons: an almost truly world-wide world war reaching levels of destruction hitherto unreached in the history of human society, was followed by five decades of wide-spread domestic, criminal, and intra-state political violence. In this chapter I will deal with a specific form of intra-state, political violence, namely civil war. And as far as civil war is concerned I will focus on one aspect: its beginning.

Throughout the past centuries another form of political violence seems to have dominated, namely inter-state war. Inter-state wars were to some extent regulated by certain norms. The formal declaration of war was one of these norms. After the Second World War, however, inter-state wars have become rare. Civil war became the typical form of war (see Siccama and Oostindiër 1995: 10). How many civil wars have broken out since 1945 is to some extent a matter of definition: what, after all, is a 'civil war'? And, in the absence of a formal declaration of war, when does it break out?

The word 'outbreak', however, hides as much as it reveals. Violent conflicts usually have a long period of gestation. They occur in a situation initially characterised merely by differences in interest. Such differences of interest may turn into conflicts, and some conflicts turn into violent ones. Lists of inter- and intra-state wars implicitly assume that there is a more or less unambiguous point in time when a conflict, until then fought with peaceful means, turns into a violent one (Franke 1994; Jongman 1995; Siccama and Oostindiër 1995). In this article I will challenge that view. I will argue that in the case of civil war rarely is there such an unambiguous turning point. In the process that eventually ushers in the use of physical violence, there are many events that can be regarded as far more decisive turning points, even though they may have quite different meanings for the various contesting parties. Although the recognition of turning points has its advantages, especially in a comparative perspective, it also obscures the dynamics of a protracted step by step process that in its course leads to violence. This is more than an academic exercise. Civil wars are rarely the concern of only a particular state at war with itself. The international political community tends to see as its responsibility the prevention of such conflict – or rather, to prevent the conflict from reaching a violent phase (Van Walraven 1998: 3).

This view of conflict prevention stresses one phase of escalation and one could argue, that by restricting the attention to the transition to violence, policy makers are too late to be effective and may be counterproductive. I will return to the issue of escalation and conflict prevention in the concluding remarks.

For reasons of length I will in the present article restrict the argument to political conflicts in Sri Lanka, but my analysis should be seen in the context of intra-state violence wherever.

Before turning to the series of events that in July 1983 led to the outbreak of civil war in Sri Lanka – and July 1983 is, in the literature on Sri Lanka, usually taken as the turning point in the so-called ethnic war in which this country has been involved ever since – there are a few conceptual issues that need clarification. This I will do in section 2 of this article. Section 3 contains the Sri Lankan case, and section 4 winds up with a few lessons.

Concepts and assumptions

The key phenomenon in this article is civil war. As far as war is concerned, the old, almost aphoristic definition of Von Clausewitz ('war is the continuation of politics with other means') is still unbeaten in its brevity and its neatness. This definition has the advantage that it views the use of weapons in a political conflict as an alternative: parties can decide to take up arms, and they can also decide to lay them down if that suits their purposes. War, civil war included, is usually part of a quite deliberate decision, not of uncontrolled emotions overwhelming one or both parties involved in a conflict. War is part of conflict strategies where decisions are taken. To resort to weapons is one of these decisions.

Yet war is much more than the actual use of weapons. A *state of war* should not be equated with actual warfare. Hobbes already knew that

> WARRE, consisteth not in Battel onely, or the act of fighting; but in a tract of time, wherein the Will to contend by Battel is sufficiently known.
>
> . . . as the nature of Foule weather, lyeth not in a showre or two of rain; but in an inclination thereto of many dayes together; So the nature of War, consisteth not in actuall fighting; but in the known disposition thereto, during all time there is no assurance to the contrary.
>
> (Hobbes 1968: 186)

A state of war (and, *mutatis mutandis*, a state of civil war) is the chance that weapons shall be used. This is more than mere play with words, for at least two reasons. First of all, civil war is often a war of a protracted kind, characterised by periods without actual fighting. In the second place, civil war almost always involves the state. A state is by definition an institution that claims the legitimate use of physical force (to quote from Weber's well-known definition). Yet a state is not continuously involved in the actual use of physical force. The possibility that violence might be used is usually quite sufficient to enforce compliance. This is the reason why it so often seems that in civil war it is a minority that begins to actually fight a 'legitimate' government. Closer scrutiny usually reveals that such minorities have been thwarted for a long time by the state using its means of control, which in the end are backed by physical violence in order to curb minority wishes and ambitions.

Civil war differs from inter-state war not only because it is waged within the boundaries of a single state. The typical civil war is fought between a central government and an ethnic minority. A high percentage of the civil wars fought at the moment are also ethnic wars waged between an ethnic minority and a government dominated by an ethnic majority. I do not mean to say that such a war is a struggle between all members of minority and majority. It is rather between a government dominated by one ethnic category and a movement that claims to act in the interests of a minority. A so-called ethnic war does not preclude good relations between numerous members of the ethnic groups involved. Ethnic differences as such are rarely, if ever, the real issue in ethnic conflict: twentieth century ethnicity is the idiom of conflict rather than its cause.

Civil war has in the field of law a very specific meaning: to be seen as war, the use of uniforms by both parties and a hierarchy are required, for instance. Such criteria are used to differentiate between various forms of intra-state violence, such as riots, *coups d'état*, and revolutions on the one hand, and civil war on the other. In practice such forms overlap. The legal requirements help to link civil war to martial law (to rights of prisoners of war, for example) and to ways of dealing with war crimes. From a sociological point of view and in order to understand processes of escalation, these criteria are less important. Seen from a processual perspective ethnic civil war is a phase in a series. Such a series can be conceptualised in a model of escalation, as has been done in Figure 9.1.

Differences in culture as such rarely, and certainly not necessarily, entail friction between populations. When such cultural differences become the vehicle or mode of expression of differential interests, then the stage is set and the language of conflict chosen, and the possibility of escalation dawns. Differences in interest may result in tension, and tension can lead to conflict between ethnic categories. Parties involved in a conflict, finally, may resort to violence. The term 'violence' in this context stands for the 'deliberate destruction of persons or property by people acting together' (Rule 1988: 11).

In reality, the arrows in Figure 9.1 may point in the opposite direction as well: in reality there is also de-escalation (see Figure 9.3, p. 193).

It is well known that conflict and tension play a role in the creation and elaboration of ethnic differences, but that is not the issue here.

At stake in this paper is the importance of the moment physical violence begins to be used on a regular scale, in an effort to solve

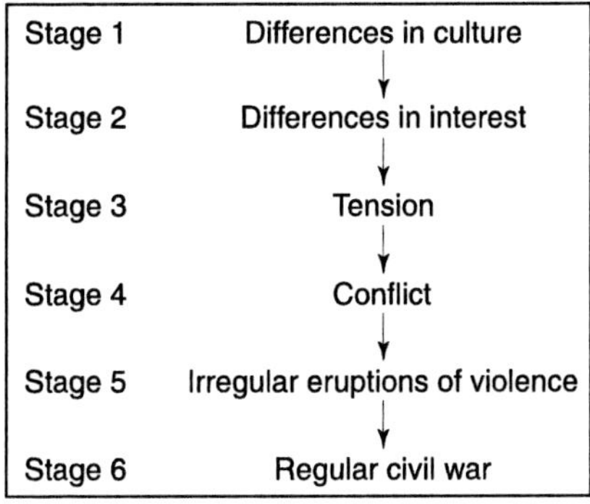

Figure 9.1 Conceptualisation of escalation to civil war.

the conflict, and whether it is useful to call this moment 'the turning point' in the process of escalation. The concerted use of violence undoubtedly turns a conflict into civil war, but the question is how important that particular moment or that particular event is for an understanding of the process. I will now turn to the post-independence history of Sri Lanka for an illustration of this process and for questioning the usefulness of the question itself.

From 'ethnic difference' to 'civil war': the case of Sri Lanka

The Sri Lankan civil war is predicated on two basic issues that surfaced during the early years of independence. I use the metaphor of 'surfacing' deliberately: both issues are a concatenation of pre-colonial differences and shifts therein during the colonial period, namely shifts in the relationship between the two main populations inhabiting Sri Lanka, the so-called Sinhala and the so-called Tamil, and the relationship between the indigenous late-colonial élite and the young, post-independence, non-élite generation (for a more extensive analysis along this line see Kloos 1997a).

The first thing to remember is that at the beginning of the colonial era there were two populations in Sri Lanka: there were Tamil-speaking people in the north and the east of the island, and there were Sinhala-speaking people in the rest. How the island was perceived at the beginning of the British occupation in 1799 by European invaders is clear from a statement made by Hugh Cleghorn, the first British Colonial Secretary of Ceylon, as the island was known at that time:

> Two different nations, from a very ancient period, have divided between them the possession of the island. First, the Cinhalese, inhabiting the interior of the country in its southern and western parts, from the river Wallouwe [Wallawe] to that of Chilaw, and secondly the Malabars [Tamils], who possess the northern and eastern districts. These two nations differ entirely in their religion and manners.
>
> (quoted in Bose 1994: 38–9)

This statement would prove to be highly volatile less than two hundred years later, because it is seen as supporting ideas of a Tamil 'homeland'.

At the beginning of the colonial era, Sinhala and Tamil were to some extent living separately, but only to some extent. Already at that time there were Tamil migrants among the Sinhala who eventually would become 'sinhalised' (I am thinking of a number of present-day castes, like the Karawa; see Roberts 1982). Moreover, the last royal dynasty of the Kandyan kingdom was Tamil, which meant that there were many Tamils living in the royal capital, Kandy (see Dewaraja 1988). Still, pre-colonial Ceylon was politically a neatly divided island, with a Tamil kingdom in the north (Jaffna) and two Sinhala kingdoms, in the southwest (Kotte) and in the central mountains (Kandy).

British colonial administration united the island politically. As a result, Tamils in particular began to spread over the entire island. One reason was that they, having earlier access to western education, had a better command over English – the language of colonial administration (including the armed forces). It also meant that they earlier and in greater numbers than the Sinhala went into the professions (medical and legal).

The Sinhala in their turn began to push into the northern and northeastern areas of the island, close to or even into hitherto predominantly Tamil areas. At the beginning of the colonial era the area between Jaffna and the central mountains, nowadays covered by the north central province, was a very thinly populated, desolate area. It had been the heartland of the ancient Sinhala civilisation, but due to wars between South Indian kings and Sri Lankan kings the old capital of Anuradhapura had been deserted, and the ancient irrigation systems had become dilapidated. What remained were small, fairly independent tank-based villages in a malaria-ridden desolation. Around 1870 the British began the restoration of, at first, small irrigation works. Later, they also began to repair the big storage tanks constructed by the kings of Anuradhapura and Polonnaruva (see Kloos 1988). In the twentieth century large colonisation schemes were implemented, resulting in migration of Sinhala into the northcentral and northeastern areas (see Farmer 1957). The migration of Sinhala into the northern dry zone was soon felt as a threat by the Tamil population. Thus, ethnic differences in interest were born.

A second division can be noted *within* both the Sinhala and Tamil populations. Both Sinhala and Tamil society are divided along caste lines. The Tamil system resembles the Indian system. The Vellala regard themselves as the highest caste, at least in Jaffna, the centre of Tamil society and culture in Sri Lanka. The Sinhala caste system is rather different from the Indian system. About half of the Sinhala belong to the highest caste, the caste of the cultivators (*govigama*). The other half consists of a variety of often quite small castes having special functions as servants, ritual servants, artisans, etc. (see for an early description of the Sinhala caste system Valentijn 1978 [1724]).

Colonial civil servants were recruited from the higher Tamil and Sinhala castes. This resulted in the nineteenth century in the rise of an in origin high caste, anglicised, often Christian, colonial élite. To this élite belonged among the Tamils also the academics, and among the Sinhala the new entrepreneurs who had become rich in liquor trading, plumbago mining and the exploitation of plantations (coconut in particular). The colonial élite had already begun to take over the administration from the British in the course of the first half of the twentieth century (Sri Lanka has had universal franchise since 1931, which is earlier than in many European states!). It is this colonial élite that finally took over the entire administration in 1947.

Both among Sinhala and Tamils there were and to some extent still are additional divisions. There are important differences between Jaffna Tamils and Tamils of the east coast (who were not subject to the king of Jaffna). Moreover, when the British introduced coffee plantations in the central highlands in the 1830s, they brought in high numbers of South Indian migrant labourers. When coffee disappeared as the result of a plant disease and tea took its place, many of these so-called Indian Tamils chose to stay in Sri Lanka. At independence in 1948, the total number of Indian Tamils was slightly higher than the number of Ceylon Tamils! The Indian Tamils (in the beginning called Malabar coolies) belonged to castes far lower than the Jaffna Vellala.

Among the Sinhala one should distinguish between Low-country and Up-country Sinhala. This distinction came into being in the course of the colonial era. Colonial history began in the early sixteenth century, with the arrival of the Portuguese. The Portuguese quickly made an end to both the Tamil kingdom in the north and to the Sinhala kingdom in the west (near Colombo). The Portuguese tried to occupy the Kandyan kingdom too. They failed, like their successors, the Dutch. The British succeeded in 1815 to occupy Kandy, and added the last Sinhala kingdom to the colony. For two centuries, however, Sri Lanka had been divided into the maritime provinces occupied by the Portuguese, Dutch and British successively, and the central mountains under the king of Kandy (Kandy is a European corruption of *kanda*, mountain). This division gave rise, after 1815 in particular, to a distinction between low-country Sinhala, and up-country, Kandyan Sinhala. In the twentieth century the distinction began to whither away – it is still there although it does not play a crucial role in politics any longer.

The distinctions between Sinhala and Tamil, and among both between establishment and the broad masses, are by far the most important ones. The first political consequences of these distinctions had already surfaced in 1948 and 1949 and had to do with the Indian Tamils rather than the Ceylon Tamils.

The first years after independence can be regarded as a period of continuation of the colonial period. After all, there had been no war of independence and there was no immediate necessity to overhaul completely the economic and political system. The national leaders of the day 'became new drivers of the existing vehicles and all the contribution they made was to make the carriage go along' (Ivan 1989: 6). Among these drivers were Sinhala politicians like D. S. Senanayake, and Tamil politicians, like G. G. Ponnambalam and S. J. V. Chelvanayakam, at that time organised in an explicitly Tamil political party, the Ceylon Tamil Congress (see Wilson 1988).

These national drivers were not quite continuing on the path that their vehicle was going. Among the earliest acts passed by the House of Representatives were the Citizen Act (1948), the Indian and Pakistani Residents (Citizenship) Act (1949), and the Parliamentary Elections Amendment Act (1949). The first two acts denied citizenship to the majority of the Indian Tamils, and the third one disenfranchised them. The political motive behind these acts was the fear of the Sinhala leaders of the electoral strength that could be exercised by the Tamil plantation workers, especially in the central province, where they outnumbered the Sinhala in several districts. Tne district of Nuwara Eliya, centre of the tea plantations, was one of them. Moreover, the Indian Tamils were suspected of sympathy for the Trotskyist *Lanka Sama Samaya Party* (LSSP) which in 1947, with ten seats, was the second party in Parliament, after the United National Party (UNP) with forty-two seats. These acts caused a split in the Tamil Congress. Some Tamil politicians, hoping to be accepted by the Sinhala majority, accepted the acts (see Wilson 1988: 34ff.). Others remained loyal to the Indian Tamils and opposed. As a result the Federal Party was formed, led by S. J. V. Chelvanayakam (see Wilson 1994).

The reaction against a still predominantly anglicised government and an equally anglicised Civil (later Public) Service came soon afterwards, during the early 1950s. The 1956 elections were won by S. W. R. D. Bandaranaike on the wave of a massive anti-English, anti-Christian, Sinhala-Buddhist nationalist platform that was supported by the Sinhala-speaking rural élites (village headmen, Sinhala teachers, Ayurvedic physicians, etc.) and by the *sangha* (the Buddhist monastic order). The first felt discriminated by a civil service, a teaching system and a medical system that was still monopolised by the English-educated colonial élite. The *sangha* felt that Buddhism had suffered severely under western rule and that it was time for redress. A convenient coincidence was that 1956 happened to be the year of the *Buddha Jayanthi*, the 2,500th anniversary of Buddhism.

Especially the issue of language set Bandaranaike on a collision course with the Tamil population. Teaching in native languages (*swabasha*) had been an issue from the early 1940s (see Dharmadasa 1992), but the slogan which won the elections was not 'native languages' but 'Sinhala only'. Because Buddhism and Sinhala were so entwined, here for the first time Sri Lanka was explicitly conceived as a Sinhala-Buddhist state. In 1956, soon after the elections, the Official Language Act was introduced. Sinhala would be the official language of Sri Lanka. The act became known as the 'Sinhala Only' Act. The proposal triggered the first ethnic riots – in one of the big colonisation schemes in the eastern province, Gal Oya, in 1956.

The Sinhala Only Act was, curiously enough, not in agreement with the Constitution of 1947, which forbade language discrimination. The act was a direct attack on an essential element of Tamil identity: language and literature. But it also greatly reduced the possibilities for Tamils to compete with Sinhala for administrative jobs. The act brought Tamil politicians, who had split as a result of the Citizen Acts, together again. As a result of fierce protests, Bandaranaike retraced his steps. He began negotiations with the (Tamil) Federal Party, and reached an agreement with its leader Chelvanayakam, in the form of a certain degree of devolution of power on a regional basis. Especially the *sangha*, however, was very much opposed to this, and due to its pressure the agreement (the so-called Bandaranaike–Chelvanayakam Pact) was unilaterally recalled by Bandaranaike. Tamil opposition to the Sinhala Only Act led to counter-demonstrations in the Sinhala areas. The prime objective of these demonstrations was to oppose any concessions to the Tamil minority (Warnapala 1974: 244). Tension erupted in the island-wide May 1958 communal riots – the second of a series of Sinhala–Tamil riots (Vittachi 1958). The Federal Party was proscribed. A Tamil Language Bill was discussed in Parliament but never presented for approval. In September 1959 Bandaranaike was assassinated (by a Buddhist monk; see Manor 1989).

Bandaranaike's ideas formed part of the programme of the Sri Lanka Freedom Party (SLFP) he established, being dissatisfied with the United National Party. The rise of the SLFP had a number of unintended consequences. The late president, J. R. Jayewardena, told me in an interview in 1996 that in the end he regarded the establishment of the SLFP as a boon, because it meant that from the 1950s onwards the political rivalry among the Sinhala became a rivalry between two wings of Sinhala establishment, and no longer a rivalry between the old establishment and parties representing the working classes, such as the Trotskyist LSSP and the Communist Party. The SLFP with its leftist leanings effectively demolished the truly leftist parties: the latter hardly survived a number of coalitions with the dominant SLFP. The new UNP/SLFP rivalry, no longer class-bound, stressed Sinhala-ness. The rise of the SLFP thus strengthened the ethnic factor in Sri Lankan politics, among Sinhala and, consequently, also among Tamils. The point is, that an entrepreneurial (capitalist) party and a working class party, however fierce their conflicts may be, in the end share a common interest. A working-class party may stage a revolution, but it will not begin a secessionist war. Ethnically based parties in the end lack a shared interest and either of them can start a secessionist war. In Sri Lanka Tamil parties did.

To understand the dynamics of conflict there is another issue that should be considered before proceeding, namely population growth and socio-economic development in Sri Lanka after independence. At independence Sri Lanka was economically relatively well off. It had received independence without having to fight for it, and due to products such as tea, rubber and cocos it enjoyed a comfortable income in terms of foreign exchange. Part of the available funds were pumped into island-wide free medical care (both curative and preventive, such as the eradication of malaria) and equally island-wide free education. As a result of medical care the mortality rate went down quickly. The birth rate went down too, but, as usual, far more slowly. As a result, the population of Sri Lanka began to increase rapidly. The new generations went to school. As a result of the post-independence relative affluence and population growth, a wave of relatively well-educated young people reached the labour market in the course of the 1960s, in search of a job. At the same time, however, world market prices for tea, rubber and cocos had begun to level off and even fall. Sri Lanka's economy began to stagnate (see Abeyratne 1998). As a result, there were no jobs for the ambitious young generation. The establishment tended to reserve economic and political opportunities for its own children. This led in April 1971 to the second major violent conflict in Sri Lanka, when the extreme-leftist *Janatha Vimukthi Peramuna* (JVP) nearly toppled the government (Alles 1976).

The JVP was a Sinhala movement, but to understand political violence in Sri Lanka one should not isolate the JVP insurgency. Two intersecting differentiations of Sri Lankan society set the scene for political violence in the 1970s and later: see Figure 9.2. The 1956 and 1958 ethnic riots and the April 1971 revolutionary insurgency have been seen as isolated events. With the knowledge we now have of a longer period, however, they should be seen as events in a systematic pattern of growing tension, conflict, and violence.

The Tamil equivalent of the JVP insurgency came one year later, in 1972. In May 1972 a new constitution was adopted. It made Ceylon a republic, henceforth called Sri Lanka. The new constitution guaranteed the supreme position in Sri Lanka of the Sinhala language and of Buddhism, at the expense of Tamil and of other religions. This led to anti-government demonstrations in Jaffna and the raising of black flags. In the wake of these demonstrations radical, secessionist youth groups were formed. The Tamil New Tigers was one of the first of these, but there were many more (see

Sinhala establishment	Tamil establishment
Ambitious non-élite Sinhala youth	Ambitious non-élite Tamil youth

Figure 9.2 Two basic schisms in Sri Lankan society.

Marks 1986). These groups began to agitate not immediately against the government in Colombo *but against the established Tamil politicians.* The rise of these youth groups meant a split in the Tamil community: between the established élite politicians who participated in the Sinhala dominated political process, and the radical and militant – often unemployed – youth. The former largely belonged to the old, English-educated high-caste élite, the latter to Tamil-educated, often lower, castes. In other words, the process that led to the 1971 insurgency among the Sinhala led in the same period to radicalisation among Tamil youth. Unemployed youths were soon willing to use violence as a political means because the Tamil political establishment proved to be powerless, even in the face of highly discriminatory measures against Tamil students, for instance. The situation in Jaffna gradually became more tense and in July 1975 the Tamil mayor of Jaffna, a Tamil supporter of the SLFP, was assassinated by the Tamil New Tigers. In 1976 this group split into two: the *Liberation Tigers of Tamil Eelam* (LTTE) and the *Tamil Eelam Liberation Organisation* (TELO).

The LTTE honoured its name by a programme of selective assassination of at first *Tamil* politicians, who were regarded as traitors, and later (Tamil) police officers. The government strengthened army presence in Jaffna.

The UNP (United National Party) government, after having won the 1977 elections in 1978 proscribed the LTTE. From that moment onwards political violence began to gain momentum (see Senaratne 1997 for a very detailed analysis of the escalation process in the years 1977–90). The August 1977 elections themselves were followed by serious riots (see Sansoni Commission 1980). In May 1978 the government began to fight the Tamil insurgent groups. Tamil insurgent groups continued their guerilla activities, more and more targeting also the Sri Lanka armed forces. Police forces and the army retaliated. The official representatives of the Tamils, organised in the Tamil United Liberation Front (TULF), were gradually losing support in Jaffna. Although they had managed to have District Development Councils introduced in 1981, these councils proved to be no real devolution of power and demonstrated that the parliamentary road was leading the Tamils nowhere.

The same year witnessed another step in the process towards civil war: after a number of political assassinations of UNP and TULF politicians in May 1981 in Jaffna by the LTTE, the Sri Lankan police and military went berserk. Massive armed force-instigated anti-Tamil riots took place in Jaffna and elsewhere. In Jaffna the public library with its invaluable Tamil manuscripts was burned down (Swamy 1994: 73)

An important threshold in the Sinhala–Tamil relations after Independence was crossed in July 1983. On 23 July the LTTE ambushed and killed thirteen soldiers (Swamy 1994: 89ff.). The LTTE had ambushed and killed soldiers before. However, what happened after the bodies of the thirteen soldiers had been brought to Colombo was a violent reaction among urban Sinhala, amounting to a veritable pogrom. In contrast to earlier riots, like the 1958 one, the Sri Lankan government for the first twenty-four hours did nothing to stop the mobs that began to attack Tamils and their property. Army and police were present in the streets of Colombo (and elsewhere in the country) amidst the mobs, but did not try to prevent either the burning and looting of houses belonging to Tamils, or the killing. Even worse, high government officials, including Cabinet Ministers, actively promoted the targeting of Tamils living in Colombo, by handing over election lists disclosing the names and addresses of Tamil voters to gangs of thugs who were taken by public transport buses to streets and neighbourhoods where many Tamils lived (see Hyndman 1984). Although the pogrom has never been subject to systematic investigation, the available evidence points in the direction of a conscious move of certain members of the cabinet (Cheran *et al.* 1993; Perera 1995).

The pogrom was swiftly followed by an amendment to the constitution: the sixth Amendment which made advocacy of a separate state on Sri Lanka a criminal offence. Tamil Members of Parliament, by their very membership of their party adhering to the so-called Vadukodai resolution of 1976 of their party, which did indeed ask for a Tamil Eelam, could not but leave Parliament (it is still a mystery why the Jayewardene government whisked the sixth Amendment through Parliament, see for comments on the decision Wilson 1988: 173, De Silva and Wriggins 1994: 565). Henceforth, Tamil separatism could no longer be discussed in the most important political arena, namely Parliament.

July 1983 is usually regarded as the beginning of permanent civil war in Sri Lanka (also for comparative purposes, see Jongman 1995, Franke 1994), but the worst was still to come. The ambush of the LTTE resulting in the July 1983 pogrom in Colombo had unanticipated results because the various Tamil militant groups profited greatly from it. The pogrom brought attention to them, also internationally. It brought support from Tamils abroad, it induced thousands of youth to become fighters, and it undermined even further the position of the parliamentary politicians. The radical LTTE eventually came to the fore as the sole custodian of Tamils interests in Jaffna peninsula after it had systematically, violently and often treacherously wiped out its rivals (see Swamy 1994: 174–98).

The Sri Lankan army had no answer to the well-organised, ruthless war machine the LTTE soon became. A number of operations of the Sri Lankan army caused the Indian government to intervene in 1987. It forced a treaty upon the Sri Lankan President, who had to accept an Indian peace keeping force (IPKF) in Sri Lanka (see for an interesting although biased inside view of Lanka-Indian relations Dixit 1998). Far from keeping peace, the IPKF soon after its arrival in July 1987 found itself in a deadly struggle with the LTTE. The Indian army too had no answer to LTTE strategies (Bose 1994).

The arrival of the IPKF, however, had an unanticipated effect: it estranged the Sinhala political élite from the Sinhala masses. The JVP returned to the political scene but now as a patriotic movement. It accused the governing élites of betraying the Sinhala motherland (*mawu bima*). Its armed wing began to attack politicians. The government retaliated. Despite the use of violence there was at first much sympathy for the JVP among the Sinhala, even in the army itself – until JVP leaders made a fatal mistake: in 1989 they threatened to attack the wives and children of the army and policemen. This resulted in the creation of secret death squads bearing names such as black cats, red dragons, etc. These events ushered in almost three years of total political crisis in Sri Lanka. The years 1987–90 saw an almost complete breakdown of Sri Lankan society. The Sri Lankan government had to cope with a Tamil secessionist movement, fought in the north by the IPKF in Sri Lanka, and with the (second) JVP insurrection among the Sinhala in the south. Official and unofficial government violence, LTTE and JVP violence, and violence perpetrated to settle private quarrels or for material gain became indistinguishable: it was no longer quite clear who killed whom and for what reason. Due to methods of killing and the tyre-burning of victims it was often not even clear who had been killed. Tens of thousands just disappeared, leaving no trace (the number of disappearances is estimated at 40–60,000 – the wide margin of 20,000 itself adding significantly to the uncertainties already implied in the word 'disappearance'). This period is referred to by Sinhala as the *beeshanaya kale*, the time of terror.

The ruthless persecution of the JVP led to the extra-judicial killing of its leadership in November 1989 (Chandraprema 1991). This proved to be a turning point towards a lessening of the political and moral crisis. The then president R. Premadasa forced the Indian army to leave the country (the last troops left in March 1990). As a result, the accusation of unpatriotic behaviour of the government subsided.

The government had to deal with the LTTE again. One of the manoeuvres of Premadasa already before the demise of the JVP leadership had been to open negotiations with the LTTE. He used these negotiations to get rid of the IPKF! After more than a year of negotiation, however, the LTTE unilaterally terminated the discussions in June 1990 and began Eelam War II as it is usually called. The LTTE was so successful that within a short period it had carved out a *de facto* Tamil state in the north of Sri Lanka, where the LTTE and no one else was in charge.

In 1994 the *People's Alliance* (*PA*) government took over from the UNP that had ruled the country since 1977. The PA government did what it had promised during the electoral campaigns: it began peace negotiations. The LTTE at first showed some interest in peace talks. In June 1995, however, it broke off the discussion with a letter from the LTTE leader Prabhakaran, and a surprise attack on Sri Lanka's navy in the harbour of Trincomalee. Thus began Eelam War III.

The Sri Lankan army resumed military activities and in 1995 occupied Jaffna peninsula. This did not bring peace. Neither did a military operation under the name Jaya Sikuru, 'certain victory', that began in 1996 and was expected to make an end to the war swiftly. It did not. It is unlikely that the LTTE can be defeated by military means. As a Sri Lanka-based secessionist movement it had already, early in its history, turned into a transnational enterprise, tapping financial and other sources wherever there are Tamils (see Kloos 1999; Gunaratna 1997). The LTTE is still a formidable foe. Although no longer operating from Jaffna but from the dry jungles south of Jaffna peninsula, it succeeded in July 1996, for instance, to overrun an army camp at Mullaitivu, some 175 miles north-west from Colombo (but close to Jaffna), killing an estimated 1,400 soldiers during a ten-day battle. In 1998, the Sri Lankan army after a very long struggle finally took a small but strategic town on the road to Jaffna, Manankulam, but at the same time lost Killinochchi, another strategically situated town closer to Jaffna. The struggle is an example of the fact that an army cannot defeat a guerilla movement as long as the latter sticks to guerilla warfare.

At the moment of writing there is no peace treaty in sight.

Concluding remarks: one turning point?

Described in this fashion the process of escalation of violence in Sri Lanka's post-independence acquires the features of a Greek *tragoidia,* in which the actors almost from the beginning choose the path inexorably leading to their doom.

In Sri Lanka there have certainly been decisions that appear to have been taken as if the main actors did have escalation in mind, yet there are no indications or testimonies that the Sri Lankan actors, whether Sinhala or Tamil, consciously planned the civil war, let alone the *beeshanaya kala*, the time of horror, of the late 1980s. Still the question remains: could this civil war have been predicted? Could – well before irreversible decisions had been taken and doom was at hand – violence have been prevented? And, if we take the recent notions of 'conflict prevention' and 'early warning' seriously, in which phase should action have been taken and by whom, and what is 'early'? Has there been a turning point in the process leading to violence?

At first sight, the anti-Tamil pogrom of 1983 and its aftermath would be such a moment. The year 1983 is usually regarded as the point civil struggle turned into civil war. I do not wish to belittle the traumatic pogrom of July 1983 but to concentrate on it amounts to overestimating one single spectacular event at the expense of understanding the logic of the whole chain of events that formed the process of escalation itself and led to the total crisis of the late 1980s. Several of these events in themselves were not at all violent as such, yet eventually led to a situation in which at least one party saw no other option than violence. Such events changed 'the disposition to actual fighting', to quote Hobbes.

However, what is the nature of the links between the various events and what is their specific contribution to escalation? Can one argue that after the acceptance in 1947 and 1948 of the discriminatory acts against the Indian Tamils by the newly elected parliament of Ceylon, civil war had become unavoidable?

Is history predetermined? The answer to this question is a matter of belief. Historical predetermination is a belief to which I personally do not subscribe. Although I *do* subscribe to the view that there are in social life law-like regularities, historical processes are, owing to elements of non-repetition and novelty, destined to be characterised by a certain degree of contingency. They are thus fundamentally unpredictable. Therefore, one cannot sensibly argue that the 1947 and 1948 acts inexorably led to civil war in the 1980s and 1990s.

However, I emphasise the qualification to 'a certain degree' of contingency. Opposing actors may in due course decide to limit each other's choice of alternatives so severely, that the possibility of prediction becomes a matter of serious consideration. There are several decisions in the Sri Lankan process that have that feature: the 1972 Constitution (which made Sinhala the official language and thus turned Tamils into second class citizens), the 1978 decision of the newly elected government to proscribe the Tamil secessionist groups, and the 1983 Sixth Amendment (which threw Tamil politicians out of parliament) have been strategic in the process of escalation. None of these decisions were violent themselves (although they were based on power, supported by the possible resort to violence). Yet in restricting the freedom of political manoeuvre of the Tamil minority, the Sinhala majority in Sri Lanka in the course of its policies left little room for the Tamil population to pursue peaceful policies with any trust. Sinhala majority politics in time left room for only one political creature: the ruthless Liberation Tiger. In this way the Sinhala majority created their own foe.

The LTTE is now classified as a terrorist organisation and the Tigers as terrorists (for example, by the United States and the government of Sri Lanka). And there is an argument to do so: suicidal bomb attacks on banks and hotels in which mainly civilians are the victims are not usually regarded as military tactics. Such attacks are regarded as terrorism carried out by groups with their back against the wall. Here, the same mechanism seems to be at work: deny the adversary all freedom to political manoeuvre, peaceful or military, and he will resort to terrorism.

From 1972 onwards, the likelihood that civil struggle would turn into violence increased sharply in Sri Lanka, and with the benefit of comparison with similar situations across the world, from that moment the possibility to predict violence increased too. Still, it is the wisdom of hindsight that gives later observers the feeling that violent politics could have been predicted.

Here the question who could have interfered becomes possible. The fateful decisions referred to were taken by successive governments of a sovereign state. Moreover, these governments had been democratically elected. From a legal point of view no one could

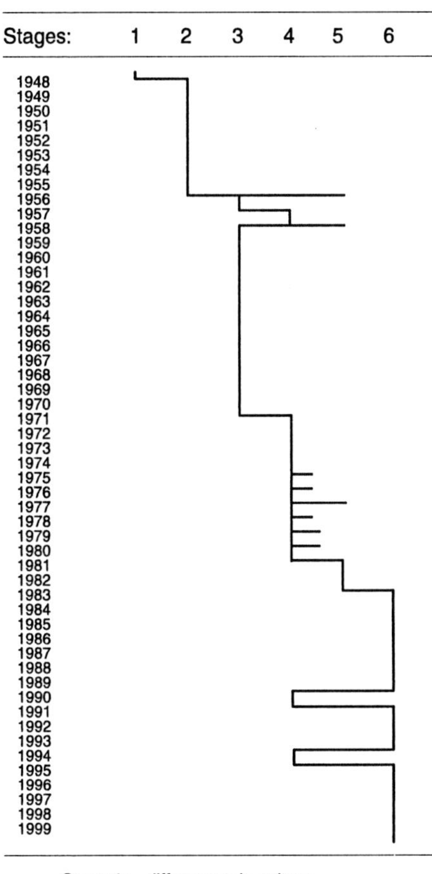

Figure 9.3 From ethnic difference (stage 1) to regular civil war (stage 6).

have interfered (even today, the government of Sri Lanka is adamant about foreign interference: the conflict is an internal one, and no one has the right to interfere[1]). Seen in this perspective the opportunities for timely 'conflict prevention' are gloomy.

A comparison with potential civil wars of the coming decades might be useful. The Sri Lankan civil war is a fairly typical example of the kind of civil war flowing from the construction of a colonial state and failing nation-building after independence. The potential civil wars of the future are of a somewhat different nature: they are related to the rise of global regimes and failure of state governments to come to terms with their minorities. Global regimes weaken state governments and allow sub-state minorities to make use of a global arena in their efforts for their wishes to be heard. If state governments refuse to accept sub-state autonomy, civil war may only be one or two steps away. I submit that governments as well as scholars everywhere have tended to ignore the violent potential of this phenomenon, even in Europe, even in prototypical states like the United Kingdom and France (see Kloos 1997b). Apparently, the possibility of differences of interest and tension turning into potential violent conflict is taken seriously not earlier than the moment weapons are procured and begin to speak. Given the contingent nature of the process this is irrational only on the basis of wisdom of hindsight.

So my conclusion is that although one could argue that conflict prevention should take place at stages 3 or 4 at the latest, the contingent nature of the escalation processes makes this not only not feasible, but perhaps even irrational.

Note

1 Using precisely this argument, in the fall of 2000 the Sri Lankan government – just before elections – turned down a Norwegian proposal to mediate for peace.

Bibliography

Alles, A.C. (1976) *Insurgency 1971,* Colombo: The Apothecaries.

Abeyratne, S. (1998) *The Economic Background of Conflict in Developing Countries, With Special Reference to Sri Lanka,* Sri Lanka Series, 7, Amsterdam: VU University Press.

Bose, S. (1994) *States, Nations, Sovereignty. Sri Lanka, India and the Tamil Eelam Movement,* New Delhi: Sage Publications.

Chandraprema, C. A. (1991) *Sri Lanka: The Years of Terror. The JVP Insurgency 1987–1989*, Colombo: Lake House Bookshop.

Cheran, R., Keller, W., Mertsch, M. and Rajanayagam, P. (1993) *A Decade of Conflict. Sri Lanka 1983–1993*, Dortmund: Südasienbüro.

De Silva, K. M. and Wriggins, H. (1994) *J. R. Jayewardene of Sri Lanka. A Political Biography Volume Two: From 1956 to His Retirement (1989)*, London: Leo Cooper.

Dewaraja, L. S. (1988) [1972] *The Kandyan Kingdom of Sri Lanka 1707–1782*, Colombo: Lakehouse.

Dixit, J. N. (1998) *Assignment Colombo*, Delhi: Vikas.

Farmer, B. H. (1957) *Pioneer Peasant Colonization in Ceylon. A Study in Asian Agrarian Problems*, Oxford: Oxford University Press.

Franke, J. P. (1994) *Die Kriege 1900–1994. Chronologie und Opferzahlen*, Hamburg: Arbeitsgemeinschaft Kriegsursachenforschung.

Gunaratna, R. (1997) *International and Regional Security. Implications of the Sri Lankan Tamil Insurgency*, St Albans, Herts.: International Foundation of Sri Lankans.

Hobbes, T. (1968) [1651] *Leviathan*, Harmondsworth: Penguin Books.

Hyndman, P. (1984) *The Communal Violence in Sri Lanka, July 1983*, Report to the Lawasia Human Rights Standing Committee.

Ivan, V. (1989) *Sri Lanka in Crisis. Road to Conflict*, Ratmalana: Sarvodaya Book Publishing Services.

Jongman, A. J. (1995) 'Contemporary conflicts. a global survey of high- and lower intensity conflicts and serious disputes', *Pioom Newsletter* 79 (1): 14–38.

Kloos, P. (1988) 'Koloniaal landbouwbeleid in Sri Lanka in de 19e eeuw: het gezichtspunt van de government agent', *Sociologische Gids* 35: 174–98.

—— (1997a) 'The Struggle between the lion and the tiger. The relevance of inter- and intra-ethnic conflict for the construction of ethnic identities in Sri Lanka', in C. Govers and H. Vermeulen (eds) *The Politics of Ethnic Consciousness*, London: Macmillan.

—— (1997b) Secessionism in Europe in the second half of the 20th century, in N. A. Tahir (ed.) *The Politics of Ethnicity and Nationalism in Europe and South Asia*, Karachi: Area Study Centre for Europe.

—— (1999) 'A Secessionist movement in an age of globalization: The liberation Tigers of Tamil Eelam of Sri Lanka', in N. Jetly (ed.) *Regional Security in South Asia: The Ethno-Sectarian Dimensions*, New Delhi: Lancers Books.

Manor, J. (1989) *The Expedient Utopian: Bandaranaike and Ceylon*, Cambridge: Cambridge University Press.

Marks, T. (1986) 'People's war in Sri Lanka: insurgency and counter-insurgency', *Issues and Studies* 22(8): 63–100.

Perera, S. (1995) 'Formation of ethnocentrism and the perpetuation of hatred: the role of socialization and media in the Sri Lankan ethnic conflict', *Sri Lanka Journal of Social Sciences* 18 (1 & 2): 55–75.

Roberts, M. (1982) *Caste Conflict and Elite Formation,* Cambridge: Cambridge University Press.

Rule, J. B. (1988) *Theories of Civil Violence,* Berkeley: University of California Press.

Sansoni Commission (1980) *Report of the Presidential Commission of Inquiry into the Incidents Which Took Place between 13th August and 15th September, 1977,* Sri Lanka, Sessional Paper; VII, Colombo: Department of Government Printing.

Senaratne, J. (1997) *Political Violence in Sri Lanka, 1977–1990,* Sri Lanka Studies; 4, Amsterdam: VU University Press.

Siccama, J. G. and Oostindiër, A. (1995) *Veranderingen in het Conflictpatroon na de Koude Oorlog: Misverstanden en Feiten,* Den Haag: Clingendael.

Swamy, M. R. N. (1994) *Tigers of Lanka. From Boys to Guerillas,* Delhi: Konark Publishers.

Valentijn, F. (1978) [1724] *François Valentijn's Description of Ceylon,* translated and edited by S. Arasaratnam, London: The Hakluyt Society.

Van Walraven, K. (ed.) (1998) *Early Warning and Conflict Prevention. Limitations and Possibilities,* The Hague: Kluwer Law International.

Vittachi, T. (1958) *Emergency '58: The Study of the Ceylon Race Riots,* London: Andre Deutsch.

Warnapala, W.A.W. (1974) *Civil Service Administration in Ceylon. A Study in Bureaucratic Adaptation,* Colombo: Department of Cultural Affairs.

Wilson, A. J. (1988) *The Break-up of Sri Lanka. The Sinhalese–Tamil Conflict,* London: Hurst & Company.

—— (1994) *S. J. V. Chelvanayakam and the Crisis of Sri Lankan Tamil Nationalism, 1947–1977,* London: Hurst & Company.

Chapter 10

Predicament of war

Sarajevo experiences and ethics of war

Ivana Maček

> Government wars aren't my wars; they've got nowt to do with me, because my own war's all that I'll ever be bothered about.
>
> Alan Sillitoe, *The Loneliness of the Long Distance Runner*

Introduction

The purpose of this chapter is to investigate how the experience of war influences and changes our perceptions about war. The war situation that is the focus of my study is the siege of Sarajevo, the capital of Bosnia and Hercegovina, during the period between 1992 and 1996.

In order to structure the otherwise opaque and often confusing experiences and materials, I shall introduce a model consisting of three significantly different modes of relating to war. I have labelled these modes the 'civilian', 'soldier', and 'deserter' modes of perceiving war, and I want to stress immediately that the meanings I ascribe to these labels differ from the common ones.[1] In the first place, these three modes represent three *ethically* different approaches towards war. They are the basis for social interaction, and they legitimise this interaction in three different ways. All three ways of perceiving wars can in practice be used by the same person. Such a mixing of ethical values is the reason behind the often-witnessed confusion and disturbing feelings towards wars which we indirectly witness in our everyday lives.

Further, we shall see that the 'civilian' and the 'deserter' modes are characteristic of the private sphere and generally of the situations invested with little, if any, *political power*. Thus, we shall find 'civilians' and 'deserters' in stories about people who were personally known by the narrator in my interviews, in the narrator himself and also in some of the foreign journalists' accounts. The 'soldier' mode is going to be characteristic of the public situations, political discourses and institutions invested with political power. Thus, the 'soldier' mode will be found in most of the books written by men in positions of political power, books written as historical documents, school books, scholarly generalisations, and when the narrator in my interviews takes a political stance. As the competition for political power in Sarajevo went hand in hand with the processes of building three antagonistic nations – Muslim, i.e. Bosniak, Serb and Croat – it is no surprise that it is within the discourse on *national identities* and loyalties that we shall find significant ethical differences between private and public, in other words, between 'civilian', 'soldier', and 'deserter' ways of reasoning.

After the introduction comes the main body of the article in which I present the 'civilian', 'soldier' and 'deserter' modes of perceiving war. In each of these modes I discuss four domains of social life that I found to be most significant in the war in Sarajevo: the character of time, the perceptions of social order, the choices made and their legitimation, and the group identities. I have chosen the account of one key narrator[2] for the purposes of illustrating attitudes and choices which were common among Sarajevans. Thus, the material on which the discussion is based consists of the key narrator's account contextualised by books on war in Sarajevo written by Sarajevans, books on war in the former Yugoslavia and in particular Bosnia and Hercegovina written by foreign diplomats and journalists, some classical works on ideas about war in the West, recent anthropological literature concerned with civilian everyday lives informed by violence, and finally my own experiences of war from a one-year period of fieldwork (see Maček 2000). This, I hope, will bring several dimensions into the portrait of the key narrator and make him and his choices more understandable and perhaps closer to the reader's own experiences. I hope that the key narrator can stand as an example of how all three modes of perception are combined in our dealing with experiences of war.

'Civilian' mode of perceiving war

The 'civilian' mode of thinking about war is characterised by the perception of war as opposite to peace, where peace is considered to be the normal way of living, civilised, moral, and with juridical routines of dealing with unacceptable destruction and manslaughter leading to punishment. War is a disruption, an interval of time which is abnormal, and generally impossible to happen to 'us'. War is something that the 'others' experience, whether it is 'others' in time or 'others' in space.

Disruption of peacetime order

To begin with, no one expects to become involved in a war. Wars happen elsewhere, to other people. No matter how near, no matter how interconnected, as long as the war stays outside of our everyday lives, we find it impossible to imagine ourselves involved in it. The best example is provided by the repeated accounts of Sarajevans of how they watched the war going on in neighbouring Croatia, and were still taken aback when Sarajevo was hit.[3]

The key narrator ignored the coming danger even when half of Sarajevo was blocked by containers and armed people with masked faces.

> X: Suddenly you couldn't go to Grbavica,[4] then they put out some containers and ramps so that you couldn't pass through to Koševsko Brdo,[5] in the middle of the day, suddenly. . . . There were some things going on, but when I think of it, I had no idea. I couldn't even imagine this sort of war happening. . . . I continued going to my firm, but you didn't really know whether to go or not. Trams were not working, and some people came while others didn't. You came to work, but you didn't have anything to do. Total chaos.

The same story was repeated by all Sarajevans driving out of the town during March 1992, coming back and being stopped at the barricades. Some ignored it, some laughed it all away. Others took it as a temporary danger and left the town, or sent their children out of it – for the summer, as they thought. As the danger of armed conflict rose, more and more people decided to temporarily leave the town. Others tried to do their best in order to prevent the conflict which was increasingly being staged as a conflict between three major Bosnian nations – Muslims, Serbs and Croats. When the shooting started, and none of the civilian actions had any effect, the war started slowly to enter the social fabric of Sarajevo. This was a gradual process of realisation that the war was no longer elsewhere, but was actually happening to 'us'.

For most people war came as a surprise, 'like a thunder from bright skies', as the key narrator put it. Accompanying it was the notion of chaos and incomprehensibility, characteristic of many war accounts describing war as 'unimaginable' (Morokvasić 1998: 66), unexperienced before (Bruchfeld and Levine 1998: 77; Vuković 1993: 14–15; Imamović and Bošnjak 1994: 17), and/or as the most cruel in human history (Kubert 1996: 141; Vuković 1993: 14–15; Imamović and Bošnjak 1994: 17).

> I do not know whether this is war. War is not an encompassing word. War has some rules of war. This is something unseen. Unseen and unexperienced forms of evildoings and dirtiness of these evildoings.
>
> (Isaković 1994: 13, my translation)

The often claimed uniqueness of the experience of one particular war, though, points to a common characteristic in these accounts: the incapacity of people to let go of their perceptions of the normal peacetime order of things. It is as if the refusal to realise the possible consequences of what is happening around them can somehow protect them from that which is feared. Even when they started referring to 'the war', Sarajevans believed that it would not last long, and that the pre-war order would soon be re-established.

Resistance to new national ideologies

The disbelief also characterised the political arena, where Sarajevans demonstrated a resistance to the political and ideological changes that were taking place. On the 6 April 1992 at least 20,000 people[6] demonstrated against the nationalist politics in front of the Parliament, pledging their loyalty to Tito's legacy of 'brotherhood and unity' (*bratstvo i jedinstvo*) and a multi-national Bosnia and Hercegovina. They stormed the Parliament, forced the resignation of the Prime Minister, took over the TV programming and put their message on the air. 'One speaker said, "Let all the Serb chauvinists go to Serbia and let the Croat chauvinists go to Croatia. We want to remain here together. We want to keep Bosnia as one"' (report by Michael Montgomery, *Daily Telegraph*, 7 April 1992, quoted in Malcolm 1994: 235). A Sarajevo woman noted in her diary:

> [In the Parliament] the speakers, unknown as well as famous, took turns speaking. Folk had whistled down Izetbegović, and

> he got terribly angry and repeated all the time: 'I didn't have to come here, but I came. . .'. In the end they allowed him to speak, in the second attempt, but his margins were small. Alija was so angry that he demanded the breaking up of the meeting of the Folk Parliament if he was to give an interview to the Youth Radio. That is what someone from the Youth Radio said.
>
> (Softić 1994: 14, my translation)

Many Sarajevans resisted national division not only through these demonstrations, but wherever it appeared, as for instance the key narrator did in his firm:

> X: In the beginning we had even secret meetings, younger people, we wanted to pursue our own line, we wouldn't allow the division, we were against national firms. Today you see how all that was naive. You thought you could do something, but you could do absolutely nothing. The centres of power where decisions were made were detached from our institution, and we were totally out of reach from those centres.

The protests, however, failed and the situation became serious. Many decided to leave, but many stayed, still not believing that a further escalation of violence was possible. Likewise, it was hard to believe that the war would be fought between Bosnian nations, which was the reason why the key narrator made sure that the units for defence were multi-national before joining them:

> X: I answered to the call to join the units for defence. Of course, I still didn't understand the situation. I asked whether all [nationalities] were represented in these units. They showed me the list and I saw that there were Croats, Serbs and Muslims on it. Naturally, since we lived in a mixed part of the town. So I volunteered and we made a sort of military formation. We met in a room, 50 souls, we had three guns, everybody was talking, no one understanding anyone. It was actually enormous chaos. There was nobody who could stand out by some qualities, as a leader. This was in our Municipal Centre. It was the beginning of May. Shells were already falling, bullets whistling, front-lines were established. It was more or less already known which territory belonged to whom. Sometimes

> we went to the lines of separation [front-lines], although these lines were protected in the first place by the people living there. They protected their hearths. There was still no consciousness formed in people.

In this account the retrospective description was made of the original 'civilian' ways of acting, and the powerlessness of that position. When the narrator referred to his naiveté and lack of consciousness, he was taking a 'soldier' stance. From the 'soldier' perspective it was naive not to realise that there was a war going on, and that the antagonistic sides in that war were different national groups, and that the group he belonged to was the Muslim, i.e. the Bosnian government's side. It was naive to think that one might have been able to change something by one's power as a citizen, because citizens might have power in peace, but in war they are powerless.

From countrymen to family

In situations of constant threat to one's existence, such as wars and the siege of Sarajevo, the essential quality one seeks in group affiliation is the protection of life and of one's standard of living. Consequently, people in Sarajevo identified primarily with the group of people with whom they could entrust their lives. This judgement was based on both their experiences and on information they could get about their situation in the war.

After the realisation that the war was happening to them, Sarajevans gradually narrowed their pre-war solidarity towards all citizens and the old political ideology of 'brotherhood and unity', to solidarity with their neighbours and friends. Because of the general collapse of civilian institutions and infrastructure, most people found themselves concerned with their own destinies and the destinies of the people with whom they were most closely related. When neighbours and friends proved not able to trust each other any longer with personal decisions, however, the solidarity group was reduced to encompass only family members. It was only within the family one could be safe, and it was only within the family that one could expect total loyalty and existential security. Later, this tight network of people became not only the focus of interest and support, but also the only reliable group one could trust with one's plans and opinions. Within this closest circle, people could rely upon each other for unconditional help with various practicalities of war life, they could share their plans of leaving town or deserting, they could express controversial political attitudes, and generally anything that might not have been seen as positive in public. As I soon discovered after coming to Sarajevo, having a family and a home to come to gave a basic feeling of (social) security.[7] The knowledge that there was someone who was going to do everything in order to help in case something happened was reassuring and necessary for normal functioning in these extremely dangerous living conditions.

'Soldier' mode of perceiving war

Accepting war as a social phenomenon controlled by human beings is characteristic of the 'soldier' mode of thinking. In this perspective, wars have their rules which are different from peacetime rules. These rules legitimate what would otherwise be socially and morally unacceptable (for instance, the killing of fellow humans and material destruction).[8] There is always a reason for a war, there are legitimate causes and aims. The knowledge that it is war makes unacceptable events and acts acceptable – it implies that this would never have happened in normal (peacetime) circumstances, so what one did (or does) does not make one a different person. It is understood that this mode of living shall end with the ending of the war.

Social memory

One of the first things we want to know about a war is when it started and when it ended. These dates and events seem to be necessary since the general idea about war seems to be that it is a limited period of time (cf. Hobbes 1997 [1651]: 70, and Jabri 1996: 34). So, in order to be able to think about a group of social events as 'war', we need to know its beginning and end. Indeed, in Western post-Second World War cultures (as well as in the former Yugoslavia), we see a firm ritualisation of war during the festivities held on these dates. Of course, the ritualisation of war takes place not only around the beginning and ending of a war, but also around some other 'key dates', 'key events' and 'key persons'. The idea of war as a limited period of time seems to arise from a need to organise the otherwise opaque and complex phenomenon of war.

The Sarajevan experience shows that it was the need to put the war events behind them, without forgetting them, which provided the ground for simplification of complexities and eventual ritualisation of events. Thus, in war 'social memory' (cf. Connerton 1989) is informed by the need to share the experience of war, and leads to ritualisation of war around those dates, events, and persons which can be filled with collectively significant meaning.[9]

As an example we can take the establishment of the first victim of the war by the Bosnian government's side – Suada Dilberović, a student. In the place where she was killed on Vrbanja Bridge, recently renamed Suada Dilberović's Bridge, there is a plate and flowers commemorating this victim. Fairly soon, in the spring of 1996, when there were practically no more new victims of the war in Sarajevo, it became clear that the death of this girl was going to symbolise all deaths and losses that occurred during the war – especially among the civilians of Sarajevo, killed by random shelling or sniper fire. That the 'first victim of the war' was a young woman, a student, and bearing a Muslim name, was hardly coincidental. A man would have been a potential soldier, and an older person would not have been regarded as having her whole life in front of her; a student symbolised intelligence and civilisation, the future of the nation; and Muslims were considered to be *the* victims in this war, especially by the official Sarajevo government's interpretation, although the same interpretation generally accepted that other groups in the conflict also had their share of suffering and losses.[10]

Another important symbol of the war took place on the 2 May 1992. On this day, Sarajevo, especially the centre, was heavily shelled for the first time. Scenes from the town on that day were played and replayed on the television, and people often reflect on what happened that day. It became a symbol of Serbian barbarism, mercilessly imprinted in the body of the destroyed town, a constant reminder of the nature of the enemy and the character of the war.

Making of the official history

With the termination of the siege of Sarajevo during the spring of 1996, the beginning of the war became more and more obviously ritualised in the state-controlled Sarajevan media, as well as in Western accounts. The war started officially on the 6 April 1992 when from the Holiday Inn sniper fire was opened on people demonstrating in front of the Parliament. The shooting was perceived as being caused by the European Union's and the United States' recognition of Bosnia and Hercegovina as an independent state. By this recognition, the results of a referendum on independence held some weeks earlier (in which most of the Muslim and Croat populations participated, and which was boycotted by the Serbian population) were given international legitimacy. The leading Serbian party, SDS, which stood behind the Serbian boycott of the referendum, took this as a threat to the Serbian population, and initiated an armed conflict by shooting at the demonstrators.

We find this account in a number of texts about the war in Bosnia and Hercegovina (Gutman 1993: xxvii; Imamović and Bošnjak 1994: 17; Imamović and Pelešić 1994: 121; Vulliamy 1994: 73ff.; Gjelten 1995: 24; Ramet 1996: 246f.), and since it has been selected for the local school books (Imamović and Bošnjak 1994: 17; Imamović and Pelešić 1994: 121), it is bound to become the generally accepted account.

Some of the authors are more vague about the exact beginning (Glenny 1992: 167; Owen 1996: 2; Rieff 1995: 17; Zimmermann 1996: 186), but they nevertheless try to pinpoint the beginning of the war to a certain violent event filled with political significance. The critique which can be directed to such ambitions to establish the exact political significance of violent war events and their dates is that the choice of events is left to the author. Consequently, the more political power behind an account, the more valid it will become, and the true story of the war will by necessity be the story of the politically empowered.[11]

Identification of sides

One of the most famous theoreticians of war, Carl von Clausewitz, described war as 'a mere continuation of policy by other means' (1997[1832]: 22), and as a sort of contest (see also Scarry 1985: 81ff.). Perceiving war as a sort of contest is characteristic of the 'soldier' mode, and it explains why identification of sides in a war, with their aims, is of central importance. We shall see that the key narrator referred to his 'beginning to understand the situation' and 'becoming conscious' when he started to accept the identification of sides in the war – Bosnian Serb Army and Army of Bosnia and Hercegovina (Muslim dominated) – an identification made in the national idiom promoted from the 'centres of power' to use his own words. A look at a school book used on the side under the Bosnian government's control can illustrate the way in which causes of the war, conflicting sides and their aims, as well as the guilt were defined:

> Bosnia and Hercegovina . . . had never experienced what Serbo-Montenegrin aggressor and domestic Chetniks did to her in the war that they started in the spring of 1992.
>
> The attack was prepared under a long period of organisation and with the help of the former Yugoslav People's Army. The extremist part of the Bosnian Serbs was also included. Their intent was to attach Bosnia and Hercegovina to Serbia, in order to accomplish the ancient dream of the Serbian nationalists to make a so-called Greater Serbia.
>
> The attack started on the 6th of April 1992. The former Yugoslav People's Army and the domestic Chetniks, armed to the teeth, started to attack the unprotected settlements and the unarmed people with the most lethal weapons. [. . .]
>
> Although the people were unarmed, they resisted fiercely. With hunting guns and hand-made weapons, Bosnian and Hercegovian fighters confronted the tanks, cannons, and aeroplanes of the aggressor. [. . .]
>
> During the early days of the aggression the people showed resistance organised in Territorial Defence and other defence formations, and then the Army of Bosnia and Hercegovina was formed. Within a short period of time it became an organised power which took a stand before its people in order to protect it from the crimes of Serbo-Montenegrin aggressors and domestic Chetniks.
>
> The intention of the aggressor was to clear the Bosnian and Hercegovian territories of the non-Serbian people, in the first place of Bosniaks, in order to create an ethnically cleansed Serbian territory. [. . .] The unseen crimes followed. Women, children and old people were slaughtered, there were rapes and episodes of plundering and burning. Villages, schools, factories, mosques, old monuments, all that was Bosniak and Muslim, disappeared in flames.
>
> (Imamović and Bošnjak 1994: 17–18, my translation)

To understand who the parties in the conflict are, their interests and goals with the war, provides an explanation of the causes of a war. Identification of the guilty side turns the otherwise appalling immorality of destruction into an organised and thus understandable phenomenon, an acceptable reality.

New national consciousness

Accepting the new social order, the rules of war, enabled the key narrator to see the reasons behind the war and its aim – the division of the population into national groups and territories. This enabled him to choose the appropriate side to express solidarity with – the Muslim side.

> X: Then the state managed to establish itself, and an army was formed . . . they took us to a location, the first encounter, with a real front. You came and saw bloody uniforms, thrown around. The people you met were retelling the stories, how someone was wounded, how someone got killed. . . . Only then did you understand the situation and what was going on. And you saw yourself in a situation of real danger. Danger to life. . . . But you didn't have any other choice. My decision to join was not in the first place because of national feelings. I told you that it was difficult and risky to leave the town, so what next. Your own decision became simply imposed on you, the decision to defend yourself, and nothing else.
>
> As time went by, more and more Serbs were leaving. Suddenly someone would not come for several days. When you sent men to see what was going on – it turned out that he had left. You know, it was war. You went with them [Serbs] to the front line and you asked yourself with whom you actually were serving. How safe you were, from that same fellow-soldier. So I went over to a unit comprised mostly of people from Vratnik,[12] where I was born. . . . These were the guys whom I more or less knew, and here were our [local] Serbs from Muslim quarters of town (*mahale*). And it is interesting that there were no cases of someone turning his back on you or running away. It might be because they knew with whom they were, and were not feeling threatened, afraid. Because those who ran away must have been scared of me as I was scared of them. It was because we didn't know each other. But here [in the new unit] the situation was different. . . . If you had a Serb with you, you knew for sure who he was.

The key narrator realised that it was war, one had to defend oneself, and one had to do it collectively, organised in army forces, in order to make an impact. The rules of war were entering personal reasoning, and the earlier unacceptable actions became accepted and necessary: bearing weapons and shooting was sanctioned, sides had to be defined and chosen, one did things because of the war and one was not personally responsible for the consequences.

At this point the 'we' group broadened. After the realisation that they were involved in a war which was part of their everyday reality, the key narrator's sense of collective security was re-established as the notion that only national solidarity could guarantee survival of the individuals.

The key narrator could identify the bloody uniforms at the front line as the real threat to his own life because, being a soldier and perceiving the war in the 'soldier' mode, he lost his individuality, and identified himself as interchangeable with any other person in the same uniform, fighting for the same government, representing the same people, and the same national cause, as Ann Norton has also noted (1988: 146, in Jabri 1996: 139):

> The army is not only collective, it formally represents the nation, the active general will. This representative character is signified by uniforms, which disguise and formally deny individuality, and by the use of the national flag and other emblems, which announce the unity of the force and its role as representative of the nation.

The essential importance of group solidarity can be understood from the choices made by the key narrator, when he changed units in order to feel safe among the people like himself, 'the guys he knew', i.e. Muslims and the local Serbs from his childhood quarters, not the anonymous Serbs whom – he felt – could have betrayed him any second. Although the growing importance of the national group membership had a destructive effect on relationships between members of different national groups, in the key narrator's account there was already a sign of the inconsistencies in the national doctrine – the 'soldier' logic – i.e. that all members of other nationalities were a threat to one's own security. The reasoning about the trust he felt towards the local Serbs he personally knew did not fit the 'soldier' logic.

The necessity of making personal choices in a war and the ways in which these are legitimated by national discourse are the key to understanding how the personal is connected and intertwined with the collective, in this case the national. Personal choices are perceived (and often also proved in practice to be) to be an existential importance – chosing between life and death. The legitimation of individual decisions by a collective ideology is always morally charged, thus giving the choices a sense of righteousness. In this way individuals become dependent on the collective blessing of their choice. The collective, on the other hand, depends on the loyalty of individuals – the individuals making the right(eous) choice.

> [A]s modern war illustrates, state interests now depended on the participation of the ordinary citizen to an extent not previously envisaged. . . . The degree of sacrifice which could be imposed on civilians had to enter the plans of strategists . . . [T]he question of the 'nation', and the citizen's feelings towards whatever he regarded as his 'nation', 'nationality' or other centre of loyalty, [was placed] at the top of political agenda.
>
> (Hobsbawm 1990: 83)

For the key narrator, the right(eous) identification was as Muslim, supporting the Muslim cause, and the government in Sarajevo, since both his family background was Muslim and the territory where he lived was under predominantly Muslim control.

War terminology

The identification with the national cause was also made easier by the war terminology. So far, the key narrator has referred to the front-lines as 'lines of separation', thus making the separation of the three Bosnian nations also a highly materialised one in the form of separated territories where 'our' territory meant life and freedom, whereas 'their' territory meant moral decay and was the source of death.

Further on in his account the key narrator used another established term for the front line, 'the line of responsibility'. It meant that the members of a military unit were responsible for the protection of a part of the front-line that was surrounding the city.

The use of the word 'responsibility' to denominate what soldiers were doing at the front-line, namely bearing weapons and shooting, successfully turned the abstract and collective nature of soldiers' tasks into an individual moral act. For an adult male in Sarajevo it was very easy to associate responsibility to protect a front-line with the responsibility to protect his own family. As the key narrator said, he had to join the Army of Bosnia and Hercegovina in order to protect his life and the well-being of his family. In this way the abstract task of protecting one's nation was turned to individually comprehensible responsibility for the family – the social roles of soldier and family father became interchangeable.[13]

Fear at the base of legitimation by nationalism

Contrary to the often stated general attitude that personal experience of violence and losses makes people into nationalists,[14] the war in former Yugoslavia had shown that it was in the first place the fear,[15] the threat of violence and losses, that made people incline towards collective protection – the urge to find a group which pledged to protect them, in this case their national group.

In my experience, the most fierce nationalists were those who mostly needed to legitimise their choices and actions – as, for example, those who avoided army service, or those who gained economic and/or political power while the majority of the population so obviously lost it. Most of the people who suffered real losses in the war did not use the official (national) rhetoric to legitimise their choices.[16] Mostly, they did not have much they needed to legitimise. Their sacrifice was obvious. Similarly, the men who did their armed service at the front-lines were often the ones who had the courage, and moral capital, to question the grand national cause and its righteousness and legitimacy. As Jabri has observed, nationalism and war are interrelated because nationalism legitimises war and choices made in it, while 'war is a constitutive element of collective identity' (1996: 139–40).

People in Sarajevo stopped making personal choices out of fear once they got used to it. When war became a way of life, the notion of fear changed its character, becoming a subdued background of life, necessary to live with. Later on in the war, choices seldom needed legitimation, which is characteristic of the 'deserter' mode of perceiving war. For example, the key narrator gave several typical accounts of the neighbours who left, and all of these accounts justified his own choices in the beginning of the war. Neighbours and friends were accused of leaving without saying that they would and the picture of unsuccessful life as a refugee was given as a justification of his own choice to stay. The picture of the scared neighbour who left made the one who stayed a brave man. Even if the key narrator thought that all things considered it was smart to leave, he still had to legitimise his 'stupidity' of staying by putting forward arguments about his consciousness of the need for national defence. On the other hand, the choice he made to 'get his ass out' did not need any explanation. By 1994 when he did it, war was a way of life in Sarajevo, and any choice to make one's life better was natural and moral.

'Deserter' mode of perceiving war

The 'deserter' mode of thinking is characterised by a realisation that the violent life-circumstances are a part of life. Every deserter has to come to terms with changes that happened in his or her life: the means of survival, the social relations, the existential threat, the religious changes, and the political changes. Deserters feel personally and morally responsible for their acts and deeds, no matter whether in peace or war. In an earlier article I have described this socio-cultural process taking place in Sarajevo during 1992–5 as 'negotiation of normality' (Maček 1997). It is a process in which all individuals, faced with unexplainable violent disruptions of their lives, constantly engage in making sense of their situation. In this mode of thinking, the differences and boundaries between war and peace become blurred – both increasingly start to resemble each other.

Fluidity of time

Tone Bringa encountered the mixing of tenses by her informants, after they had been expelled from their village by violent means. She observed that 'they were living in a time, a dramatically and constantly changing time, which was neither in the past, the present, nor the future' (1995: xvii). What Bringa had witnessed was the character of time in war, hard to express by peacetime means. Owing to the same reason, the beginning of a war cannot be pegged to a precise point in time by those whose lives are affected by the war experience. For them, time has a fluid character characteristic of the 'deserter' mode. The disruptions of peacetime life happen gradually, mounting the changes one upon another, until at one point a realisation is reached that the life circumstances have changed so drastically that they no longer can be perceived of as peace. Only when that realisation is reached is it possible to look back at the past disruptions of peace, and decide which of these disruptions bear most significance in relation to events that were to come. At that point, a 'civilian' mode characteristic of peacetime existence turns into a 'soldier' mode.

Written material from and about the war in Sarajevo shows a difference between individual and official political choices in the ascription of significant meaning to certain events. As opposed to foreign authors and local history books trying to pinpoint the real beginning of the war among political and military events noted on the international level, the war almost invariably began for Sarajevans on the day that they experienced their first heavy shelling. A letter by a young woman in Sarajevo to her sister in Zagreb on the 6 April 1994 can illustrate this:[17]

> Do you remember how nonplussed the neighbours in Radićeva were when we, immediately after we came, asked them what their cellar was like and to show it to us? Funny, on that 7th of April '92 the war had not yet seriously started for them only because no shell had yet fallen in their courtyard. But we, who lived only twentyish minutes further away, had already had the experience of forty hours spent in a cold cellar, crowded with neighbours, from babies to seventy-year-olds.
>
> (Softić 1994: 11–12, my translation)

Although surely accepting the date and the events on the 6 April 1992 as the real beginning of the war, most of the people I talked to, when asked about the beginnings of the war, would start somewhere in March 1992, or even earlier. People invariably described and reflected on their first encounters with *unlawful violence*, such as the barricades in March, set up by the masked people who later on became identified as Serbs, especially as the out-of-town Serbs, i.e. the villagers, the uncivilised, primitive, the 'others'. They reflected on their first encounters with signs of *Serbian nationalism* such as the splitting of the firm along national lines as we saw the key narrator's account, or an unexplainable and provoking display of Serbian symbols as in the Serbian wedding-party that was shot at in March. People also reflected on the beginning of the *dissolution of the legal political structures*, as was the case with national politics and national interests which took over the joint Bosnia and Hercegovina's Parliament. Finally, when talking about the beginning of the war, Sarajevans also reflected on the *dissolution of the life circumstances they were used to*, such as the breakdown of public transportation, disappearance of work and dissolution of the neighbourhood.

So, for an individual, the beginning of war had a complex character – it was experienced as an increase of intangible and disturbing events ('civilian' mode), it was in retrospect fixed on the date of the first realisation of acute physical danger ('soldier' mode), and it was going to be publicly remembered and commemorated on the date of some political or military event ('soldier' mode). As an individual experience, most people will try to forget the war, because the opaque character of these experiences (e.g. the beginning of the war gradually sneaking up on their civilian lives) makes it hard to incorporate them into their contemporary life situations ('deserter' mode).

A meaningless disruption

The 'soldier' notion that wars are logical events controlled by humans, sometimes even honourable,[18] ordered by laws of war, with legitimate aims and clearly opposing sides, becomes untenable for the people experiencing a war because war experiences, almost without exception, are unexpected. The logic behind fear, violence, and destruction becomes insignificant (cf. Nordstrom and Martin 1992: 13; Green 1994: 250; Warren 1993: 3; and a number of anti-war fiction books and films[19]). The key narrator gave me an example of a situation where the disruption of life – a death – could not be justified by any rules or logic of war:

> X: I can tell you one case. In my old unit there was a boy from the orphanage which was near our headquarters. In the orphanage he had a younger brother and sister. A fine boy. Good person. Scared and young. He had just turned eighteen years of age. After I changed units I heard that he got killed, somewhere in Vogošća.[20] They were going, naively, over a field, and an anti-aircraft cannon (*PAT*) was shooting at them. He got hit in the groin. They couldn't evacuate him so they

> hid for some time, and he bled to death. There was a colleague with him who tried to help him, they had bread with them so the colleague tried to stop the bleeding by pressing the bread against the wound. But he died. What hurts is that the brother and sister he was taking care of – he was their mother and father – they lost him.

The experience of a dear person getting killed felt so unjust that no cause could be seen as worth it (cf. also Morokvasić 1998: 66). The longer a war goes on, and the more experience one gains, the more obvious it becomes that the 'soldier' mode of thinking does not hold. This, it could be argued, is when the 'deserter' mode begins to emerge.

Inconsistencies and disappointment

The inconsistencies with the 'soldier' mode were most often found on a personal level of experiences and relations. Here the notions of insecurity as to what was right or wrong, as to why all this was happening, and an understanding of others' choices although opposite from one's own, dominated.

Many people realised that the national defence and unity in whose name they were fighting, were just words in the mouths of politicians who were not sacrificing themselves for the same national cause. People began to understand those who were not willing to fight for any cause, and they began to see that the enemy (or, the enemy soldiers) were probably in a similar situation to their own. The neat division into a Serbian and a Muslim side, and the guilt of all Serbs, as well as the meaningfulness of being a soldier, became questioned by the key narrator. When it came to his neighbours and his fellow combatants, he gave an account full of understanding for the reasons behind their decision to leave, for their feelings of fear, for their decision not to take up arms. Here, the war ceased to make sense, and the 'soldier' mode explanations did not work.

> X: A Serb neighbour left, but he left later on in the war. The man simply didn't want to go to the army, so they said, very well, you won't carry a gun but then you'll dig trenches. He probably didn't like it so he left. . . . The digging of trenches was worst for people who were not soldiers. Why? Because they

came to a totally unknown terrain. When I was on the 'line-of-responsibility' I knew where I was sheltered and where I was visible. . . . But these people came from outside and they didn't know the terrain. The ones guarding the line didn't tell them what they needed to know. You know, they exposed themselves, and got hit by a sniper or a grenade. . . . There were these units of Civilian Defence that came to dig trenches for us. But their digging of trenches was meaningless. They caused more damage than they were useful. But, I understand them. They just wanted to get through that day, they came for one day to dig. Mostly, we soldiers dug too, all of us. You got your part for digging. OK. We dug trenches for ourselves. The deeper and better you dug, the better it was for yourself.

When an anti-tank shell hit [flew through] my apartment, this Serb neighbour was the first one to come and help, to clean it up. He, and another neighbour who left with his family. Two fine people. Not because they helped me, I thought the same also earlier. The Serb neighbour was a man who knew how to fix many things, he was an electrical engineer. He had tools, so when I needed something I went to him, and if I didn't know how to do it he would show me. And he was always ready to help.

In the account about another Serb neighbour, the key narrator shows the human understanding in his moral judgement of the neighbour's decisions to leave. In fact he admits that his own decision to join the Army of Bosnia and Hercegovina was a wrong one:

X: They left by the end of summer, 1992, so they were here for some time. It is strange, but he wasn't mobilised anywhere. But I don't know, these were the subjects which you couldn't openly ask people about, because there were many people hiding from the army, not only Serbs but also Muslims. Smart people, really. Smart, not smart, I don't know. Yes, they are smart, now. From today's perspective, when you add all things up, when you see that most of the politicians talk about one thing, and do something else. All politicians hid their sons or placed them abroad, or had them employed somewhere where they were far away from, from . . . dangers. So it was not characteristic only for Serbs. The majority, well not a majority

> but a large number of people, tried to avoid the gun [armed service], of course, in order to protect themselves. Especially in the beginning, because they couldn't grasp the entirety of the situation. Because what happens if you wait, rely on someone else? Who is that 'else'? I mean, if you don't join the forces and resist, your destiny is clear. He'll come to your house, into your apartment. Beside all the moral dilemmas.

In this passage the key narrator demonstrated the moral dilemma and the burden of his own choice. After giving the description of the unsustainability of the national cause, and the righteousness of the choice to avoid the armed service, he once again used the Bosnian government's arguments in order to justify his own choice to become a soldier. This moral pendulum, between 'deserter' and 'soldier' moralities, is characteristic of war accounts by people existentially involved in a war.

When he reached the conclusion that those people who avoided military service did the right thing, the key narrator had completely 'deserted' the 'soldier' cause. Eventually, he also managed to act in accordance with this new realisation:

> X: Until 1994 I was on these 'lines of separation'. After that I continued in the same unit but not in the fighting formation. I went over to the command, to the finance, as an accountant, I did some programming. Basically I saved my ass. I got myself out of the way.

The 'desertion' of the key narrator thus consisted of disappointment in the national cause, which also meant giving up on moral judgement of people around him based exclusively on their nationality – Serbs could be good, trustworthy people, and Muslims could be bad and cheat on you. The 'desertion' from the armed service was only the consequence of the 'desertion' of the national cause and its 'soldier' (national) moral.

Blurring the civilian–soldier divide

Not only did the sense of justice became shattered as the war went on, but also the clear-cut borders between front life and domestic life became blurred in the key narrator's account, proving again that the division into civilians and soldiers (as in the 'soldier' mode) did not correspond to the experience of war:

> X: We went to the lines of separation [front-lines] in shifts – 5 days on the line and 10 days rest [at home]. . . . Coming home was chaos. You came from terrible hygienic conditions, sleeping for 5 days in a half-destroyed, deserted and filthy house, making fire in ovens that were falling apart, digging trenches but not being able to wash yourself. . . . So, when you came home your first thought was to take a bath. And what did that bath look like! There was no electricity, and no gas to warm the water. You had a bit of wood. . . . I always took off all my clothes immediately in the hall, and went into the bathroom which was freezing in winter time. You washed yourself quickly. . . . Then all the domestic activities would wait for you. . . . The first thing I would do after coming from the front was to fetch water. I needed a whole day for this. And the same before leaving for the front. . . . There was always a crowd waiting for water. People were nervous, there was shelling. It was interesting when a shell would fall, you didn't leave the queue, because if you had already waited for two hours, what then? You had to have water. . . . That was really worst, bringing water from the Brewery.

The difference between the soldiers' and civilians' experience of the war gradually became artificial. As the key narrator described his experiences of war as both a civilian and a soldier, it became obvious that the great divide was blurred. His life was threatened in both cases, but the worst violation was fetching the water as a civilian. On the other hand, he satisfied his social demands better as a soldier:

> X: I didn't go to the neighbour [where mostly women gathered] for coffee and a chat. I was tired of all the talking. . . . I got the social component [of needs] satisfied on the line. In 5 days you had time to talk enough, to change the flow of thoughts in your head. So I'd stay at home and listen to the news, meditate in the dark, pointlessly.

Powerlessness and humiliation

As the evidence of the unsustainability of the 'soldier' mode of structuring the war grew, the war became meaningless time, passing in a struggle for survival, intertwined with feelings of helplessness, powerlessness, and humiliation. In order to survive, people developed some qualities that they never would have dreamt of having – the capacity of living with a constant knowledge that every minute could be the last one and yet, in the evenings, falling into bed and asleep at once, dead-tired, not reacting to explosions, or being unmoved by daily reports about the dead. As they tried to maintain as much of their pre-war lives as possible, they were ashamed and perplexed by their insensitivity to danger and death, as well as by other humiliating circumstances of their lives, feelings they had, and actions they took. Feelings of humiliation were characteristic of the situations where something that was considered to be a part of normal (decent) human life, was disrupted.

Alternative solidarities

With the realisation of the reasons behind choices that Serbs made, and with the disappointment in the Muslim national cause, the 'we'-group identification changed from 'we-Muslims must protect ourselves from Serbs' to 'we-educated middle class Sarajevans' or 'we-who do not want to carry weapons'. As those who officially were defined as 'others' once again became perceived privately as one of 'us', the division into warring sides became blurred, and the official legitimation of the national causes and explanations of war became harder to sustain.

This frame of mind allowed for other types of collective groupings to emerge. One of the two most powerful ones was the bond through living in Sarajevo during the entire war. The other powerful social bond was between the pre-war citizens of Sarajevo. It was a social reaction to the dramatically changed demographic structure of the town due to the approximately 150,000 so-called 'internally displaced people' who, according to the United Nations, came to the town during the war. Most of these people were Muslims from east Bosnian villages, something that awakened a lot of resentment among the secularised Sarajevan citizenry.

Predicament of war

At the beginning of this chapter I posed a question about how the experience of war changes our ways of perceiving it. In order to answer it, I have introduced a model of three ethically different ways of perceiving war which constitute the basis for different ways of personally choosing one's social actions and their legitimation. While the 'civilian' and 'soldier' mode could be found everywhere, the 'deserter' mode of perceiving the war and acting on it proved to be specific to the people who had experienced the war. Thus, the experience of war changes our ways of perceiving it by adding an additional third ethical mode to it. Moreover, during the war in Sarajevo, I observed the mixing of the modes, depending on the context and the point that was being made. The more public and official the context, the more 'soldier-like' the moral. I therefore conclude that the experience of war forces us to make our own individual ethical choices in every given situation. If we recognise this fact, it becomes very hard to escape the personal responsibility for the choices we make and the actions we take.

I have found a somewhat similar argument in the works of one of the great contemporary social analysts of the Holocaust, Zygmunt Bauman (1989, 1991, 1992, 1993). To some, Bauman's insistence on a 'pre-societal' origin of human 'moral duty' based on 'the essential human responsibility for the Other' (1989: 198–9) might appear essentialist, or at least scientifically unproved and a matter of belief rather than scientific analysis. This may be true to an extent, but we should be careful not to dismiss some ideas as matters of faith and not science only because they are not yet sufficiently proven. I have taken up Bauman here, because I feel that his attempt to tackle the seemingly irrational behaviour of people who chose to help the 'Others' while risking their own lives during the Holocaust is connected to my analysis of Sarajevan material. In the first place, we share the idea that individuals are faced with the *choice* of the social actions they are going to take and the ethics (i.e. ethical mode) they are going to use to legitimise these actions. And second, we have witnessed the existence of an unrecognised political force (or forces), which appears *irrational* if we consider the known social and political explanation frames. In the case of Sarajevo this became apparent in the emergence of the 'deserter' ethics and perception of war.

The 'deserter' mode is generally non-existent in official and politically recognised discourses. As Elaine Scarry has shown, in a war situation, those who have the power over injuring, are also the ones with the power of defining the truth, i.e. *the* ethics. This leaves the ordinary people usually with very little power, which is exactly what the politico-military élites desire, because it is a necessary prerequisite for successful engagement in a war. What the analysis of my Sarajevan material showed, however, is that those with no power over injuring, are by no means completely at the mercy of the politico-military élites, but that they indeed do have the power to act and change their living conditions. A case in point was the desertion from the Army of Bosnia and Hercegovina which became accepted as a life-sustaining strategy among Sarajevans. It became accepted on the local collective level, which in its turn forced the state politicians to treat desertion mildly, and eventually introduce a general amnesty.

Had it not been for the similarity of Bauman's ideas based on another huge human catastrophe of this century, I would have perhaps been satisfied by a description of the 'desertion'. As the case is, I am tempted to suggest a possible explanation. It might not necessarily be the primordial pan-human morality that was the foundation of the 'desertion' in Sarajevo, but the ethics of 'desertion' certainly grew out of a force, a potential political power that was opposed to the officially recognised political powers. Perhaps it can be described as the political power of socio-cultural life which is most often perceived as politically powerless. I propose that it is this political power that we should look for in order to better understand and eventually start to change contemporary wars.

Notes

1 Thus, I shall use quotation marks every time I use the terms in my own sense.

2 The key narrator (X) is a man with whose family I got acquainted in spring 1995. Since they were a fairly young and modern Sarajevan family, consisting of parents in their early forties and a teenage daughter and son, we did not have much difficulty in finding a common language of interests and sense of humour. I spent quite a few late evenings at their apartment, eating, drinking and chatting – socialising, as Sarajevans would say. As the key narrator had joined the Army of Bosnia and Hercegovina (the armed troops under the Sarajevan government's control) in the beginning of the war, I asked him if he was willing to talk to me about it, and if I could tape that conversation, something to which he agreed. In this account he described his war-experiences and the choices he made: from a civilian turning into a soldier, and from a soldier finding ways of avoiding the armed service.

3 See, for instance, Softić (1994: 6).

4 Grbavica is a fairly central part of Sarajevo, held by Bosnian Serbs during the war, reintegrated in March 1996.

5 A part of Sarajevo on a hill, near his home.
6 The reports vary between 20,000 as in Magnusson (1993: 23) or Gjelten (1995: 2), and 50,000 to 100,000 as in Malcolm (1994: 235).
7 This was why I developed a very special relation with the couple I was staying with – I became their 'war-kid' (their own daughter was in Sweden), and they became my 'war-parents'.
8 Indeed, there is an entire body of terminology developed in order to obscure the moral unacceptability of the rules of war. As Scarry (1985: 67) put it: 'The language of killing and injuring ceases to be a morally resonant one because the successful shelling of the bodies of thousands of nineteen-year-old German soldiers can be called "producing results" and the death of civilians by starvation and pestilence following an economic boycott is called "collateral effects" . . .' Some other expressions of the same kind are 'low intensity conflict' (cf. Taussig 1992: 22) and 'ethnic cleansing'.
9 Connerton (1989: 3) posits that as long as the memories of their society's past diverge within a group of people, they cannot share their experiences – which would go against the basic needs of people suffering the living conditions of war. Furthermore, it is important to note that 'images of the past commonly legitimate a present social order' (ibid.) which makes 'social memory . . . a dimension of political power' (Connerton 1989: 1). This is of course 'a crucial political issue' since the 'control of a society's memory largely conditions the hierarchy of power' (Connerton 1989: 1).
10 Hedetoft's definition of a 'hero' as a 'cluster of national meanings' (1993: 281–300, in Jabri 1996: 140) applies well in this case, as the making of Suada Dilberović into a hero was a part of the Muslim national constitution which took place during the war. Only a week after her death, Suada Dilberović was referred to as 'the first heroine of Sarajevo's defence' (*Preporod* 15 April 1992, my translation).
11 Interesting is the parallel that Scarry (1985: 56ff.) makes in her analysis of the war as a contest of injuring. She points to an inverted reciprocity between the power of the injurers (those in control of the means of injuring) and the pain of the injured. Translated into the circumstances of the war in Bosnia and Hercegovina, the more the population suffers the larger the power of the politico-military élites which control the conscripts and weapons. Or the other way round, the larger the power of the politico-military élites (largely gained by international diplomatic recognition), the larger the suffering of the population. Thus, the suffering of the unarmed would have been diminished if the international community had boycotted those in control of injuring, thus diminishing their power. Or, had one stopped the injuring of the unarmed, one would have diminished the power of the ones who had the control of weapons.

12 Vratnik is an old part of the town with a predominantly Muslim population and the Muslim town-character.

13 A similar result was achieved during the Second World War with *Ustaše* in Croatia which were using the military slogan 'For home – ready!'.

14 Here, I think of all the reports, especially during the first years of the war, which promoted the idea that the reason for the war in Bosnia and Hercegovina was to be found in the impulse, or the need, to revenge for atrocities experienced during the Second World War and earlier. Or even worse, that bloodshed was in the nature of the people living in the Balkans, as for example suggested by Kennan: 'the strongest motivating factor involved in the Balkan wars [of 1913] was . . . aggressive nationalism . . . [which] drew on deeper traits of character inherited, presumably, from a distant tribal past . . . And so it remains today. . . . It is the undue prominence among the Balkan peoples of these particular qualities, and others that might have been mentioned, that seems to be decisive as a determinant of the troublesome, baffling, and dangerous situation that marks that part of the world today' (Kennan 1993: 6).

15 For more about fear, see Green 1994 and Taussig (1992:2).

16 Although, of course, there were people who used the national rhetoric in order to explain their loss. This was where nationalism could profit from the people in mourning, because they were bound to desperately look for any kind of explanation for their personal tragedy.

17 See also Bringa (1995: xvi) and Lagumdžija (1995: 11). This is what makes the diary of 'Sarajevo's Anne Frank', Zlata Filipović, inauthentic as a diary. Under the date of 6 April 1992 she writes '. . . war is here!' (Filipović 1993), which is a fact that was not yet established at the moment she was supposedly writing it. Although inauthentic as a diary, her writings are nevertheless representative of events and some general attitudes in Sarajevo during the war.

18 See Rieff (1995: 17) and Jabri (1996: 98–9).

19 Pat Barker's *Regeneration*, Remarque's *All Quiet on the Western Front*, Hemingway's *A Farewell to Arms*, Heller's *Catch 22*, Mailer's *The Naked and the Dead*, and Salinger's *For Esmé – with Love and Squalor*, can stand as examples. In the film genre the post-Vietnam subjects dominate. Among the most familiar ones are *Apocalypse Now*, *Platoon*, *Forrest Gump*, *Born on the Fourth of July*, and the post-Cambodia films such as *The Killing Fields.*

20 Vogošća is a Sarajevan municipality slightly outside of town, held by Bosnian Serbs through the war, reintegrated in March 1996.

Bibliography

Bauman, Z. (1989) *Modernity and the Holocaust*, Ithaca, NY: Cornell University Press.

—— (1991) *Modernity and Ambivalence*, Cambridge: Polity Press.

—— (1992) *Mortality, Immortality and Other Life Strategies*, Cambridge: Polity Press.

—— (1993) *Postmodern Ethics*, Oxford and Cambridge, Mass.: Blackwell.

Bringa, T. (1995) *Being Muslim the Bosnian Way: Identity and Community in a Central Bosnian Village*, Princeton, NJ: Princeton University Press.

Bruchfeld, S. and Levine, P. A. (1998) *. . . om detta må ni berätta . . . En bok om Förintelsen i Europa 1933–1945* (Tell ye your children. . . . A book about the Holocaust in Europe 1933–45), Stockholm: Regeringskansliet.

Clausewitz, C. von (1997) [1832] *On War*, Ware, Hetfordshire: Wordsworth Classics of World Literature.

Connerton, P. (1989) *How Societies Remember*, Cambridge: Cambridge University Press.

Filipović, Z. (1993) *Dnevnik Zlate Filipović* (Diary of Zlata Filipović), Sarajevo: Međunarodni centar za mir.

Gjelten, T. (1995) *Sarajevo Daily: A City and Its Newspaper Under Siege*, New York: Harper Collins Publishers.

Glenny, M. (1992) *The Fall of Yugoslavia*, London: Penguin.

Green, L. (1994) 'Fear as a way of life', *Cultural Anthropology* 9(2): 227–56.

Gutman, R. (1993) *A Witness to Genocide: The First Inside Account of the Horrors of 'Ethnic Cleansing' in Bosnia*, Shaftersbury, Dorset: Element.

Hedetoft, U. (1993) 'National identity and mentalities of war in three EC countries', *Journal of Peace Research* 30(3): 281–300.

Hobbes, T. (1997) [1651] *Leviathan*, New York and London: W. W. Norton & Company.

Hobsbawm, E. (1990) *Nations and Nationalism since 1789: Programme, Myth, Reality*, Cambridge: Cambridge University Press.

Imamović, E. and Bošnjak, J. (1994) *Poznavanje društva 4. razred osnovne škole* (Understanding Society for the Fourth Grade of Primary School), Sarajevo: Ministarstvo obrazovanja, nauke, kulture i sporta.

Imamović, M. and Pelešić, M. (1994) *Historija 4. razred gimnazije* (History for the Fourth Grade of Gymnasium), Sarajevo: Ministarstvo obrazovanja, nauke, kulture i sporta.

Isaković, A. (1994) *Antologija zla* (Anthology of Evil), Sarajevo: Ljiljan.

Jabri, V. (1996) *Discourses on Violence: Conflict Analysis Reconsidered*, Manchester and New York: Manchester University Press.

Kennan, G. F. (1993) 'The Balkan crisis: 1913 and 1993', *The New York Review of Books*, July 15: 3–7.

Kubert, J. (1996) *Fax from Sarajevo: A Story of Survival*, Milwaukie: Dark Horse Books.

Lagumdžija, R. (1995) *Biljezi i ožiljci* (Marks and Scars), Sarajevo: OKO.

Maček, I. (1997) 'Negotiating Normality in Sarajevo During the 1992–1995 War', *Narodna umjetnost* 34(1): 25–58.

—— (2000) *War Within: Everyday Life in Sarajevo under Siege*, Uppsala: Acta Universitatis Upsaliensis.

Magnusson, K. (1993) *Den bosniska tragedin* (The Bosnian Tragedy), Stockholm: Utrikespolitiska institutet.

Malcolm, N. (1994) *Bosnia: A Short History,* London: Papermac.

Morokvasić, M. (1998) 'The logics of exclusion: nationalism, sexism and the Yugoslav war', in N. Charles and H. Hintjens (eds) *Gender, Ethnicity and Political Ideologies,* London: Routledge.

Nordstrom, C. and Martin, J.A. (1992) 'The culture of conflict: field reality and theory', in C. Nordstrom and J. Martin (eds) *The Paths to Domination, Resistance and Terror*, Berkeley: University of California Press.

Norton, A. (1988) *Reflections on Political Identity,* London and Baltimore: Johns Hopkins University Press.

Owen, D. (1996) [1995] *Balkan Odyssey,* London: Indigo.

Preporod (1992) 15th April, Sarajevo: Mešihat Islamske zajednice Bosne i Hercegovine.

Ramet, P. S. (1996) *Balkan Babel: The Disintegration of Yugoslavia from the Death of Tito to Ethnic War*, Boulder, Colorado: Westview Press.

Rieff, D. (1995) *Slaughterhouse: Bosnia and the Failure of the West,* New York: Touchstone.

Scarry, E. (1985) *The Body in Pain: The Making and Unmaking of the World,* New York and Oxford: Oxford University Press.

Softić, E. (1994) *Sarajevski dani, sarajevske noći: dnevnik i pisma 1992–'94* (Sarajevan Days, Sarajevan Nights: Diary and Letters 1992–94), Zagreb: V.B.Z.

Taussig, M. (1992) *The Nervous System,* London: Routledge.

Vuković, Z. (1992) *Ubijanje Sarajeva* (Killing of Sarajevo), Podgorica: Kron.

Vulliamy, E. (1994) *Seasons in Hell: Understanding Bosnia's War,* London: Simon & Schuster.

Warren, K. B. (1993) 'Introduction: revealing conflicts across cultures and disciplines', in K. B. Warren (ed.) *The Violence Within: Cultural and Political Opposition in Divided Nations*, Boulder, San Francisco and Oxford: Westview Press.

Zimmermann, W. (1996) *Origins of a Catastrophe: Yugoslavia and Its Destroyers – America's Last Ambassador Tells What Happened and Why,* New York: Random House.

Index

abduction 167, 170–2
Afro-Caribbean religion 88, 92, 94
age grade 129, 132, 134, 137
Albania 98–100, 105, 106, 109–11, 113
Albert, B. 69
Alés, C. 69
Allen, T. 161
Althusser, L. 43
antagonism 1, 10, 12, 16, 29, 35–42
anthropophagy 77–80, 84; *see also* cannibalism
Apache 144–54, 156, 157
Appadurai, A. 11
Arawak 51, 79, 83
Arens, W. 80
Atchei *see* Guayaki

Bantu 'Somali' 162, 167, 168, 171
Barkow, J. 132
Bauman, Z. 219, 220
Behrend, H. 12–13
Bertran de Born (in Ezra Pound's 'Sestina: Altaforte') 36
besa 101, 113
Bhabha, H. 82
blood-feuding 49, 50, 60; *see also* *kanun*
Bois-Caïman ceremony 87, 88, 91
Boldinger, G. 63
Bosnia and Hercegovina 197, 198, 200, 205–6, 210, 213, 215, 220
Boucher, P. 81
Bourdieu, P. 140
Bourgois, P. 13
bow-fighting 60
bratstvo I jedinstvo ('brotherhood and unity') 38, 200, 202
bravery 149; concept of 147
bride-robbery *see* women's robbery
Bringa, T. 211, 222
Burma 35
Buss, D. 139

Campbell, D. 9
cannibalism 32, 52, 76–85, 88–92; *see also* anthropophagy
Cariage, P. 50, 59, 65
Carib 50, 51, 79, 83
Carib-speaking Indians 50, 51, 72
Caribbean 76, 77, 79–85, 92
caste 181, 182, 187
Chagnon, N. 69
Chisholm, J.S. 140
Cibecue Battle 151
civilians 162, 197, 198, 204, 212, 213, 217, 219
Clastres, P. 28–30, 32–4, 42–4
Clausewitz, C. von 1, 177, 205
colonial discourse 80–2, 85, 89
colonialism 80, 82, 84, 153
Columbia 51
commodisation of despair 161

competition 2, 4, 7, 15, 19, 36, 143, 155, 198
conflict, causes of 1, 5, 9, 143
conflict prevention 177, 191, 194
Connerton, P. 204, 221
Cremony, J.C. 144–5
Croatia 199–200
cultural archive 161, 170, 172

Dalmas, A. 87–8
Daly, M. 125, 133, 138
Dar es Salaam 162, 164, 167, 168
Davisson, L. 153
Dean, B. 32
deserters 197, 198, 210–13, 216, 219
Dizi 124–5, 127, 130, 131, 136, 137, 140
Draper, P. 139
duel 49–64, 66, 68–9, 129, 132–4, 136
duelling, ceremonial 129, 133–4
Durham, E. 101, 105

Elezi, I. 104
Elwert, G. 5, 113, 115
enemy image 144, 148
escalation 177, 179–80, 187, 191, 192, 194, 201
ethic (ethical mode) 197, 198, 219, 220; *see also* modes of perceiving war
Ethiopia 123–4, 127, 138
ethnicity 11
ethno-ethnohistory 144
ethnohistory 144, 156
event 144, 149, 151, 152, 155, 157, 203–5, 212, 213; violent event 1, 9, 12, 13, 18, 205, social events as war 203, 213
evolutionary psychology 126, 127, 132
exchange theory (logic of exchange) 29–30, 33–5, 53, 56, 59, 69
experience 4, 6–8, 12, 15–17, 19, 37–8, 41, 150–4, 161, 165, 166, 168, 170, 172, 197–200, 202–4, 212–14, 216–20; experience of rape 166, 167, 173; experience of war violence 161, 165, 172

family 202, 213, 209, 210
fear 210, 213, 214, 222
Ferguson, R.B. 4, 69
'fitness' 126, 134, 135, 136, 138, 139
Fogelson, R. 144, 156
Foucault, M. 43
Fox, R. 128, 129, 135, 137

Galla 170
Garde, P. 38
Girard, R. 8, 22
'globalising' forces 128
Goodwin, G. 146, 148, 151, 154, 156
Guayaki 32–3, 35, 37
gumlao 35
gumsa 35
Gusinde, M. 71
Guss, D. 52, 65

Haberland, E. 140
Haiti 87–9
Hamilton, W. 127
Hann, C. 139
Harpending, H. 139
Harris, M. 69, 78
Harrison, S. 33–6, 42–4
Hasluck, M. 107–9
Hercegovina *see* Bosnia and Hercegovina
history 9, 11, 16, 20, 97–9, 111, 151, 152, 154, 155, 204, 212
Hobbes, T. 177, 191, 203
Hobsbawm, E. 209
Hoffmann, L.-F. 87–8
holocaust 219
homicide 98, 125, 129, 134, 137
honour 5, 101, 102, 105, 107–9, 114, 117

Hulme, P. 80–5, 93
human sacrifice 12, 76, 90, 91
humiliation 109

Ideological State Apparatuses (ISA) 32, 43
incest 53, 57
Israeli–Palestinian conflict 6

Jabri, V. 210
JVP (Janatha Vimukthi Peramuna) 186, 189, 190
Juba river 162, 167, 170, 171

Kachin 35
kanun 101–11, 113, 117
Kessel, W.B. 152
kidnapping 108, 114, 167
Kosovo 98, 106, 110, 114–17
Krohn-Hansen, C. 12

Laclau, E. 36–7, 42
Leach, E. 35, 43–4
legitimacy 6, 8, 9, 14, 155, 205, 210
legitimation, of nationalism 210, 218; of personal choices (of individual decisions) 198, 209, 210, 219
Levi-Strauss, C. 43, 53; on reciprocity 53
LTTE (Liberation Tigers of Tamil Eelam) 187–90, 192
Lizot, J. 69
Ljubljana (Slovenia), regional elections in 40
Lowland South America 49, 50

Manambu (Sepik region of PNG) 33–6; Avatip men's cults among 35
Maroon 86
Mason, P. 79
Mastnak, T. 39
memories, of men 165; of rape 166; of the past 167; of torture 167; of violence 167; of war violence 161, 165, 170, 171; of women 165
memory 8–11, 16, 103, 109, 161, 165, 166, 168; social 4, 16, 20, 152, 162, 171, 203, 204, 221
Mencinger, J. 39
Métraux, A. 86
Moeran, B. 87
Moore, J. 141
motivation, theory of 123, 126
Mouffe, C. 36–7, 42
Mursi 140
myth 52, 53, 77, 87, 91; of creation 70

narrative 7, 9–11, 13, 17, 19–21, 90, 102, 144, 146–8, 151–4, 157, 166, 169–73; of violence 32; of the past 167, 169, 172
nationalism 11, 41, 210, 212, 222
Nordstrom, C. 7, 12
normality, negotiation of 211
Nyangatom 128, 130, 131, 135, 136

obeah 85, 86, 94
Oromo *see* Galla

Pavlowitch, S. 38
performance 6, 9, 10, 12, 27, 105, 107, 135, 136; violent 123
Peteet, J. 6, 10
Pima 144–5, 148
pogrom 188, 189, 191
power 3–6, 8–11, 20, 29–31, 35, 40, 41, 60, 66–9, 82, 86–9, 109, 110, 112, 115, 116, 143, 144, 148, 153, 154, 202, 205, 219–21; political 197, 198, 205, 210, 221
powerlessness 202, 217, 218
Prabhakaran, V. 190
prestige 5, 60, 66, 67, 106, 108, 110, 113–15, 117, 126, 132, 133, 135–7; prestige competition 137

'primitive' society, Clastres' definition of 28–9; as a society against exchange 29; war in 30, 33
'primitivism' 28

raid 70, 115, 129, 130, 132, 136, 137, 146–8, 152, 153, 169–71
Ramet, P. 40
rape 32, 163–9, 171, 172; *see also* memories of rape
reciprocity 53–57, 59, 126, 127, 129, 132, 138, 221
refugee camps *see* refugee settlement
refugee settlement 162–6
Reichel-Dolmatoff, G. 49, 59, 69, 71
religion 8, 44, 77, 78, 80, 85–8, 91–4
Repressive State Apparatuses (RSA) 32, 43
reproductive chances 125, 126, 132
resistance 80, 86, 88, 94, 200
revenge 4, 15, 57, 58, 61, 68, 99, 103, 126, 129, 134, 146–7, 149–50, 168, 222
Richards, P. 123
Riches, D. 3–4, 6, 12, 14, 26–7, 68, 76, 129, 139
riot 179, 185, 187, 188; ethnic 184, 186
ritual 10, 33, 36, 44, 49, 60, 66, 79, 81, 86, 88, 91–3, 101, 103–6, 109, 117, 124, 129–38
Robben, A.C.G.M. 7, 12
Ruddle, K. 51
Rule, J.B. 179

Sagan, E. 78
Sarajevo 197–200, 202–4, 209, 212, 218, 219
Scarry, E. 32, 205, 219, 221
Seabrook, W. 90–1
Serbia 200
Sierra de Perijá 51
silence 167, 168
Simmel, G. 1, 20
Sinhala 180–9, 191–2
slave 77, 86–9, 91, 94, 167, 170, 171; African 85–7, 91, 92
slavery 86, 88, 94, 167, 170, 172, 173
social contexts, of violent behaviour 50; of war 61; of vendetta 61; of duels 61; of suicide 64
sociality 28, 29, 33–5, 42, 129, 140; idea of 129
socio-cosmological differentiation, mythical 52, 53
soldier 161, 163, 171, 197–8, 202–4, 208, 210, 212–14, 216, 217, 219
Somali 166–8, 170–2; *see also* Bantu 'Somali'
Somali Bantu *see* Bantu 'Somali'
Somalia 161–3
Southern Somalia 161, 163, 168
Sri Lanka 177, 180–2, 184–2, 194
St John, S. 89–91
stories *see* memories
suicide 49, 50, 63–7, 71
Suri 123–5, 127–40
symbolic capital 66, 161
Symons, D. 139

Tamil 180–92
terrorist 192
Tito, Marshall (Joseph Broz) 38–40, 200
Toposa 130, 131
torture 32, 165, 166, *see also* memories of torture
tourism 128
trauma 166
Trivers, R. 127
Tupinamba 79
Turton, D. 140

Ugrešić, D. 5

Van Wees, H. 139, 177
vendetta 49, 50, 60–1, 63–4, 66, 68–70
Venezuela 49, 51, 70, 72

Verdery, K. 99
violence, as ritual 129; culture of 129, 138, 140; 'defensive' 32; etymology of 25–6, 28; goal-oriented 125, 129; observers of 12; perpetrators of 12; pre-emptive 12; results of 8; sexual 168, 170; symbolic dimension of 6; triangle of 12, 80; victims of 12; and restraint 129
violence, forms of: notion of 50, 67; legitimate vs. illegitimate 31, 67; legal and illegal 50, 67; negative-reciprocal 59, 61, 63, 66, 67; reciprocal 59, 61, 63, 67; self-referential 67; symbolic notions of 50
violent imaginary 9–11, 77
violent practice 11, 50, 84, 85, 93
Viveiros de Castro, E. 78
Vodou 76, 77, 85–93
Voodoo *see* Vodou

war: as event 144; as disruption of peace 198; civil 176–80, 188, 191–4; concept of 4, 20, 144; cultural construction of 1, 144, 147; definition of 5, 15, 176–7; ethics of 197; experience of 197; memories 161; modes of perceiving war 198, 203, 210, 211, 218, 219; perceptions about war 197; war dance 147
warfare 49, 50, 69, 70, 136, 144, 146, 151, 152, 154, 155, 157, 177, 191; as events of the past 151
Wavrin, M. de 62
Weber, M. 8, 67, 178
Wehrheim-Peuker, M. 82
Western Apache *see* Apache
Weule, K. 21
Whitehead, N. 79, 82
Wilson, M. 125, 133, 138
witch 82
women's robbery 67, 108
wound marks 67
Wright, R. 126

Yanomami 49
young male syndrome 133, 138
Yugoslavia, Socialist Federative Republic of 21, 37–42, 198, 203, 210
Yukpa 49, 50; etymology of 54, 55; difference between Yukpa/Yuko 54–5; internal distinctions 54–8; mythology 52; creation of the world 52; establishment of the incest tabu 53; social organisation 50, 54

Zigula 162, 167–73
Zizek, S. 41

Printed in the United States
64629LVS00002B/119